COMPARABLE WORTH:
Issues and Alternatives

Edited by
E. Robert Livernash

EQUAL EMPLOYMENT ADVISORY COUNCIL

Washington, D.C.

FOREWORD

As our society moves into the 1980's, the question of whether discrimination in employment will be eliminated is no longer in issue. The wide-ranging efforts, both voluntary and involuntary, of individuals, private organizations, educational institutions, business and government are having an undeniably positive effect. To those of us whose work experience began before World War II, statistical proof of this fact is unnecessary. Indications of the marked progress being made in eliminating employment discrimination against women and minorities can be found in almost every aspect of working life from the make up of a routine business meeting to the consideration now given most personnel decisions. Obviously, these are only symbolic. It would be foolish to argue that all forms of discrimination have been eliminated completely.

The questions facing the 80's are more difficult and complex, however, because they involve issues on which there is no consensus. They deal not with "whether" but with "how" and "when" and "at whose expense." Will employment discrimination be eliminated primarily through voluntary action or through government defined and enforced equality? Will it be done through affirmative action that creates opportunities and provides needed training or through meeting goals that are indistinguishable from quotas? Will society accept true mobility in employment as the essence of equal opportunity or must parity in employment be achieved? And, if parity is to be the answer, how and by whom will it be defined and how quickly must it be reached?

The three basic groups with the most immediate interest in resolving these questions are the protected groups, government equal employment enforcement officials, and the employer community. All seek similar goals, but their roles differ. Leaders of the protected groups constantly seek better mechanisms to eliminate discrimination more rapidly. The constituencies which pressure them to take vigorous, and sometimes even radical, action also restrict their capacity to make the compromises necessary for practical results. Government administrators, motivated by personal and professional commitments to end discrimination, seek similar mechanisms, but must restrict their choices to those which are politically unobjectionable to legislators, legally compatible with judicial interpretations of our laws, and socially acceptable to the general public.

From a practical standpoint action is stimulated by the protected groups and regulated by the government but, as is often the case, the action itself is taken by employers. Employment is furnished by employers. If equal opportunity in that employment is to be achieved, it must be supplied by employers. And, fundamental as is equal employment opportunity, it must be provided in the context of conflicting interests and forces. These include the expectations of shareholders, the minority labor force and majority workers; the goals of union representatives and myriad regulatory agencies; and the availability of dispute resolution systems and skilled workers. In today's troubled economic climate, the cost of disrupting existing methods of determining compensation is a basic problem that cannot be ignored. Consequently, while employers also seek efficient mechanisms for eliminating discrimination, there is no possible way that their actions and decisions can ignore the economic realities in which their respective organizations operate.

In the search for appropriate mechanisms, experience has shown that often the most touted scheme is one which is based on some basic, numerical comparison. Any method of simple statistical analysis which can be used both to identify and eliminate discrimination has great appeal, because it enables leaders of protected groups to counteract unreasonable constituent pressures, minimizes enforcement burdens for the government, and provides understandable symbols to tally progress. The rapidly developing interest in comparable worth is an illustration of this trend for, when viewed in simplistic terms, it appears to meet the criteria listed. Whether this mechanism is an effective means for proving discrimination is the focus of *Comparable Worth: Issues and Alternatives.*

There are a number of threshold problems which should be recognized before discussing comparable worth. First, the premises upon which comparable worth rests are more discernable than its definition. Briefly stated, proponents contend that the marketplace has historically discriminated by establishing lower rates of compensation for jobs held predominantly by women and, in some instances, by minorities. They argue that any job has a certain inherent "worth" to the employer, or perhaps to society at large, and that it is therefore possible to compare these "worths" even though they do not require the same skill, effort and responsibility and are not performed under similar working conditions (the Equal Pay Act standards). If this comparison indicates that a position held predominantly by women is paid less than a "male" job of comparable worth, the difference in pay rates is presumed to be exclusively the result of past societal discrimination. Consequently, proponents argue that it is necessary to devise a common measuring system which is capable of assigning a numerical worth to each job, so that jobs which are dissimilar can be compared and their pay rates analyzed for possible discrimination.

While these premises are clearly subject to question, there is an even more basic reason for uncertainty. As Professor Livernash points out in the lead paper, the concept of comparable worth has never been defined in operational terms or associated with any measurement device. EEOC Commissioner J. Clay Smith, Jr., in an address to the Biennial Conference on Civil Rights of the Ohio AFL-CIO on February 6, 1980, indicated a similar view when he said, "Of course, all definitions of comparable worth are in a state of flux."

A second threshold problem concerns disagreement as to whether comparable worth is even the issue which should be discussed. For example, EEOC's first major effort in this area was to contract with the National Academy of Sciences (NAS), in late September, 1977, to prepare a report which would "Assess [the] feasibility and desirability of developing and implementing a system for evaluating the comparability of jobs according to the skills, responsibility, and effort required." Two interim reports have been prepared by NAS for EEOC, only one of which has been made public. ("Job Evaluation: An Analytical Review" by Donald J. Trieman, National Academy of Sciences, February 1979.) A final report, due September 30, 1979, has not yet been issued. The emphasis in the NAS contract, interim reports, and early comments by EEOC officials appeared to focus on an examination of job evaluation systems as a means of disclosing job discrimination.

By 1979, however, the comparable worth concept had become the focus for discussion and, more recently, the terms "job segregation" and "wage discrimination" are being used. This ambiguity as to the real issue involved seems apparent in statements by several EEOC Commissioners and in the announcements of the Commission's public hearings on Job Segregation and Wage Discrimination under Title VII and the Equal Pay Act. In October, 1979, EEOC Chair Norton predicted that comparable worth, more than hiring or promotion, will be the women's issue of the 1980's. (See DLR 211, Oct. 30, 1979.) Similar sentiments were expressed by Commissioner Smith several months later. (See DLR 28, Feb. 8, 1980.) Nonetheless, in the last of the announcements rescheduling the public hearings, EEOC stated that several responses to earlier notices dwelt on issues other than whether the wages of segregated jobs are discriminatorily depressed. It then commented that:

> The Commission, of course, recognizes that remedying job segregation must include the traditional remedies of access and mobility. But in this hearing the Commission intends to focus only on the more narrow issue of whether such segregated jobs have been discriminatorily assigned depressed wages. The Commission is not specifically exploring any theory that would compare the worth of

different jobs by some abstract standard determined and administered by the government, as is sometimes implied in the concept of 'comparable worth.' (See Fed. Reg. Vol. 45, No. 36, Thursday, February 21, 1980, p. 11659.)

Regardless of the term used—comparable worth, bias-free job evaluation, job segregation or wage discrimination—basic to all is the premise that not only can the worth of each job be measured independently of the market but also that the worth of dissimilar jobs can be compared and any resulting differences in pay rates can be attributed to discrimination.

Third, there is a question as to the extent to which comparable worth is relevant in dealing with equal employment opportunity. This involves what many believe is a fundamental difference between employers and the Congress on the one hand and EEO enforcement officials on the other as to what is meant by eliminating employment discrimination. The language of Title VII of the Civil Rights Act of 1964 is stated in functional terms that deal with a variety of personnel actions, e.g., hires, discharges, compensation, deprivation of opportunities. Its thrust is to eliminate discrimination by assuring equal treatment in job *mobility*—that is, equal *opportunity*. By making certain that full mobility is available to all, Congress felt that the effects of past discrimination would gradually be eliminated. Most employers have accepted this view. The enforcement agencies, on the other hand, interpret Congressional policy as requiring more than mobility, that what should be done is to eliminate the effects of past discrimination *immediately*. In other words, job *parity* or a numerical equivalency in the number of jobs *held* and levels of compensation *received* must be achieved at once rather than awaiting the effects of equal opportunity. Comparable worth would seem to have particular application to questions of parity. Its value, if any, in assessing the presence or absence of mobility is not readily apparent.

Because of threshold problems such as the above, employer concerns are not limited merely to the use of comparable worth as a mechanism for enforcing equal employment laws. Of equivalent, or perhaps greater, significance are the potential consequences for society and the economy generally. In other words, is the adoption of comparable worth as an enforcement technique more important than competing interests and forces? Can the concept be defined in operational terms with standards that can realistically be applied? Is it necessary if job mobility is the essence of equal opportunity? These considerations are of paramount importance to employers for, as this book shows, the potential consequences, both economic and social, of disruption of the multiplicity of wage determination systems used throughout industry, without sufficient consideration of the impact of market forces, collective bargaining, and similar factors, would be enormous.

Serious misgivings about EEOC's approach to the issue began to develop soon after the NAS contract was made. The NAS study was perceived as the beginning of an EEOC search for an enforcement mechanism which had implications reaching far beyond issues of equal employment. As a result, the Equal Employment Advisory Council concluded that an independent study should be initiated that would explore the area in question, not only from the standpoint of the feasibility of use of comparable worth and related matters as a means of dealing with employment discrimination, but also from the more basic premise of whether it is desirable. Its primary purpose would be to give those interested an objective reference point from which to assess the validity of EEOC's assumptions about the use of job evaluation and comparable worth in discrimination cases.

This book is the result of the study. The papers included analyze each of the major premises on which comparable worth is based and the judgment of the authors as to the impact of the doctrine if used as a method of proving discrimination in employment. Also included are a thorough examination of the legislative history of the controlling statutes, judicial reaction to its use, and foreign experience with similar concepts. The particular topics which are covered were suggested both by the authors and by industry equal employment and compensation experts. E. Robert Livernash, one of the pre-eminent academic authorities in the field of job evaluation, played a dominant role in selecting and refining the topics and in choosing the authors for each paper. He also prepared an overview of the book, which contains a brief review of the papers of the other authors as well as his own conclusions. The positions expressed by the authors of the various papers are their own and do not necessarily represent the views of the Equal Employment Advisory Council, its member companies and trade associations, or any other employers or their organizations.

It would be a serious omission if this foreword did not emphasize that employers are more interested than most in a simple, understandable, objective and accurate means of determining compliance with equal employment laws and regulations. One of the most serious difficulties they have had throughout the existence of anti-discrimination laws is ascertaining what is expected of them. As pointed out above, employers generally face the most immediate ramifications of federal rules and regulations which are either ambiguous or impractical, and they are first to bear the cost of requirements which are established without consideration of the consequences of their implementation. Protected groups, which play such a critical role in the formulation of federal regulations, and the government, which dictates how they are to be met, share no similar responsibility, no similar penalty.

Commissioner Smith, in his Biennial Conference address, asked "Will the economy of the 80's create an adversarial relationship in Civil Rights?" Characterizing himself as an optimist, he expressed the belief that ". . . people of goodwill and good intentions can meet the challenge of the 80's head on." His optimism is shared by some and hoped for by most, but optimism alone is insufficient to meet this challenge. What is necessary is, first, a thorough examination of the substance and consequences of each regulatory proposal as it is presented and, second, a willingness on the part of protected groups, the government, and the business community to maintain their commitment to the elimination of discrimination within the context of the economic realities of today's world. We hope this study will be useful in this examination.

Kenneth C. McGuiness
President
(June, 1980)   Equal Employment Advisory Council

ACKNOWLEDGMENTS

This study was prepared under a special unrestricted grant from The Business Roundtable. The contributing authors were encouraged to express their own judgments and opinions and they are responsible for the accuracy of all material developed in their papers. The Roundtable exercised no editorial control over the study and did not otherwise participate in its preparation.

Special recognition should be given to the contribution of the Ad Hoc Committee of the Equal Employment Advisory Council, which managed the project, and to Kevin S. McGuiness and Lorence L. Kessler, who edited the final manuscript.

TABLE OF CONTENTS

AN OVERVIEW
by
E. Robert Livernash

E. Robert Livernash is the Albert J. Weatherhead Jr. Professor of Business Administration Emeritus at the Harvard School of Business. A graduate of the University of Colorado in 1932, he received his M.A. from Tufts College in 1934 and his Ph.D. in economics from Harvard University in 1942. From 1943 to 1945 he was the Wage Stabilization Director, then Chairman of Region I of the War Labor Board. After serving as the Director of Research for the J. F. McElwain Co. for seven years, Dr. Livernash began his teaching career in 1953 at the Harvard Business School, retiring his fulltime position at the school in 1975. From 1972 to 1975 he was also the President and a professor at the Iran Center for Management Studies. Dr. Livernash is well known for his work in the areas of labor economics and job evaluation and his numerous articles and books. He was a member of the State Personnel Commission for the State of New Hampshire, which developed a job evaluation plan for all state employees. He was the author of "The Internal Wage Structure" in *New Concepts in Wage Determination* (McGraw-Hill, 1958); "Job Evaluation" in *Employment Wages in the United States* (Twentieth Century Fund, 1953); "Wage Administration and Production Standards" in *Industrial Conflict* (Arno Press, N.Y., 1954); and with Sumner Schlicter and James Healy, *The Impact of Collective Bargaining on Management* (The Brookings Institution, 1960).

AN OVERVIEW

The purpose of this "overview" paper is closely related to the objectives of the study itself. It is intended to identify and analyze the compensation issues embedded in the concept of comparable worth, as defined by its supporters, and then suggest what is believed to be a more appropriate alternative response.

The fundamental issue is rather simple. Supporters of the comparable worth theory believe that differences between the compensation rates currently paid for jobs and positions predominantly held by women and those paid for jobs and positions predominantly populated by men are indicative of sex discrimination. They would implement the theory to revamp structural wage and salary relationships in order to eliminate or reduce this allegedly discriminatory disparity. However, for the variety of reasons developed in this study, it is impossible to achieve the ends desired by the means proposed. In so far as a problem of sex discrimination continues to exist in professional compensation systems, it relates essentially to relative earnings and not to relative rates of compensation. In other words, it is not evaluated job rates which need correction but the distribution of women within the employment and compensation hierarchy. As a result, the viable method for correcting the relative shortfall in female average earnings when compared to male earnings is through the increased upward mobility of women. Clearly, the above issue also relates to minorities and to a lesser degree to the occupational pattern of employment.

This over-simplified summation of the conclusions which flow from this study does not imply that rates of compensation are "equitable." In fact, as will be made clear in the substantive papers, equity cannot be identified unless it is assumed to be reflected in market rates combined with job evaluation standards. There is simply no known technique by which job "worth" in any intrinsic sense can be measured. The papers emphasize the necessity of basing relative rates of compensation on a combination of market rates and job evaluation and that a failure to do so will lead not only to highly arbitrary and controversial results, but also to an administrative quagmire.

This study should not be perceived, however, primarily as support for existing, professionally practiced compensation procedures and techniques, since the debate over comparable worth involves a variety of questions as to the equity of compensation systems. The major purpose of the study, in fact, is to provide helpful insights to those responsible for the administration of compensation systems and to those with authority for the review and oversight of such systems, particularly persons in regulatory agencies, in the legislature and in the judiciary.

Aside from the legal paper, the authors of this study are academic professionals, each working in a scholarly manner within an individual framework of value judgments. While the purpose of the project is not to produce an academic treatise, all of the authors hope that their papers will make an academic contribution and that the study will be useful to students taking relevant courses, particularly on the graduate level.

An overview paper is just that, an introduction to and an overview of the study as a whole. There will be no attempt to summarize each of the individual papers, because each is far too complex for simple condensation. An effort will be made, however, to state the primary thrust of each author's work, to capture the major aspects of each paper, and to state the issues embedded in the comparable worth concept. Naturally, this distilling process will result in the making of some rather dogmatic statements, and the richness of the papers and the depth of their respective analyses will not be captured adequately. It is hoped, therefore, that this introduction will serve both as a capsule review of the study and as an inducement to read all of the papers. It should be noted, however, that the opinions and ideas found in this overview should not be taken as representative of sentiments of all of the authors who participated in the study. While such unanimity would be gratifying, it is not likely. This paper will provide some individual conclusions based on the analyses of the others.

AN INTRODUCTION TO THE STUDY

This study contains seven substantive papers. In this overview, the seven papers are reviewed briefly and then discussed in accordance with the following topics:

    I. The concept of comparable worth;
    II. The nature of job evaluation and market rates;
    III. The institutionalization of compensation systems;
    IV. Foreign experience with comparable worth;
    V. The statistical analysis of discrimination within an organization;
    VI. The legal controversy and the potential regulatory quagmire.

The overview will end with, first, several personal conclusions as to the merit of implementing a comparable worth approach to job evaluation and, second, a discussion of the alternative approach of increased upward mobility.

The first paper, which was written by George T. Milkovich, concerns the "emerging debate" over pay differences between men and women. One major thrust of the Milkovich paper is an analysis of how pay should be determined. Should pay be based on equal pay for equal work, including traditionally evaluated payment relationships, or should pay be equal for jobs of "comparable worth"? In the discussion of this question, two issues are treated; the first is whether the currently accepted standard, equal pay for equal work, is discriminatory. The second involves the persistent gap between the earnings of men and those of women. The implication of this second issue is that if average earnings of both sexes were equal, pay would be free of sex discrimination. Milkovich structures his discussion by using both an equity analysis of compensation objectives, systems and practices, with special emphasis on the implications of job evaluation techniques, and a synopsis of the similarities and differences between the Equal Pay Act and Civil Rights Act of 1964. The reader is specifically referred to the discussion of comparable worth on pages 36 to 38.

Another important thrust of the Milkovich paper is a discussion of the measurement of the earnings gap and the gap's relation to the question of discrimination. The weaknesses and the analytical difficulties inherent in the use of regression analysis are ably described in both their "macro" and "micro" dimensions.

Milkovich imparts to the reader a strong statement of and feeling for "the case for" comparable worth and, at the same time, a strong statement of the substantial difficulties in the measurement of discrimination when confronted by the real world of compensation objectives and practices, with its multiplicity of institutional and environmental surrounding circumstances. Finally, the reader is urged to read Milkovich's "concluding observations" beginning on page 46. Clearly, comparable worth will not escape controversy.

The second paper in the study, which was written by Donald P. Schwab, has as its primary task the analysis of job evaluation. Schwab also relates job evaluation, however, to the concept of comparable worth, drawing upon a wide range of relevant research.

A most noteworthy aspect of the paper is Schwab's comparison between "job evaluation prescriptions," which appear to assume that evaluation through its system of compensable factors measures the worth of a job to an organization, and "job evaluation as theoretically prescribed is a mechanism for identifying worth based on job content. In fact, however, no definition of worth has been established, much less accepted." (See page 62.) In contrast, job evaluation as practiced "identifies and differentially weights compensable factors to maximize the relationship between them and the wages for key jobs which are assumed to reflect the market. Thus, the actual criterion of job evaluation is not worth in a job content sense, but market wages. The model (compensable factors and weights) emerging from this process is then applied to non-key jobs for purposes of establishing a wage hierarchy.'' (See page 63.)

As Schwab makes quite clear, job evaluation as practiced will not serve the supporters of comparable worth, and it is most difficult to discern how the technique could be fundamentally altered. Schwab's paper is a rich one, and his analysis is essential to any discussion of comparable worth.

George H. Hildebrand's wide-ranging paper concentrates on "the nature and significance of external labor markets as they relate to official efforts to alter particular internal wage structures to conform to the now-emerging theory of equal pay for jobs asserted to be of comparable worth." (See page 81.) Hildebrand pursues his analysis through the following topics:

1. Evolution and meaning of the theory of comparable worth;
2. The meaning of the notion of a labor market;
3. Comparable worth, job evaluation, and the external market for labor;
4. Key jobs and the external market for labor;
5. What is the worth of a job?
6. Some legal and economic aspects of the doctrine of comparable worth; and,
7. Some potential economic and political impacts of the comparative worth approach.

Each and every one of the above topics could be singled out for special emphasis. In point of fact, his final topic dealing with potential impacts of comparable worth will be relied upon heavily in the overview discussion of the potential regulatory quagmire.

Rather than attempt to deal in a cursory manner with Hildebrand's various topics, two quotations will be given, unfortunately out of context, to indicate two dimensions of the unintended consequences of a potential regulatory endeavor. The first is as follows:

> Two additional observations should be made. First, the contemplated extension of the principle of equal pay for substantially equal work to encompass the vague rhetoric of comparable work is directed in essence to the reconstruction and the regulation of the wage and salary structures of defendant firms and their component parts throughout the country. Potentially, the scope for this exercise has no limits beyond the personnel and administrative capacities of the government agencies that would enforce it. In short, even assuming that the full achievement of such control might take several years, the proposal leads directly to administrative wage control for the entire American economy. (See page 83.)

As to social consequences, Hildebrand states:

> In summary, economic theory tells us that if comparable worth is
> put into effect (1) unemployment rates for females will rise, (2)
> unemployment of females also will rise, (3) the major victims will be
> the poorest female workers, (4) welfare dependency will grow, (5)
> female youngsters will be large losers of job opportunities, and (6)
> there will be some withdrawal of discouraged women workers from
> the labor force, precisely because official policy, in the purported
> service of a peculiar concept of social justice, will have destroyed
> their jobs for them, despite their own efforts to be productive and
> self-supporting citizens. (See page 106.)

The fourth paper in the study was written by Herbert R. Northrup. It effectively captures both the logic of and the feeling for the institutionalization of job evaluation, and it contains a significant section on parity employment and comparable worth.

As Northrup describes in some detail, management developed job evaluation primarily in response to the rapid growth of unionism after the passage of the National Labor Relations Act in 1935. Job evaluation was developed in part to avoid unionization and in part to meet the challenge of collective bargaining. Some of the most significant plans, such as basic steel, became joint programs. During this period, the organizational hostility of the new industrial unions was demonstrated in many ways, not the least of which was in the perpetual flood of wage grievances exacerbated by the War Labor Board's constraint on general wage increases. Northrup ably portrays the events and trends of this period, especially in his discussions of the "Southern California Aircraft Industry" (page 112) and his analysis of "The Basic Steel Program." (See page 115.)

The fifth paper, by Janice R. Bellace, analyzes foreign experience with comparable worth. She begins her analysis with a discussion of Article 119 of the Treaty of Rome, which mandates equal pay in the European Community, and ILO Convention No. 100, Equal Remuneration between Men and Women of the International Labour Organisation. Bellace then reviews the various legal provisions in nine countries in the European Community, namely, Italy, Ireland, Denmark, France, Belgium, Luxembourg, Netherlands, Germany, and the United Kingdom, and in four other countries, Sweden, Canada, Australia, and New Zealand.

The paper by Harry V. Roberts deals with the statistical analysis of discrimination within an organization, concentrating on the statistical biases in the measurement of employment bias. In his analysis, Roberts uses factual data from the Harris Bank case, in which he served as an expert witness for the defendant. The essence of the results of his analysis is that the shortfall in female earnings is fully explained when the data have been adjusted for three biases. In other words, the adjusted data are more consistent with an assumption of nondiscrimination than with an assumption of discrimination.

The seventh and final paper in the study, which was written by Robert E. Williams and Douglas S. McDowell, concerns the legal framework of the Equal Pay controversy—equal work versus comparable worth. The authors base their review of the controversy on an extensive analysis of the legislative history of the Equal Pay Act of 1963 and of Title VII of the Civil Rights Act of 1964. The paper allows the reader to assess the extent to which the issues raised in the substantive papers in this study were captured in the legislative debates. In point of fact, the fundamental administrative difficulties in implementing comparable worth were well stated in the Congressional debates.

I. THE CONCEPT OF COMPARABLE WORTH

In its simplest terms, any discussion of comparable worth involves three fundamental facts. First, comparable worth has not been operationally defined by its supporters. Second, it is improbable that it will be so defined and, third, a non-arbitrary wage structure requires the use of job evaluation and market rate standards.

One of the most basic analytical points to be made with respect to the concept of comparable worth is that to date it has not been defined in operational terms. This is true with both the term "worth" and the term "comparable." All of the papers in this study stress this fact either by elaborating upon the non-operational character of comparable worth or by discussing the concept's decided ambiguity. Milkovich, for example, notes parenthetically that "no operational, practical definition seems to exist" (page 36) and he further states:

> Even if such a bias were empirically verified, the absence of a workable definition of comparable worth is particularly troublesome. Without a workable process akin to collective bargaining or to job analysis, evaluation and wage surveys, it is unclear how employers, unions, courts and agencies can apply comparable worth.[1]

Other papers make similar statements. For example, Hildebrand in his discussion of job evaluation states:

> It is important to note at the outset, however, that no 'value-free' system of evaluation has yet been shown to exist. To date, the notion of comparable worth involves sheer rhetoric alone; that is, it lacks operational meaning. (page 83).

---

[1] Milkovich appears to hold out some hope that further study and research may lead to operational definition. See his section on "comparable worth," page 36, particularly page 38. The present author regards this outcome as quite improbable.

Obviously, until comparable worth has been associated with some measurement device, the concept cannot be applied in any comprehensive or systematic manner. Any attempt to apply it without operational definition would result not only in endless debates but also in quite arbitrary results. In fact, without an operational definition, the concept cannot be analyzed or even discussed except in vague and philosophical terms.[2]

Turning to the second point noted above, it also appears quite improbable that comparable worth will be defined in operational terms. Supporters of the concept apparently reject measurement devices and standards which are now used in compensation systems, namely, traditional job evaluation techniques and wage rates prevailing in the market. As Milkovich points out in an insightful discussion (see pages 36-37, they are clearly ambivalent in their attitude toward job evaluation. On the one hand, they reject traditional job evaluation approaches as being dominated by market rates which they feel reflect discrimination. Implicit here is the additional rejection of market rates as a direct guide for the establishment of structural wage or salary relationships. On the other hand, these supporters still hold out hope for the development of a "bias-free" evaluation technique, which is improbable when related to the fundamental character of the job evaluation process. Existing job evaluation plans establish their dominant structural wage relationship from market rates, a point developed by the Schwab paper. As a result, without the use of traditional job evaluation and market standards, it is most difficult to understand how non-arbitrary structural wage and salary relationships can be established.[3]

The above paragraph states the essence of the third point initially made, namely, that a non-arbitrary wage structure appears to require the use of traditional job evaluation techniques and market rates. The plain fact is that no alternative standards are known to exist, and as has been stated, without operational standards, debate would be endless and the results of any attempted implementation would be quite arbitrary.

Such an assessment may appear extreme, but anyone who has worked in the development and administration of job evaluation systems is very much aware of the subjective nature of skill and responsibility requirements, as well as the difficulty of making comparative judgments as to working conditions and physical effort. When rating jobs with distinctly different types of skill, the rater is consciously and unconsciously guided by market rates. Consequently, if these judgments are reasonably valid, so-called bias-free evaluation would confront serious implementation as well as definitional issues.

----

[2] Superficially, the concept may be made "operational" by plotting separately on a scatter diagram average earnings for predominantly male and female jobs, drawing the respective lines of relationship between average earnings and evaluated points, and advocating that the earnings gap be closed by raising female rates of compensation as in the state of Washington study. (A relevant analysis of the earnings gap is contained in the paper by Harry V. Roberts.)

[3] This point is considered in more depth in the section of this paper on job evaluation and market rates, which begins on the following page.

Naturally, the question of alleged discrimination is the ultimate issue with respect to this paper and the project. From a logical basis, it is impossible to prove that a set of given structural wage or salary relationships are or are not discriminatory. Absent specific evidence showing employer intent, there is no universally accepted value system. Also, it is impossible to prove completely a negative, even though statistical inference, as developed by Harry Roberts, would strongly support a non-discriminatory explanation of salary relationships at least in the organizations studied.

On a less sophisticated level of analysis, however, it is very doubtful that viable, structural wage or salary relationships can be established except through use of evaluation and market standards. It is similarly doubtful that correctable salary *rate* discrimination exists in carefully administered wage and salary systems. Inappropriate *earnings* differentials can be corrected by increased upward mobility, and many organizations have greatly increased the rate of promotion of women employees, and thus their average earnings, initially under the stimulus of affirmative action programs. Clearly, increased upward mobility is an appropriate approach for corrective action.

II. THE NATURE OF JOB EVALUATION AND MARKET RATES

In almost all organizations, wage and salary structural relationships are determined by formal or informal job evaluation systems. Where the more informal job classification and individual rate systems prevail, they still follow evaluation procedures and standards, though no doubt less rigorously than in formal evaluation approaches.

At first, job evaluation was introduced primarily in response to the direct or indirect challenge of unionism. The fundamental purpose was to create "equitable" and "rational" wage and salary structures. Jobs were first described, then evaluated, and finally, wage rates were attached to the structure in a systematic manner. In point of fact, vastly improved wage and salary structures were developed and have been maintained. While wage and salary structures are again under challenge and review, it is doubtful that the fundamental characteristics of the systems can be changed.

The fundamental character of job evaluation, as developed by Schwab, is the integration of market rate and job content standards. He states:

As practiced, it serves the important administrative function of linking external and internal labor markets. Indeed, by using market key jobs as the actual criterion, job evaluation establishes a correspondence between the market and non-key job wage rates. No alternative procedure has been proposed that better performs this function. (See page 68.)

In formal point systems of job evaluation, this integration is achieved by a trial and error "best fit" approach, which relates points for key jobs to both the labor market rates for these jobs and the points used to score the jobs on the compensable factors which have been chosen for use in the evaluation system. In this integration process, various semi-independent or "non-competing groups" of jobs are put together into a single system.

In developing this skeletal point system for key jobs, the relationships have to make sense from a compensable factor point of view. Point relationships also must correlate reasonably well with market rates for key jobs and also with rates currently being paid on the jobs. If a job is a poor statistical fit from either a compensable factor or a labor market point of view, it is abandoned as a key job. Again, to achieve an improved statistical fit, the weight and average point scores given to the jobs on the various factors may require adjustment. In the evaluation process, "skill" is normally the dominant factor. "Responsibility" may have a reasonably heavy weight, while "physical effort" and "working conditions" tend to carry relatively low weights.[4]

As Schwab makes clear, market rates are dominant in this integration process, implying that relative skill is in fact judged by its assessment in the market. The rating process as applied through group judgment tends to make sense although there is in fact no way to measure or judge skill objectively. It is also true that individual judgments vary considerably. Individuals tend, from the point of view of their own values, to believe that the market undervalues their own type of skill or the types of skill with which they are most familiar, and probably, much of the philosophical argument surrounding comparable worth relates to this point. Clearly, whether market assessment of skill is in fact "equitable" can be endlessly debated, yet no alternate non-arbitrary standard has been devised.

In systems of job evaluation it could be argued that "responsibility" serves virtually as a *fudge* factor to modify skill ratings to fit the market. In basic steel, for example, skilled maintenance jobs are roughly at the middle of the point range, primarily because "skill" ratings are modified by the relative ratings on "responsibility." Similarly, "physical effort" and "working conditions" alter relative placement only by one or two labor grades in the typical evaluation system and again tend to achieve an improved "fit" with the market.

As several of the authors point out, payment systems have multiple objectives and a number of dimensions apart from job evaluation which bear upon the compensation of individuals. Among the additional factors bearing upon the pay of individuals are the following:

1. *The general level of wages and salaries.* The higher the general level the greater is the structural freedom from market constraints.

---

[4] Weighting is a complex topic which is not developed in this overview paper. See Schwab's discussion of job evaluation as practiced, particularly page 63.

2. *The size and comprenensiveness of the benefit package.* There is considerable variation in the division of compensation dollars between wages and benefits. Relatively high benefits may offset relatively low pay.

3. *The number of labor grades and the related wage or salary and point spread of these grades.* The fewer the labor grades within a given wage range, the less is the wage or salary differentiation among jobs. The wider the monetary spread of the labor grades the greater is the scope for payment distinctions among individuals working on the same job.

4. *The design and content of jobs and their related employee requirements.* The tasks of employees may be grouped into a relatively small number of broadly defined jobs or into a larger number of more specialized jobs. The design of jobs is highly particular to the individual organization.

5. *The nature of the reward system for the compensation of individuals within rate ranges, that is, the relative emphasis on merit or seniority.*

It is impossible to guess how far a regulatory agency would penetrate into the last three of these areas in an attempt to establish structural wage and salary relationships based on a particular interpretation of comparable worth. The above characteristics of payment systems are highly particular to a specific industry and organization and reflect value judgments on the part of those managements and unions directly involved. Federal or state regulations of these areas could readily inhibit managerial discretion and lead to quite arbitrary decisions. The belief is that potential equal employment challenges have already led employers away from merit based decisions. Promotion policies based on promotion of the "senior qualified" employee are tending to supplant merit policies, and "merit increases" within rate ranges have probably become more seniority oriented. Fred E. Foulkes' recently published study of personnel policies in leading nonunion companies indicates a surprising degree of seniority emphasis in so-called merit increase policies in these companies. There is no known research, however, which analyzes changes in these policies over the relevant years.[5]

Regulatory agencies, in an endeavor to move toward "bias-free" evaluation plans, also might modify the compensatory factors now used in traditional plans. For example, in industrial job evaluation wage plans, the commonly used compensable factor of "physical effort required" might be a target for removal as has been the case in Germany. In so far as such a factor improves the correlation of evaluation scores with market rates, however, it would be difficult to support such a change on other than philosophical grounds.

---

[5] Fred E. Foulkes, *Personnel Policies in Large Non-Union Companies* (Englewood, New Jersey: Prentice-Hall Inc., 1980).

Perhaps the most far-reaching change which regulatory agencies might attempt to achieve could be the substitution of a single evaluation plan for the multiple plans now used in different administrative units within an organization. The use of different office and factory evaluation systems is now widespread. Comparable worth, however, might be regarded as requiring direct comparison of blue and white collar jobs.

Job evaluation is a flexible administrative mechanism. A primary requirement, the integration of a market rate and compensable factor standard, can be achieved reasonably well by using either a single system or multiple systems, although it can be argued legitimately that a better evaluation point fit and a better wage fit can be achieved with multiple systems than with a single system. On the other hand, having worked with a single system that applied to all employees of the State of New Hampshire, this author recognizes that an adequate fit can be achieved by applying a single system to a wide variety of blue and white collar employees. The decision as to the use of a single or multiple systems should be made primarily, it is believed, on whether one or a number of administrative units are involved. For example, union and nonunion employees should not be combined in a single system. Technically, however, whether a single or multiple systems are used is not fundamental so long as the system is anchored to market rates.

It should be kept in mind that potential regulatory changes are not being contemplated against a background of relatively irrational and unplanned structural wage and salary relationships, as was the case when job evaluation was first introduced. Today's structural relationships are the result of well developed compensation systems. Also, current systems are decidedly institutionalized, a point which is developed in the paper by Northrup. As a result, any change directed at implementing some aspect of comparable worth would meet very substantial resistance and would be highly disruptive.

In the foregoing discussion, the terms "market rates" and "market rate standards" have been used as though such rates and standards were precise and easily ascertainable. This is far from the case, as is developed in the paper by Hildebrand.[6] Hildebrand notes that labor markets may be classified according to categories developed by Clark Kerr. Two types of markets are perhaps the most useful in establishing "key" jobs, although simply noting these two types does not do justice to a complex topic. The first type is the "'neo-classical market,' in which competition is effective enough to establish uniform market-clearing rates for well-defined occupations, and there are no unions." The second type is an "institutionalized market" in which collective bargaining establishes, at least roughly, a going rate. At times, however, it is necessary to use rates from "natural markets" in which

---

[6] Hildebrand's excellent wide-ranging paper will be used as the basis for the subsequent discussion of a potential regulatory quagmire. The present discussion of market rates as used in job evaluation will be held to bare essentials and will lean heavily upon his section, "Key jobs and the external market for labor." (page 89 ff.)

"competition is weak, occupations are poorly defined, and rates of compensation show much dispersion, even for comparable work." (See page 90.) While this is subject to various complexities, Hildebrand notes:

> The point should now be clear. Certain jobs are standardized, usually due to technology, across many firms in a given local labor market; in fact, they may reach across several industries as well. For example, on the blue-collar side, there are machinists and millwrights, or computer programmers, secretaries and accountants on the clerical side. These jobs provide the basis upon which the wage curve can be built, precisely because they tie the external and internal markets together. For these reasons, they are called key jobs. (See page 91.)

It may be appropriate in the circumstances of a given case to use only a small or a larger number of key jobs in linking the external and internal markets, but it is not necessary for the purposes of this discussion to consider the matter in greater detail.

III. THE INSTITUTIONALIZATION OF COMPENSATION SYSTEMS

As stated in the introductory remarks on Northrup's paper, job evaluation was developed primarily by managements to avoid unionization and to meet the challenge of collective bargaining. As noted earlier, some of the most interesting programs, such as basic steel, were jointly developed and implemented. The institutionalization of compensation systems was one phase of a developing union-management accommodation. Northrup notes the process of adjustment and the relationship of the institutionalization of compensation systems to it as follows:

> Collective bargaining requires that conditions of employment be determined by a set of rules—'a system of industrial jurisprudence,' as the late Professor Sumner H. Slichter termed it. Wage structure relationships are at the center of these rules, fundamental both to wage setting and administration and to the orderly establishment and handling of almost all other terms and conditions of employment. Job evaluation or other wage classification schemes not only determine the relationships of tasks and therefore wage differentials, but also provide for a means of orderly job progression and transfer. As a result, the methods for determining such relationships are inextricably intertwined with seniority, promotions, layoffs, training, and all other aspects of intraplant mobility. Unless the relationship of jobs is agreed upon, any orderly disposition of labor-management issues, both in negotiating new contracts

and in administering existing ones, becomes extremely difficult. Moreover, once agreed upon, job relationships change as technology improves, methods are perfected, or products or tasks are altered and, thus, a satisfactory relationship of jobs and compensation requires that the parties to a collective agreement design a system to settle disputes between the contract's effective dates. (See page 109.)

The institutionalization of job evaluation and other compensation systems required the incorporation of these systems directly or by reference into the labor agreement. But the essence of the institutionalization process was holding constant all wage and salary rates during the term of the labor agreement except in the case of new or changed jobs. With respect to new and changed jobs, job evaluation became an orderly procedure for establishing their rate of compensation and thus, continuous wage grievance turbulence ended.

IV. FOREIGN EXPERIENCE WITH COMPARABLE WORTH

No attempt will be made to discuss the richness of detail in Janice R. Bellace's paper. The perspective the reader receives from her review of foreign experience, however, is highly suggestive of possible future developments in the United States.

A first and major conclusion from her analysis is that none of the countries has attempted a comprehensive program to implement comparable worth. As a matter of fact, many are at a stage of removing or reducing blatantly discriminatory sex differentials for identical or highly similar work. It also should be noted that evaluation systems are not nearly so common in most foreign countries as in the United States, and structural wage differentials are established on the basis of quite broad and general occupational classifications. There are, nonetheless, a few countries where job evaluation is widely practiced and is even more pervasive than in the United States.

As in this country, there is no foreign definition of comparable worth, nor is there uniformity as to the definition of "equal value," a term commonly found in European statutes and international agreements. As a result, there are similar problems with the lack of an operational definition. Unlike the United States, however, it would seem that the foreign countries have in fact consciously or unconsciously appreciated this difficulty and have not attempted comprehensive programs.

A second conclusion worthy of note is that comparable worth would seem to have limited value for countries with highly egalitarian wage policies. Where all wage differentials have been drastically narrowed, only limited discrimination could conceivably exist. In such countries there has not been widespread interest in comparable worth, but this also appears to be true of most of the foreign countries reviewed.

The most suggestive dimension of foreign experience is the approach being taken in those countries most actively concerned with the topic, particularly Germany and the United Kingdom, and readers are urged to study Bellace's analysis of trends there. In those countries, the attack on existing wage structures has been limited to particular issues and situations. For example, in Germany the use of physical effort as a compensable factor in job evaluation is being questioned, as has been the creation of "light work" labor grades as disguised discrimination. An enforcement approach in the United States requiring similar modifications in job evaluation systems would have a widespread and disturbing impact.

V. THE STATISTICAL ANALYSIS OF DISCRIMINATION WITHIN AN ORGANIZATION

Robert's paper on statistical bias in the measurement of alleged discrimination, as well as his more detailed Harris Trust and Savings Bank study, make an essential contribution to this project by dispelling the apparent widespread notion of discrimination in pay. Statistical studies of alleged discrimination in rates of pay are meaningful from a regulatory point of view only when carried out, as in the Roberts' study, within the confines of an organization. The necessity to conduct appropriate analysis within an organization is based on the fact that it is only within an organization that the individual rates of pay used in compiling male and female averages can be adjusted for differences in seniority and other productivity or equity variables associated with an individual's pay. Also, study within an organization is necessary to restrict comparison to individuals working on the same or closely similar jobs. Possible discrimination in rates of pay, as distinct from possible discrimination in average earnings, can exist in a meaningful sense only among individuals performing essentially the same work. Average earnings, on the other hand, aggregate all types of work, both similar and dissimilar. They represent a hierarchy of evaluated labor grades. Thus, differences in male and female average earnings could arise from barriers to upward mobility, and can and should be corrected not by adjustment of rates of pay but by appropriate training and promotion policies. Positive programs to correct this type of shortfall in female earnings are increasingly effective.

Roberts makes three bias adjustments in the Harris Bank data. One is for seniority (length of service), a technical correction. As Roberts states: "Of course, any technical inadequacy of regression can distort conclusions. In my experience, however, the main technical inadequacy that is likely to lead to a biasing effect is the flawed treatment of seniority." (See page 194.)

The purpose of this bias adjustment is to achieve a proper mathematical fit in the relationship between seniority and rate of pay. See his section II, beginning on page 179, more particularly the section beginning on page 193.

A second bias adjustment is needed to confine the analysis to individuals performing similar work. This adjustment is carried out by restricting the analysis to employees within "non-competing" groups. In the Harris case, these "non-competing" groups were established by agreement with the regulatory agency. (See the Roberts' discussion, page 192, "Noncompeting Groups and 'Job Segregation'.") The third and most important of the bias adjustments is the "underadjustment bias." (See page 183.) The technical aspects of this adjustment will not be discussed here, but its purpose is to correct for differences in seniority, age, experience, and years of education. It is decidedly interesting that these variables are so significantly related to pay. From a job evaluation perspective, a simple explanation of the purpose of this adjustment is to correct for differences in pay rate variation among individuals working on the same or similar jobs to achieve a more accurate comparison of male and female job rate averages.

While the statistical complexities involved in carrying out the corrections for the three biases are rather forbidding, the results are decidedly impressive. The comparison in male and female earnings after adjustment is more consistent with an assumption of nondiscrimination than with an assumption of discrimination.[7]

Although Roberts avoids any generalization beyond his data, it is reasonable to presume that most companies with professional wage administration would be found to have a nondiscriminatory wage and salary structure. Problems associated with merit systems of individual compensation are more formidable, but these systems too should typically be non-discriminatory. They are either increasingly meeting the challenges of an open climate and grievance procedure or are giving way to seniority-based systems. Today, companies with personnel policies worthy of the name are rapidly removing the vestiges of any past discriminatory practices.

VI. THE LEGAL CONTROVERSY AND THE
POTENTIAL REGULATORY
QUAGMIRE

If the Equal Pay Act of 1963 had in fact required equal pay for comparable work, that is, if it had adopted the comparable worth concept, a

---

[7] The reader wishing to pursue the statistical analysis is strongly urged to study Roberts' longer analysis: Roberts, Harry V., "Harris Trust and Savings Bank: An Analysis of Employee Compensation," Center for Mathematical Studies in Business and Economics, University of Chicago, (1979).

veritable regulatory quagmire would have been created. It is by no means clear, in the first place, how the law would have been implemented or how a regulatory agency actually would have carried out its mandate from a procedural standpoint. For example, the future status of existing wage provisions in labor agreements is not known. Most wage agreements, as has been noted earlier, currently require that wage rates for particular jobs remain fixed for the duration of the agreements except in the case of new or changed jobs. It is possible the law would have reestablished the right to challenge job rates at any time and, undoubtedly, there would have been numerous administrative issues concerning the scope and timing of comparable worth challenges and decisions, including the question of whether one could compare rates in union and nonunion administrative units. Almost regardless of how these procedural issues were resolved, the end result would have been highly disruptive.

Moreover, the scope and difficulty of the regulatory task would have been enormous, a factor which Hildebrand discusses in "Some Potential Economic and Political Impacts of the Comparative Worth Approach." (See page 102.) Essentially, regulation would have involved the wage and salary structural relationships of the entire labor force. Also, the administrative agency charged with this regulation would have been asked to determine what constituted comparable work without the benefit of any operational standards. As Hildebrand notes, the only somewhat similar administrative task was the War Labor Board's regulation of "intraplant inequity." But, in point of fact, the War Labor Board did not attempt to pass upon the merits of these cases.

During World War II, the Board, particularly the regional agencies, received vast numbers of requests either by employees or jointly by employers and unions for adjustments in wage rates for one or at most a few jobs which involved more than a small number of employees. Technically, the wage analysts in the regions were required to pass upon the merits of these cases and determine whether an inequity existed which warranted correction. In reality, however, such a process was impossible. Decisions often were routine. For example, a wage analyst sitting in Boston would be charged with deciding whether a request for a wage adjustment on some specialized job, such as a position in a metal working plant in Springfield, Vermont, warranted an upward adjustment of ten cents an hour to remove an inequity resulting from a comparison between that job and some other specialized position in the plant. Since the inflationary impact of these individual adjustments was relatively small, any plausible reason was accepted by the analysts and such adjustments were normally approved. Given the actual experience of the War Labor Board, it is not difficult to speculate that an attempt to make *legitimate* decisions, all of which would be controversial, to implement a law requiring "equal pay for jobs of comparable worth," and without operational standards, would be utterly hopeless.

Fortunately, the legislative debate, as developed by Williams and McDowell, shows that Congress recognized the wisdom of requiring equal pay for equal (substantially similar) work. As these authors state:

> To summarize the legal precedents, it can be stated that Title VII and the Equal Pay Act, read together, provide a statutory scheme whereby qualified female employees are guaranteed access to all jobs. At the same time, Congress intended that federal agencies and the courts should not become involved in evaluating the relative worth of dissimilar jobs. (See page 204.)

A thoroughly developed description of the legislative debate can be found in the Williams and McDowell paper. At the very least, the reader is urged to read Section VIII., "Summary and Conclusion." (See page 244.) As the authors state:

> Among the advantages Congress found in the more limited "equal work" concept were: (1) that it is less vague than the "comparable work" approach, and not as difficult to enforce; (2) that it recognizes the expertise and experience of private parties in job evaluation matters; and (3) that it would not inject federal regulators and the courts into an area where they had little expertise. (See page 244.)

And finally:

> Application of the "equal work" standard involves primarily factual determinations and does not require the courts to engage in extensive comparisons of dissimilar jobs. The inquiry, rather, is whether or not the jobs in question are the same. (See page 246.)

Not only is the equal work standard easier to regulate, it also effectively eliminates direct sex discrimination in compensation since it applies to each and every job.

VII. SOME CONCLUSIONS

There are two broad conclusions to be drawn from this study. First, any attempted implementation of comparable worth would encounter substantial difficulties and would have disruptive and undesirable consequences; and second, there is a viable alternative—the accelerated promotion of women, particularly within the managerial and professional hierarchy, which is being effectively pursued by many companies.

The various difficulties inherent in any attempted implementation of comparable worth begins with the ambiguous character of the concept and its lack of operational definition. Comparable worth is based upon a rejection of traditional job evaluation plans and market rate standards and would substitute in their place some undetermined form of bias-free or value-free job evaluation. Support for such an approach fails to appreciate the realities of how evaluation procedures actually operate, an analytical consideration which is the central focus of the paper by Schwab. In fact, any approach to the establishment of structural wage relationships, which is not based on market rates and job evaluation as practiced, is difficult to comprehend. Additionally, if some way were found to surmount the serious difficulties with implementation, the various "harsh consequences" enumerated by Hildebrand gradually would follow, not the least of which would be an administrative quagmire.

Nonetheless, logical difficulties and potential problems will not halt the political and social pressures to correct the alleged discrimination associated with the world-wide rise in female participation rates. At the very least, some proposed changes in job evaluation systems are likely to gain official support, a development which already has occurred in several foreign countries, particularly Germany and the United Kingdom. It is impossible at this time, however, to state what the specific developments in the United States will be, or to predict even generally their consequences. Much may depend upon the vigor with which upward mobility programs are pursued and their impact upon relative average earnings.

Clearly, the increased upward mobility of women within the employment and compensation hierarchies is a logical method of raising the relative average earnings of women, and is not attended by the problems and difficulties associated with comparable worth. The principle objection to its use, however, is that it is far too slow to be effective.

In fact, this objection may not be as compelling as it seems initially. Recently, there have been statistical indications of a substantial upward mobility of women, as well as changes in labor force participation patterns which portend further future advances for females.[8] Census data indicate, for example, that the number of women employed as managers and administrators (non-farm) increased from 1.0 million in 1970 to nearly 2.6 million in 1979. The significance of this increase is highlighted by a comparison with the number of females in the clerical workforce. In 1970, there was one woman employed as a manager for every ten females employed in clerical positions. From 1970 to 1979, however, for each increase of ten in the number of female clericals, the number of women employed as managers increased by four. In 1970, women filled approximately 16 percent of all manager positions, but by 1979 the number had risen to 24.4 percent. Another example is seen in the dramatic increase in the number of female lawyers and judges from 13,182 in 1970 to more than 61,000 in 1979. Women accounted for 4.8 percent of all individuals working as lawyers and judges in 1970; by 1979, this figure had

---

[8] 1970 Census of the Population, Employment and Earnings, January 1980.

risen to 12.8 percent. During this same period, both the percentage of craft workers who are women and the percentage of service workers (excluding private households) who are women remained about the same. Indeed, the strong upward trends have been in select professional and managerial employments.

Moreover, there have been very interesting changes in the age pattern of participation of women. For example, about 38 percent of women born during 1886–1895 participated in the labor force when they were 20–24 years old. The participation rate of these women fell to about 26 percent when they were 25–34 and then increased only slightly as they grew older. Very few of these women who had left the labor force to have children re-entered as they grew older.

A sharp contrast with the above is seen in the pattern of labor force participation by younger groups, *i.e.,* those born in 1896–1915, 1916–1925, 1926–1935, 1936–1945, and 1946–1955. Among these age groups three trends emerge:

1. With each younger age group the participation rate at age 20–24 increases, rising from about 38 percent for those born in 1886–1895 to 60 percent for those born in 1946–1955;
2. The decline in participation rates at age 25–34 becomes much less marked, in fact disappearing for those born in 1946–1955; and
3. The re-entry pattern becomes much steeper. For example, about 47 percent of the women born in 1936–1945 participated in the labor force at age 20–24. This participation rate fell to only about 45 percent at age 25–34 and has increased to more than 60 percent at age 35–44.

As the above data demonstrate, the dramatically increasing participation rates for younger women and the emerging favorable employment trends demonstrate that mobility is working. Similar trends exist for minorities. The fact that upward mobility is working does not, however, obviate the necessity to continue to strengthen training and promotion policies and practices and to meet remaining elements of actual and alleged discrimination through effective personnel policies. The "bottom line" in the management of human resources is to create a positive and open climate for employee relations. In such an environment, allegations of discrimination will receive a positive response regardless of the specific content of the complaint or whether it arises in a union situation. Both formal and informal grievance procedures are important feedback mechanisms in creating a positive employee relations climate, and a positive managerial response through such mechanisms represents social advance. Given the success of and the continued potential for upward mobility, and the problems associated with the implementation of comparable worth, it is most doubtful that new legal or regulatory controls are appropriate.

THE EMERGING DEBATE

by
George T. Milkovich

Professor Milkovich identifies the principal issues underlying the emerging debate over the pay differences between men and women and the systems used to determine wages. Focusing on the question of how pay should be set, he compares the currently accepted standard, equal pay for equal or substantially similar work, with the notion of comparable worth and then discusses the measurement of the earnings gap between men and women. He notes that a preliminary analysis of comparable worth has never been produced and that there is no common understanding of the relationship between contemporary compensation systems, such as job evaluation and market surveys, and female/male wage differences. Similar confusion exists concerning the consequences of governmental intervention into the wage determination process. Professor Milkovich concludes that, until these fundamental issues are more fully understood, existing pay differences should be resolved through the vigorous application of equal opportunity and affirmative action.

George T. Milkovich is a Professor of Human Resources at the Center for Human Resources Research in the School of Management at the State University of New York at Buffalo. After receiving his Ph.D. in Industrial Relations at the University of Minnesota in 1970, he was a Professor at the University's Graduate School of Business and a Visiting Professor at the School of Industrial and Labor Relations at Cornell University and the Graduate School of Management at UCLA. Dr. Milkovich is a member of the Industrial Relations Research Association and the Academy of Management and currently is the President of the latter's Human Resources Division. He has written extensively in the areas of compensation theory and equal employment opportunity, and his publications include a chapter with Frank Krzystofiak entitled, "Equal Employment Issues: A Perspective," in *Human Resources Management Readings* (Prentice Hall, 1979); and "The Concepts of Equity in Compensation, EEO and Job Evaluation" in *Job Evaluation and Equal Opportunity* (Industrial Relations Counselors, 1979). Dr. Milkovich is the co-editor of *Affirmative Action Planning Concepts*, an upcoming book based on papers presented at OFCCP's Conference at Cornell University, and he is preparing a text on compensation administration for Business Publications, Inc.

THE EMERGING DEBATE

A significant national debate over the pay differences between men and women and the systems used to determine wage rates has emerged.[1] While all the questions have yet to crystallize, two basic issues seem to underlie the controversy. The first is whether the currently accepted standard, equal pay for equal work, is discriminatory, and if so, should it be replaced with another standard, equal pay for work of comparable worth. Underlying this issue is whether wage differences observed in labor markets should continue to serve as a factor in the determination of the relative value of work. The challenge to the equal pay for equal work standard also questions whether current compensation systems, specifically job evaluation and market surveys, simply perpetuate the discriminatory practices alleged to be reflected in the market.[*]

A second, perhaps more basic issue in the debate, involves the persistent gap between the earnings of men and those of women. The oft-quoted datum, "The average earnings of fully employed women in 1978 ($8,583) is 58% of the fully employed male average earnings ($14,790)" is used in the popular press to highlight the issue. Some assert that this earnings gap is proof of discriminatory compensation practices, the implication being that if average earnings of both sexes were equal, society would have achieved employment relations free of sex discrimination. The focus is on differences in rates for jobs traditionally dominated by women (e.g., office and clerical) versus rates for male-dominated jobs (e.g., managerial and crafts). The underlying question, therefore, is whether the relatively lower average wages paid for clerical, office, and operatives jobs is attributable to work-related factors, such as the job's relative contributions to the production of goods and services, the degree of unionization, and employer and industry characteristics? Or are the differences in wages principally a result of discriminatory traditions that "crowd" women into traditional jobs, which in turn depress the wage rates for those jobs?

---

* Comments of Jerry Newman, Frank Krzystofiak and the other authors of the study on an earlier draft of this chapter are greatly appreciated.

[1] Pay in this chapter refers to all payments, direct and indirect.

The potential resolution of these issues will have far-reaching consequences'. Society in the 1980's, through governmental and judicial interpretation of existing legislation and through possible additional legislation,
faces at least two basic policy options. One is to reduce the earnings gap between men and women by requiring employers and unions to raise the rates
for relatively lower paid jobs (in which larger proportions of women have
traditionally been employed) to match rates for higher paid, "male
dominated" jobs. The other is to avoid tampering with the vast array of
wage structures and wage determination systems found in the economy and,
instead, rely upon the removal of discriminatory barriers that have
historically hindered women's entry into the higher paid jobs, through
vigorous enforcement of equal employment and affirmative action practices.

This paper will serve to introduce the issues in this debate. It will examine the differing standards of equal work versus comparable worth and
the implications for contemporary pay practices. Also, it will analyze the
"earnings gap" and the models and research that underlie much of our information about this "gap." Subsequent papers in this study examine
specific aspects of these issues and other related issues in greater detail.

I. EQUAL PAY: FOR EQUAL WORK
OR FOR WORK OF COMPARABLE WORTH?

Equal work and work of comparable worth represent very different
standards on which to base pay. Equal work, a standard underlying contemporary compensation systems, has a reasonably well-accepted interpretation in labor-management relations, within the judicial system, and
among compensation experts. By contrast, the notion of comparable worth
does not have as clear a definition, and perhaps therein lies some of the confusion and concern. Comparable worth appears to take on different mean-
ings to different people. It seems to have become a rallying cry for those who
perceive the "earnings gap" as an example of the social injustice present in
United States society. For others, comparable worth is a behavioral or social
science construct, akin to "organization climate" or "quality of working
life," for which researchers may attempt to develop measures and conduct
investigations. This section of the paper examines equal work and comparable worth, their respective definitions, and their implications for pay decisions.

A. *Equal Work*
Equal work is work of similar content, requiring that similar work
behaviors and tasks be performed under similar working conditions, and re-

quiring similar responsibilities, efforts, and abilities. The entire focus of equal work is job-related. Within contemporary compensation systems, the objective is to pay jobs of equal work content equally and, just as importantly, to pay jobs with different work content differently, based upon the relative value of the work to the organization's objectives.

At this point, some background in contemporary compensation practice is necessary to appreciate more fully the role of the equal work standard in the process of the determination of pay.[2] Most compensation systems have multiple objectives; for example, those listed in Figure 1, "to influence employee decisions to join, to remain, and to work efficiently in a cost-effective manner" are commonly found in corporate compensation policy manuals.

Figure 1

**COMPENSATION SYSTEM: BASIC CONCEPTS,
COMPONENTS AND OBJECTIVES**

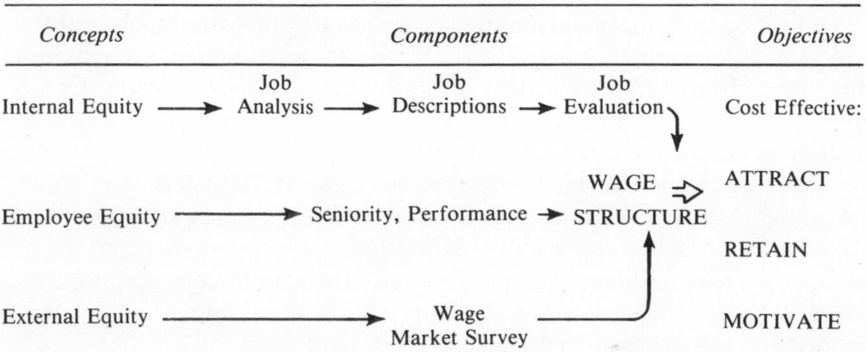

Concepts	*Components*			*Objectives*
Internal Equity →	Job Analysis →	Job Descriptions →	Job Evaluation ↘	Cost Effective:
			WAGE ⇒	ATTRACT
Employee Equity ⟶		Seniority, Performance →	STRUCTURE	
			↑	RETAIN
External Equity ⟶		Wage Market Survey		MOTIVATE

While compensation systems have multiple objectives, these objectives may differ among employers generally, or even within the same employer at different locations or at different times. Some organizations, for example, may not try to influence workforce productivity with pay for performance or with incentive pay systems, but will emphasize the attraction and retention of a competent workforce as the principal objectives. Still other organizations may simply focus on minimizing costs, and thus set as low a wage as possible.

1. *Internal Equity.* To achieve these objectives, compensation systems are designed to balance at least three concepts of equity in setting pay rates; internal, external and employee equity. Internal equity refers to the relationships of different jobs within an organization. How, for example, does the

---

[2] Entire textbooks examine compensation systems in considerable detail. The interested reader is urged to refer to these more detailed treatments. David W. Belcher's *Compensation Administration* (Englewood, New Jersey: Prentice Hall, 1974) is acknowledged as a classic.

work of the key punch operator compare to the work of the computer operator to the programmer to the systems analyst? The relationships among jobs yield the job structure or the levels of work found in an organization. They reflect the fact that the content of one set of tasks and behaviors (a job) is either equal to or different from another set of tasks and behaviors. Furthermore, the relative value of the contributions of these jobs is based on their work content and its contribution to the accomplishment of the organization goals. For example, the contribution to the organization of a systems analyst who designs a new inventory or production control system is greater than the contribution of the job that programs the system or that key punches the program. Thus, internal equity, or the relationships among jobs within the organization, has two aspects: (1) the relative similarities and differences in work content of jobs, and (2) the relative value or contribution of the work to the organization's goals.

Internal equity is operationalized in compensation systems through a sequence of processes. The first of these is job analysis, which is the systematic collection of information about the tasks performed, the abilities and behaviors required to perform them, and the environment under which they are performed.[3] The results of job analysis are summarized in job descriptions or work descriptions, which usually consist of a one- or two-page summary of the job.

Job evaluation, the third process in the sequence for determining internal equity, is the systematic evaluation of job descriptions (summaries of job content) to determine a job structure based upon the contributions or value of the jobs to the organization's goals. Through these procedures, internal equity is translated into a structure of jobs based upon the work performed and the value of this work to the organization.

Job evaluation has received special attention in the debate over equal work and comparable worth, as evidenced by the National Academy of Sciences' contract with the Equal Employment Opportunity Commission.[4] The other two processes, job analysis and preparation of job descriptions, have received less attention in the debate, though it can be argued that both are crucial. It is only through proper job analysis that the job-relatedness of most pay decisions, and for that matter, most human resource decisions, can be justified.

---

[3] While internal equity, through job analysis, job descriptions and job evaluation, focuses on the job and not on the individual employee, it is incorrect to assume that employee skills and abilities do not enter into the design and tailoring of work. The notion that people are somehow fixed and matched to jobs as pegs to holes is antiquated. Jobs are designed and tailored to fit workforce capabilities and employees seek out education and are trained to match job requirements. It is a dynamic interplay between job content and employee qualifications.

[4] See Donald J. Treiman, "Job Evaluation: An Analytical Review," (Interim Report to the Equal Employment Opportunity Commission, Washington, D.C. National Academy of Sciences, 1979). Also see D. P. Schwab's paper in this volume.

As the following list indicates, perceptions of job evaluation seem as diverse as the blind men viewing the elephant:

1. Aids in determining the essential similarities and differences in job duties, tasks and action.
2. Within a job family or occupation, determines the relative contribution or value of jobs to an organization.
3. Aims at providing a systematic-objective basis for the comparison of job contents.
4. Is a method which helps to establish a justified rank order of jobs—it is only one of the starting points for establishing the relative differentiation of wage rates.
5. Is to establish a mutually acceptable criterion of equity.
6. Aim is to establish on an agreed logical basis the relative values of different jobs in a given plant or industry. Job evaluation does not, of course, take the place of established procedure for bargaining between employers and workers, but use of a system of job evaluation may facilitate the development and maintenance of an equitable relationship among different jobs.
7. Is an attempt to determine and compare the demands which the normal performance of particular jobs make on normal workers without taking account of the individual's abilities or performance of the work concerned.[5]

Two basic aspects of job evaluation emerge from these views:

1. *A measurement aspect:* That job evaluation, properly developed and administered, is a relatively objective, systematic, analytical process which assesses both the similarities and differences in the *content of work*, and the *relative value of the work* to the organization;
2. A "rules of the game" or *process aspect:* That job evaluation, properly administered, provides procedures through which various interested parties interact and exchange views pertinent to the content of work and its relative value.

Under the former view, the premise is that the two key constructs, work content and relative value of the content, can be assessed in some acceptable, objective manner. The view is not new; in the 1930's and 1940's, industrial engineers, psychologists, and management scientists worked toward developing job evaluation as a relatively objective approach to

---

[5] For these and other views on job evaluation, see *Job Evaluation* (Geneva: International Labour Organisation, 1960).

measuring the content of work and its relative value.[6] Renewed interest in the measurement aspects of job evaluation again appeared in the 1970's, and Schwab's chapter in this volume reflects this interest.[7]

There is a need to distinguish between a job evaluation plan as originally developed and the plan as it is applied and used over the years. At the time of its development, a job evaluation plan is designed to model the existing pay structure. In so doing, the plan is intended to incorporate the external economic forces as well as the existing customs and conventions of the work environment. Over time the pay differences may change as well as the norms and relationships of job content. Several studies have found that the weights and factors originally developed to mirror the prevailing pay structures had been modified through the application of the plan.[8]

The other characteristic of job evaluation, the process to achieve a consensus on differences in pay, emphasizes the non-measurement, "rules of the game." In this view, Livernash observed that "Job evaluation is not a rigid, objective analytical procedure. Neither is it a meaningless process of rationalization. Job evaluation must produce acceptable results. The results may be judged from two bases: wage relationships among key jobs or relationships within clusters. Job evaluation is tested by the degree of correlation achieved between points of key jobs and acceptable wage relationships."[9] He further points out that historically job evaluation was developed to bring some order and acceptance to the hodgepodge of unrelated wage rates that existed in the 1930's and 1940's.

To gain acceptance of pay differences, the job evaluation process involves the various parties concerned about pay differences. In some situations this includes union and management representatives; in others it involves compensation committee representatives from various functions or divisions of management to higgle over the appropriate slotting of jobs into a pay structure. To effectively achieve acceptance of pay differentials, the

---

[6] For example, see Jay L. Otis and Richard H. Leukart, *Job Evaluation*, 2nd edition (Englewood Cliffs, New Jersey: Prentice Hall, Inc. 1954); C. H. Lawshe, Jr. and R. F. Wilson, "Studies in Job Evaluation: 6. The Reliability of Two Point Rating Systems," *Journal of Applied Psychology*, 31, (1947), pp. 355–65.

[7] The U.S. Civil Service Commission recently completed an extensive revision of their classification systems. The techniques and research designs used reflected the state-of-the-art in measurement. For example, see J. M. Madden, *An Application to Job Evaluation of a Policy Capturing Model for Analyzing Individual and Group Judgment*, Technical Report PRL—TDR—63—15, AD—417—273, Lackland Air Force Base, Texas (1963); R. C. Mecham and E. J. McCormick, *The Use in Job Evaluation of Job Elements and Job Dimensions*, Purdue University, Occupational Research Center (1969); David D. Robinson, et al., "Comparison of Job Evaluation Methods," *Journal of Applied Psychology*, 59, (1974), pp. 633–37; L. R. Gomez-Mejia, R. C. Page and W. W. Tornow, *Traditional vs. Statistical Job Evaluation* (Minneapolis: Control Data Corporation, Research Report 169-79, 1979).

[8] W. M. Fox, "Purpose and Validity in Job Evaluation," *Personnel Journal*, (October 1962) pp. 432–37.

[9] E. Robert Livernash, "The Internal Wage Structure," in G. W. Taylor and F. C. Pierson (ed), *New Concepts in Wage Determination* (New York: McGraw-Hill, 1957), pp. 140–72.

job evaluation process must be relatively open to the participation of all relevant parties. Perhaps current and future plans must include wider participation of various employee groups. However, the prospect of wider participation raises such issues as which employee groups to include, how to insure fair representation, etc.

2. *External Equity.* The second aspect of equity shown in Figure 1, external equity, refers to the relationships among jobs among employers in the external labor market. The basic issues to be answered in external equity are how do other relevant employers pay for equal work, and how do we wish to pay for it? External equity is established by determining the going rate for similar work in relevant external labor markets. These rates for jobs are usually established through a process of surveying the practices of other employers, yet the process is more involved than it may seem. It requires that the following sequence of decisions be faced:

1. Which employers should be included in the survey?
2. Is the work content of the jobs described by surveyed employers equal?
3. How is "pay" to be defined?
4. Which wage policy is consistent with the organization objectives?[10]

The question of which employers to include in the survey process is a critical decision in the wage determination process. Should all those employers who use the jobs under question be included, regardless of size, industry and geographic location? A partial answer involves the definition of the relevant labor markets for each specific job for each employer. These labor markets are based in part on the product/service markets in which the employer competes, as well as the type of skills and abilities the job requires. It is of some interest to note that the process for establishing the relevant external labor markets, and the relevant employers to survey has not been raised in the debate over equal work versus comparable worth; nor, it would seem, has the process been systematically researched by wage and salary experts.[11]

Another decision which must be faced in the determination of the going rate is whether the content of the jobs to be surveyed are similar to those under analysis. For example, does the work content of a programmer position in one organization require knowledge of only the BASIC language, whereas the job in the employer surveyed require proficiency in a range of languages including BASIC, COBOL, and PL 1? In the latter case the two "programmer" jobs are dissimilar and should not be matched in the survey.

---

[10] For greater detail on the survey process, see David W. Belcher, *Compensation Administration* (Englewood Cliffs, New Jersey: Prentice Hall, 1974).

[11] It should also be noted that other compensation decisions, such as the process of establishing pay grades, ranges and progression schedules, require additional analysis.

Other decisions, such as determining precise definitions of "pay" and statements of wage policy, are also critical in the process of establishing going rates. The need to define pay is apparent if one realizes that actual rates paid for work may differ from pay ranges, that total or gross pay (including the opportunity to accumulate overtime pay) differs from base pay, and that some employers offer superior benefit packages and less "pay" than others. The concern in establishing the going rate is to ensure comparison of "apples to apples."

The wage policy issue refers to the decision to set wage rates at a rate that matches, leads, or follows the going rate established in the market. While the rationale underlying each policy is beyond the scope of this paper, it is relevant to note that employers differ in their approach to the market. For example, some employers adopt a "wage leader" policy; that is, they set their rates above going rates for equal work in the market to insure that a highly qualified and efficient workforce will apply for their job opportunities. These differences in approaches to the labor markets reflect the high degree of decentralization and uniqueness that exist in wage determination procedures.

3. *Employee Equity.* Employee equity is the third aspect of equity incorporated in compensation systems. Employee equity focuses on the relationships among individual employees employed in similar work within an employer. For example, should one programmer be paid differently from another if one has greater seniority and/or superior performance, or should all programmers receive the same pay? This aspect of equity focuses directly on the individual employees in relationship to the work performed. Merit or "pay for performance" and seniority or "automatic progression" are common practices designed to recognize work-related differences among individuals performing equal work.

The standard of equal pay for equal work is a factor in all three aspects of equity. Internal equity focuses on the assessment of equal and different work through the operations of job analysis, job description, and job evaluation. The concerns for matching specific work content, "apples to apples," in the wage and salary survey process insures that equal work is being compared across employers when the "going rates" in the relevant labor markets are determined. Finally, the equal work standard is seen in the use of performance and seniority or experience to determine pay differences. Such systems recognize that differences in performance and/or experience within equal jobs can be recognized with pay. Thus, the equal work standard is a critical factor in the wage determination process.

The previous discussion was intended to provide a brief overview of contemporary compensation systems. The danger is that a reader will conclude that a simple, uniform set of practices exists. In a society and economy as diverse as the United States, compensation practices and wage decisions are equally diverse and complex. These may include the absence of any formal system, or job analysis plans, multiple job evaluation systems, multiple wage surveys, differential geographic allowances, group and individual incentive and bonus arrangements, lump sum awards, seniority, merit, COLA increments, international arrangements, varying wage policies, and arrangements in which employees participate in a variety of compensation committees.

The above list includes only some of the direct compensation systems; indirect compensation or benefit systems are equally diverse. Furthermore, the influence of unions has not been discussed; obviously, they play a critical role in the determination of wage settlements, establishing wage patterns, and even influencing, in some cases, the details included in job analysis, job descriptions, and evaluation. The role of collective bargaining in wage determination is examined in the Northrup paper in this collection.

B. *Equal Work Among Occupations*

In the current debate over equal work and comparable worth, it is important to consider the process by which occupational pay differences evolve. For example, what are the bases for wage differences between key punch operators versus programmers, or typists and secretaries versus electronic component assemblers versus plumbers or electricians? One criticism of the equal work standard is that while processes such as job evaluation, job analysis, performance evaluation and incentive pay may perform a reasonable function within job families or groups of jobs related in work content, they are not as useful in the establishment of wage rates among jobs with diverse work content. The fact that some organizations use multiple job evaluation systems, e.g., one for office and clerical jobs, another for manufacturing, and still another for managerial jobs, seems consistent with this argument. A possible explanation lies in the fact that different types of work possess different factors which contribute to the organization goals.[12]

The problem is to develop measures, common denominators, that permit or facilitate comparison across the diverse types of work found in the U.S. economy. It is the problem of comparing the value or contribution of apples versus oranges to one's health, or of comparing a ton of copper with a ton of steel in the wealth of a nation's natural resources; a common yardstick is required. In contemporary compensation systems, that yardstick has been found in the wage rates generated in the market place (external equity)—by the interactions of the employers' demand for labor expressed as job opportunities, and the workers' willingness to fill these opportunities under the terms and conditions offered. Adam Smith observed:

---

[12] Research using quantitative job analysis, which seeks to identify basic elements of work and workers' abilities and behaviors in dissimilar jobs, may be applicable here. See, for example, F. Krzystofiak, J. Newman, and G. Anderson, "A Quantified Approach to Measurement of Job Content," *Personnel Psychology*, 32, 2 (Summer 1979), pp. 341-57; and M. D. Dunnette, "Task and Job Taxonomies as a Basis for Evaluating Employment Qualifications," *Human Resources Planning Journal*, Vol. 1, 1 (1977).

There may be more labour in an hour's hard work than in two hours's easy business; or in an hour's application to a trade which cost ten years' labour to learn, than in a month's industry at an ordinary and obvious employment. But it is not easy to find any accurate measure either of hardship or ingenuity. In exchanging indeed the different productions of different sorts of labour for another, some allowance is commonly made for both; it is adjusted, however, not by an accurate measure, but by the higgling and bargaining of the market, according to that sort of rough equality which though not exact, is yet sufficient for carrying on the business of common life.[13]

Yet it is precisely the wage rates generated in the market, this common denominator, that advocates of the comparable worth notion maintain are inherently biased against women and minorities. The market, its imperfections, and its role in the wage determination process are discussed in a later section and in detail in the Northrup, Hildebrand and Schwab papers.

C. *Equal Work: A Brief History*

The debate between equal pay for equal work and equal pay for work of comparable worth is embedded in legislative history and court decisions on the Equal Pay Act and Title VII of the Civil Rights Act of 1964. A detailed account of the legislative and legal history of this issue is contained in the Williams and McDowell paper; however, a brief overview helps understand the debate.

1. *Equal Pay Act*. Both statutes have the same fundamental objective of remedying discriminatory compensation. Generally, the Equal Pay Act requires that women and men receive "equal pay for equal work" and states:[14]

No employer having employees subject to any provisions of this section shall discriminate, within any establishment in which such employees are employed, between employees on the basis of sex by paying wages to employees in such establishment at a rate less than the rate at which he pays wages to employees of the opposite sex in such establishment for equal work on jobs the performance of which requires equal skill, effort, and responsibility, and which are performed under similar working conditions, except where such payment is made pursuant to (i) a seniority system; (ii) a merit system; (iii) a system which measures earnings by quantity or quality of production; or (iv) a differential based on any other factor other than sex: Provided, That an employer who is paying a wage

---

[13] Adam Smith, *The Wealth of Nations* (London: Book I, C.V. 1776).
[14] 29 U.S.C. § 206(d).

rate differential in violation of this subsection shall not, in order to comply with the provisions of this subsection, reduce the wage rate of any employee.

Thus, the "equal work" standard under this Act establishes quite specific standards to judge whether employers paying differing wages to men and women are illegally discriminating. The standards include:

- Within the same establishment;
- Jobs the performance of which require similar skills, efforts and responsibility; and
- Performed under similar working conditions.

Four exceptions (affirmative defenses) were provided that permit inequalities in pay. Thus, inequalities are permitted if they are caused by:

- A seniority system;
- A merit system;
- A system which increases earnings by quality or quantity of production; or
- Some factor other than sex.

Under judicial interpretation of the Equal Pay Act, the work content of jobs does not have to be equal but only "substantially equal." Furthermore, the Courts' findings have emphasized first, the actual job behaviors, tasks, and work content performed, instead of simply job titles and second, the skills and abilities required to perform the job content, rather than the skills possessed by the employee. Thus, equal pay for equal work has been translated into equal pay for performance of substantially equal job content requiring substantially equal skills within the same establishment.

2. *Title VII.* Title VII, a much broader law, also deals with inequalities in pay and, specifically, with its relationship to the Equal Pay Act. The amendment to 703(h) of Title VII, known as the Bennett Amendment, provides:

> It shall not be an unlawful employment practice under this title for any employer to differentiate upon the basis of sex in determining the amount of wages or compensation paid or to be paid to employees of such employer if such differentiation is authorized by the provisions of section 6(d) of the Fair Labor Standards Act of 1938, as amended (29 U.S.C. 206 (d)) (i.e., the Equal Pay Act).

A key issue in the equal work/comparable worth debate is the precise interpretation of the Bennett Amendment. The debate centers around whether both features of the Equal Pay Act—(1) four affirmative defenses permitting inequalities in pay and (2) the substantially equal work standard— are included in Title VII. On the one hand, the Bennett Amendment can be construed as including both features in the Civil Rights Act. Alternatively, it can be interpreted as including only the four affirmative defenses and not the equal work standard. This is a vital difference. If the equal work standard is not included in the Civil Rights Act, then another may be used. The most likely substitute is the standard of comparable worth—that jobs of comparable worth must be paid equally.

D. *Comparable Worth*

"Comparable worth is the most difficult issue that has arisen under Title VII and, ultimately, it could have the same impact on the nation as school desegregation did in the 1950's," EEOC Chair Norton is reported telling a recent conference.[15] The notion of comparable worth, for which no operational, practical definition seems to exist, holds that whole groups of jobs, such as those in clerical and nursing work, are traditionally underpaid because they are held by women, and that these lower wage rates amount to sex discrimination under Title VII. Proponents of substituting "comparable worth" as the standard for wage determination maintain:

- Women have historically been "crowded" into certain occupations through discriminatory practices in society;
- The labor market reflects this crowding and thus the employment discrimination that caused the crowding; and
- If the labor market is discriminatory, so too are pay systems based on it.

Thus, existing pay systems based on the labor market mirror present and past discrimination. The following excerpt perhaps reflects the basic position of comparable worth proponents:

> Additionally, the practice of setting wages according to job families (occupation) is a sure way of producing sex-biased results. It is clear that the market place is biased against women; therefore to use the market place as a basis for paying clerical workers less than maintenance workers, for example, is to perpetuate discrimination.[16]

Proponents of comparable worth also see an immediate need to eliminate the external labor market's influence in wage setting. "To the extent bias does exist in the marketplace, and as long as it remains uncor-

---

[15] "Fair Employment Practices: Summary of Latest Developments," No. 383 Washington, D.C.: Bureau of National Affairs, Inc. (November 8, 1979). A more recent speech seems to suggest a modified position.

[16] H. Remick, "Strategies for Creating Sound, Bias Free Job Evaluation Plans," *Job Evaluation and EEO: The Emerging Issues* (New York: Industrial Relations Counselors, Inc., 1978), p. 91.

rected, many women are involuntarily contributing each paid day to maintaining the high salaries which exist in predominantly male jobs."[17]

Even if such bias were empirically verified, the absence of a workable definition of comparable worth is particularly troublesome. Without a workable process akin to collective bargaining or to job analysis, evaluation and wage surveys, it is unclear how employers, unions, courts, and agencies can apply comparable worth.

Some may suggest that employers' hiring, selection, and upgrading procedures have undergone modification under Title VII. These modifications were also "particularly troublesome." Why not similar modification of equal pay for equal work? In the former case, work-related procedures were available, test validation procedures and non-discriminatory programs were already developed and in use by many employers. Thus far, no workable procedures exist to translate comparable worth into practice.

How is one to determine the difference between comparable worth vs. non-comparable worth? What factors and measurement procedures are to be used? Some have suggested that quantitative job evaluation and job analysis, properly conducted, might provide the answer.[18] In fact, proponents of comparable worth see job evaluation in two veins:

1. As a potential tool to determine comparable worth within organizations, thereby solving a major limitation of the concept; or
2. As another example of administrative rules and procedures steeped in the traditions and customs of the work place, mirroring the pay inequalities in the external market, and simply perpetuating the historic discrimination found in the employment relationship.

On the one hand, if job evaluation can operationalize the concept of comparable worth, it has potential for ferreting out current biased pay inequalities; on the other hand, if job evaluation does nothing more than mirror the past, it may itself be a source of discrimination. As discussed earlier in this chapter and as later chapters in this volume will demonstrate, job evaluation is only one of several processes involved in wage determination systems. It is highly unlikely to be useful as a measure of comparable worth.[19]

Job analysis, as discussed earlier, has yet to be examined as a possible answer to the current inability to operationalize comparable worth. Quantitative job analysis analyzes jobs in terms of basic behaviors and tasks required to perform a job.[20] The notion of comparable worth implies that the

---

[17] Remick, p. 122.

[18] Donald J. Trieman, "Job Evaluation: An Analytical Review," Interim Report to the Equal Employment Opportunity Commission (Washington, D.C.: National Academy of Sciences, 1979).

[19] See, for example, the paper by Donald P. Schwab in this volume, p. 49.

[20] See footnotes 7 and 12.

job content and/or the qualifications required to perform the work establish value. Under the comparable worth theory, the content of diverse types of jobs must somehow be judged in terms of "comparability." Consider, for example, how one could compare the content of specific jobs such as electricians, registered nurses, elementary school teachers, plumbers, foundry workers, bus drivers, systems analysts, tellers and employment recruiters, across a variety of employers, in various geographic locations, in different industries, under different union situations. Perhaps job analysis approaches can identify dimensions of work content and behaviors which are universal across all jobs; considerably more research is required to evaluate this option—to date it seems unlikely.[21]

Lost in the debate over a workable definition of comparable worth is the more basic issue of whether the current standard, equal pay for equal work, should be replaced with comparable worth. Even if quantitative research in job evaluation and analysis would yield a universal taxonomy or a set of guidelines for determining comparable worth, the basic issue confronting society is a value judgment. The absence of a clear meaning of comparable worth tends to obscure the debate over the possible consequences of discarding the equal pay for equal work standard.

II. THE DIFFERENCES IN MEN'S AND WOMEN'S PAY

The force underlying the emerging debate over pay determination seems to be the disparity in male/female earnings: the "earnings gap." As reflected in Table 1, the median earnings of women are substantially less than men's, across occupations.

The very existence of this "gap" is considered by some to be evidence that society and contemporary compensation systems discriminate against women. Further, the "gap" may be growing; women's median full-time earnings in 1955 were 64% of men's, yet by 1973 women's median earnings were only 57% of men's earnings.[22] During the last decade a number of research studies have begun to investigate the factors which may be related to the earnings gap. While a detailed review of all the academic work is well beyond this paper's intent, some background in the work is vital to understanding more fully what is and is not known about the "earnings gap,"

---

[21] Perhaps an answer can be found in developing a process that can be applied. Existing taxonomies, such as those found in Functional Job Analysis or derived from the Position Analysis Questionnaire, could be considered, though this author's experience with PAQ suggests it lacks the specificity required for compensation decisions, and the FJA lacks the rigor that should be required in contemporary compensation systems.

[22] "The Earnings Gap Between Women and Men," Women's Bureau, Employment Standards Administration (Washington, D.C.: U.S. Department of Labor, 1975).

Table 1

**MEDIAN 1972 EARNINGS OF
FULL-TIME YEAR-ROUND WORKERS
BY OCCUPATION AND SEX GROUP**

| | Median Earnings | | Women's Median Income as Percent of Men's |
	Women	Men	
Professional & Technical Workers	$8,796	$13,029	67.5%
Managers & Administrators (except farm)	7,306	13,741	53.2
Sales Workers	4,575	11,356	40.3
Clerical Workers	6,039	9,656	62.5
Craftsmen & Kindred Workers	5,731	10,429	55.0
Operatives (including transport)	5,021	8,702	57.7
Service Workers (except private household)	4,606	7,762	59.3
Private Household Workers	2,365	—	—
Nonfarm Laborers	4,755	7,535	63.1

Source: U.S. Department of Commerce, Bureau of the Census, Current Population Reports. Series P-60, No. 90, 1973.

and more importantly, how much of the gap is attributable to discrimination. The plan for this section is to discuss briefly the general model used to investigate pay differences and then examine some of the complexities involved in the measurement of discrimination in male and female pay differences.[23]

A. *General Model: The Earnings Gap and the Role of Discrimination*

The general approach for determining the degree of discrimination in the wage determination process is deceptively simple. The portion of the male/female differential attributable to discrimination is determined by:

1. Estimating the portion of the difference that is attributable to work-productivity related factors;
2. Inferring the remaining, unexplained portion of the differential to be wage and employment discrimination.

---

[23] For an excellent treatment of pay differences from an economic and sociological perspective as well as cross cultural, see H. Phelps Brown, *The Inequality of Pay* (University of California Press, 1972).

An illustration may aid in the explanation of this "residuals" approach. Assume the following information:

	Average Wage	Average Education
Males	$10,000	12 years
Females	$ 5,800	9 years

Also assume that the following empirical model has been derived based on data for males.

$$\text{Male Wage} = \$1,000 + (\$750 \times \text{Education})$$

It is clear that not all of the gap between the male and female average wage is attributable to discrimination. Part of the difference may be attributed to the lower average education of women, and the remainder would be inferred to be discrimination. If women were paid as if they were men, under this approach they would receive $1,000 plus $750 for each of their nine years of experience, for a total of $7,750. The difference between men's actual earnings ($10,000) and women's *expected* earnings, had they been compensated as if they were males ($7,750) reflects a nondiscriminatory productivity difference ($2,250 = (12 years − 9 years) × $750 per year). The difference between women's expected earnings ($7,750) and their actual earnings ($5,800) reflects that difference which is not explained by differences in education and thus, is assumed under this approach to be the result of sex discrimination ($7,750 − $5,800 = $1,950).[24]

---

[24] The most common technique used in the study of male/female pay differentials is regression analysis which takes the following general form:

$$Y_i = B_0 + \sum_{j=1}^{n} B_j X_{ji} + U_i$$

where Y_i is the level of wages or earnings; $X_{1i}, \ldots X_{ni}$ are the n work-productivity factors used to explain Y.

To compare two groups such as male/female wages, the usual approach is to estimate this equation for each group:

$$\text{Males:} \quad Y_i^m = B_0^m + \sum_{j=1}^{n} B_j^m X_{ji}^m + U_i^m$$

$$\text{Females:} \quad Y_i^f = B_0^f + \sum_{j=1}^{n} B_j^f X_{ji}^f + U_i^f$$

A detailed discussion on the use of these formulas appears in A. S. Blinder, "Wage Discrimination: Reduced Form and Structural Estimates," *Journal of Human Resources*, 8, (1973),

Review of studies that use this general model conclude that the portion of the earnings gap not attributed to work-productivity factors (i.e., attributed to discrimination) ranges between 12% and 70%.[25] These differences in results may be accounted for by differences in the samples, time periods, methods, and sources of data used. In general, however, the more factors considered to be related to work-productivity, the smaller the "residual" portion of the earnings gap and the smaller the role inferred to discrimination.

One factor, differences in the occupation in which males and females are employed, is often the most significant factor in explaining the male/female earnings gap. Some argue that to include a person's occupation in the model ignores the effects of employment discrimination. Bergmann and Oaxaca, for example, assert that women and men have unequal access to occupations caused by the traditional sex-role stereotyping of occupations, traditional barriers to educational opportunities, and the discriminatory employment practices of employers and unions.[26] Unequal access contributes to the "over crowding" of women into certain occupations, which itself tends to dampen pressures for wage increases. Thus, the effects of including occupation affiliation in any model of the earnings gap is to mask effects of occupational discrimination, and hence, to ignore the alleged role that discriminatory hiring and promotion practices may play in the determination of wage differences.

Conversely, to exclude the job in which a person is employed from any model of wage differentials is to argue that differences in occupations are not related to wage differences! The unresolved dilemma facing researchers is how to separate that portion of differences in occupations that may be related to productivity and thus, wage differences, from the portion that is the product of discriminatory employment practices. Translated to a somewhat more practical level, this dilemma surfaces in litigation over wage discrimination. The issue boils down to which factors are permitted in a model of the wage determination process. Plaintiffs advocating the comparable worth

---

pp. 436–55. The process is to compare the portion of the male/female differential explained by the productivity-related factors and the constants; the residual is attributed to discrimination. An additional step in the analysis is to examine the work-productivity related variables associated with females and value them as if they were male factors. The difference between the wage females would *expect* if their work-productivity attributes were valued as if they were males and the *actual* wages paid to females is treated as discrimination.

[25] See, for example, Kahne and Kohen, "Economic Perspective on the Role of Women in the American Economy," *Journal of Economic Literature,* 13 (1975) pp. 1249–74; and I.V. Sawhill, "The Economics of Discrimination Against Women: Some New Findings," *Journal of Human Resources,* 8, (1973) pp. 383–95.

[26] B. R. Bergmann, "Occupational Segregation, Wages and Profits When Employers Discriminate by Race or Sex," *Eastern Economic Journal* (1974), pp. 103–10; R. L. Oaxaca, "Sex Discrimination in Wages," *Discrimination in Labor Markets,* A. Ashenfelter and A. Rees (eds.) (Princeton, New Jersey: Princeton University Press, 1973).

theory tend to argue that to include occupational affiliation factors, such as job and the level of the job in an organization, simply masks the discriminatory effects of the hiring and upgrading practices. Defendants would be expected to argue that jobs and the level of jobs in the organization are productivity-related and must be included in any model of the wage determination process.[27]

B. *Complexities Related to the Measurement of the Wage Determination Process and Discrimination*

Several troublesome issues confront the "residuals" approach to assessing the role discrimination may play in the wage determination process. To begin, four issues must be addressed.

1. *The models underlying the analysis.* Discrimination under the "residuals" approach is inferred. To do this with any degree of confidence requires that the model include all other significant work-productivity related factors. Omitting any of these factors will incorrectly inflate the unexplained residual and, thus, the role discrimination is assumed to play. Figure 2 lists some of the factors that must be considered in any model of wage determination. These include:

1. Work related differences in male/female characteristics (e.g., seniority, skills, and abilities);
2. Differences in employee work behaviors (e.g. performance, absenteeism, turnover);
3. Differences in the content of the work performed (e.g. budgetary responsibilities and skills required);
4. Differences in union membership and union characteristics (e.g. belonging to a relatively powerful pattern leader);
5. Differences in employers and in industries (e.g. profits, size, willingness to pay, capital/labor intensive);
6. Differences in labor market conditions (e.g. vacancies by ability/skill level).

While many of the recent studies of male/female wage differences include some of these factors, *none* of the published studies include all of them. This is not because researchers are not aware of these factors; the omissions are due in large part to two problems. First, there is a lack of adequate, publicly available data, and second, proxies are often used which, on their face, seem to include most factors, but on closer examination reveal that much of the information is too abstract. For example, few studies include differences in job performance because the data are difficult to obtain. Yet

---

[27] See *e.g.*, *Presseisen v. Swarthmore College*, 14 FEP Cases 1312 (E.D. Pa. 1976), 15 FEP Cases 1466 (E.D. Pa. 1977); *James v. Stockham Values & Fittings Co.*, 559 F.2d 310, 15 FEP Cases 827 (5th Cir. 1977).

Figure 2

**POSSIBLE DETERMINANTS OF
FEMALE/MALE PAY DIFFERENCES**

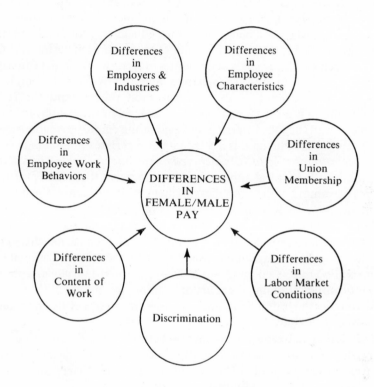

many compensation systems pay different wages for differences in performance. Data for other employee work behaviors such as absenteeism and turnover are equally difficult to obtain and typically are excluded. Differences in "content of the work" is another troublesome factor. Most studies attempt to account for differences in work content by including the "occupation" in which the job is classified. However, the occupational codes used, such as clerical, sales, managerial, professional, crafts, operatives, etc., are so broad that they do not account for differences among the types of work within each occupation. All managerial jobs are not alike, nor are all crafts, sales, etc. Yet differences in work content do account for differences in wages.

2. *Most models assume a "macro" perspective.* While actual pay decisions are made at the level of the employer and union, with few exceptions most economic analyses of the earnings gap are conducted at the national, market, or perhaps industry level. It is simply incorrect to assume that all the critical factors which go into wage determination in all establishments across the United States, are reflected in such aggregate analysis. Unfortunately, aggregate models often do not adequately include such "micro" factors as differences in employee work behaviors; in the education, skills and abilities to perform specific jobs; in the specific content of the work; in the interaction or match between employee skills and abilities and the work; in the employer's wage policies; or, in union objectives and relationship to employers. Research and modelling of the compensation process and the role of discrimination in it must be performed at the level of the establishment, the department, and the job. Inferring and evaluating employer-union behavior from existing aggregate data is inadequate and perhaps misleading.

3. *Measurement of factors included in the models.* Table 2 lists some of the factors and the typical approach used to measure these factors. It is important to examine closely the measurement of each factor, since it is the measure that is actually used in the model. For example, training is an aspect of "Employee Qualifications," and differences in "training" seem to be an important factor to consider in the study of male and female pay differences. Note that, if included, training is usually considered to be vocational training, and is measured as a dummy variable—yes or no—and hence, ignores the field of vocational training, the years of training, the quality of training and, finally, whether the training was even required for the job in which the person is employed!

The models also omit the interaction between an individual's qualification and the job in which she or he is employed. Consider for example, education; every published study of male and female wage differentials includes this variable as a productivity-related factor. Education, as a concept, conjures up thoughts of levels of education (high school, college, vocational school) and fields of education (content of course work, and training), yet the most common measure of education used is years of schooling. Hence, it may omit differences in fields of education, and more importantly, whether the education obtained has any relationship to the job. The fact that the author has a Ph.D. doesn't mean that the qualification is required in my job. The mere fact of possession of a qualification does not mean it is work related. Examples of cab drivers, typists, locomotive engineers, painters, etc. with college degrees are numerous.

Finally, most studies revert to the use of "proxies" for factors which cannot be measured directly. Thus, for example, years of education serves as a proxy for all the differences in a person's skills and abilities, or performance is measured by absenteeism, or the content of the work by major occupational classifications, or differences among employers by major

Table 2

POSSIBLE DETERMINANTS OF MALE/FEMALE PAY DIFFERENCES: COMMONLY EMPLOYED MEASURES

Determinants	Common Measures Employed in the Models
EMPLOYEE QUALIFICATIONS	
Seniority/Experience	Time spent in Civilian Labor Force, frequently omitting seniority within job or employer
Skills/Abilities	Omitted
Education/Training	Years of education, vocational training coded 0, 1; omitting worker relatedness
Health	Some work limitations
EMPLOYEE WORK BEHAVIORS	
Performance	Usually omitted, occasionally proxies such as absenteeism
Absenteeism	Usually omitted
Turnover	Usually omitted
Part-time/Full-time	Usually included, coded 0, 1
Hours worked	Usually included as hour/week
UNION MEMBERSHIP	Usually coded 0, 1; union characteristics omitted
CONTENT OF WORK PERFORMED	Usually coded as major occupational categories; Managers, Professional, Clerical, Sales, Crafts, etc.
Tasks/Behaviors Required	Omitted
EMPLOYER/INDUSTRIES	Usually coded by major industrial classifications such as Agriculture, Mining, Construction, Durable/Non-durable Manufacturing, Finance, Communications, etc.
Profits/Size/Wage Policy	Specific employer characteristics are typically omitted.
MARKET/REGION	
Market Conditions	Typically coded as high/low unemployment and high/low wages; more detailed aspects of market typically included in employer market surveys are omitted
Regions	Typically coded as Northwest, South, West, etc.
OTHER FACTORS	Macro-economic studies may include such factors as marital status, family background, whether or not a person has migrated once since age 16, and age.

Sources: R. Oaxaca, "Sex Discrimination in Wages," *Discrimination in Labor Markets*, A. Ashenfelter and A. Rees, (eds.) (Princeton, NJ: Princeton Press, 1973); A.S. Blinder, "Wage Discrimination: Reduced Form and Structural Estimates," *Journal of Human Resources*, 8, 4, (1973) pp. 436–55; Francine Blau, *Equal Pay in the Office* (Lexington, MA: Lexington Books, 1977); I.V. Sawhill, "The Economics of Discrimination Against Women: Some New Findings," *Journal of Human Resources*, 8, (1973), pp. 383–95; H. Sanborn, "Pay Differences Between Men and Women," *Industrial and Labor Relations Review*, 17 (1964) pp. 532–50; R. Oaxaca, "Male-Female Differentials in the Telephone Industry," in *Equal Employment Opportunity and the AT&T Case*, P.A. Wallace (ed.) (Lexington; MIT Press, 1976); J.E. Buckley, "Pay Differences Between Men and Women in the Same Job," *Monthly Labor Review*, 94 (1971) pp. 36–39.

industrial classifications. The use of proxies simply abstracts much of the detailed, work-relatedness found in contemporary systems of wage determination that may account for differences in wages.

4. *Lack of publicly available data.* The point has already been made that publicly available data tends to be useful for only aggregate economy, industry, or occupation-wide analysis. This level of analysis misses the diversity and complexity of wage decisions made at the employee/employer level. Most data banks generated by public agencies such as the Michigan Survey Research Center's "Panel Study of Income Dynamics," or the Census Bureau's "Summary of Economic Opportunity" lack the specificity required. Measures of employee qualifications, job content, and employer and union characteristics are not included. Hence, also lacking is the capacity to relate precise differences in qualifications, job requirements, employers and labor markets to wage differences.

Thus, existing empirical formulations and methodologies have not adequately modelled the wage determination process and hence do not adequately account for the role of discrimination. This is principally due to: (1) the omission of significant work-related factors in most models; (2) the lack of focus on the employer—union and individual job interaction as the level of analysis; (3) the absence of adequate measures for the factors; and (4) the lack of micro, publicly available data to perform such analysis.

III. CONCLUDING OBSERVATIONS

The present chapter serves to introduce the principal issues related to equal pay, comparable worth, and the earnings gap. The debate over substituting comparable worth for equal work as the standard for wage discrimination hinges on two issues: (1) the current lack of a workable definition of comparable worth, and (2) more basically, the lack of any systematic analysis of the possible consequences of its application. What, for example, are the consequences of raising the wages paid for those jobs dominated by women to correspond to some "national average" of the rates paid jobs dominated by men? Is it analogous to an OPEC increase in oil prices, which passes through all stages of the economy and is reflected in increased costs of living? Will those currently employed in higher paid occupations perceive their wages to be unfairly low, and will future workers be less likely to invest in the training and education required for some of these jobs? How important are wage differentials in the allocation of the labor force? How will changing the occupational wage differentials affect individual decisions to choose one job over another, one career over another, or one employer over another? These and other questions related to the possible consequences of abandoning the equal work standard must be thoroughly examined if the solutions are to be arrived at on other than emotional grounds. On the other hand, the formulation and application of alternative policy options should not be held up until these questions are examined. An example of this is that women will remain concentrated in the lower paid occupations without the vigorous application of equal opportunity and affirmative action practices by employers.

This paper also addresses the problems faced in modelling the wage determination process, and in isolating the role of discrimination in it. These problems include the lack of a well developed and tested model of the wage determination process at the level of the employer/union, the need to refine the process for identifying and measuring productivity-related factors, the need to parcel out the effects of employment or occupational discrimination from the analysis without ignoring the productivity effects of job differences, and the need to make job, employee and employer data publicly available. Of these, the major missing piece is the lack of a well developed model of the employer wage determination process. This is particularly unfortunate, since the public debate focuses on issues that can be most effectively addressed through such a model.

Finally, the hope is that the debate over equal work/comparable worth will help generate the much needed research into the wage determination process. Many of the concepts and techniques used in contemporary compensation systems were developed and refined in the 1930's and 1940's. It is time to re-examine them; perhaps the challenges to current practices will rebuild the links between practice, policy and research in the field.

JOB EVALUATION AND PAY SETTING: CONCEPTS AND PRACTICES

by
Donald P. Schwab

Professor Schwab's paper concerns the methods that employers use to set wages and the feasibility of using job evaluation as a means for identifying the worth of jobs. His thesis is that, while theoretical descriptions of job evaluation often imply that it measures job worth, in practice it measures compensable factors of jobs to maximize the relationship between the wages assigned to each job covered by the evaluation system and the wages for key jobs, which are assumed to reflect the market. Professor Schwab then explains how job evaluation fits into the total compensation process and shows that organizations often use pay to accomplish a variety of personnel/human resource objectives. He concludes that job evaluation is not likely to be helpful in identifying worth in any way which differs from the market and that any assumption that pay differences between employees is due to job evaluation or any other single pay procedure probably will be incorrect.

Donald P. Schwab is a Professor at both the Graduate School of Business and the Industrial Relations Research Institute at the University of Wisconsin-Madison. An H. I. Romnes Faculty Fellow, he also is the Director of the Center for Personnel/Human Resource Management and has taught at both the University of Kentucky and the University of Minnesota. Dr. Schwab is a member of several professional organizations, including the Industrial Relations Research Association and the Academy of Management. He is an editorial consultant for the *Journal of Applied Psychology* and *Organizational Behavior and Human Performance* and serves on the editorial board of the *Academy of Management Journal.* A prolific writer, he has co-authored several books on related topics including, *Performance in Organizations: Determinants & Appraisal* (Scott Foresman & Co., 1973), *Perspectives on Personnel/Human Resource Management* (Irwin, 1978), and *Personnel Human Resource Management* (Irwin, 1980). Professor Schwab received his B.B.A., M.A. and Ph.D. in industrial relations from the University of Minnesota.

JOB EVALUATION AND PAY SETTING: CONCEPTS AND PRACTICES

Recently, the notion of comparable worth and its probable value for the reduction or elimination of potential wage discrimination, especially between the sexes, has begun to receive attention.* At issue are many questions including the meaning and measurement of comparable worth. The present paper deals primarily with these questions: What is comparable worth and can it be measured?

These questions are addressed from the perspective of current wage setting practices within organizations. In particular, comparable worth is examined within the context of job evaluation, which has been suggested as a potential mechanism for identifying the *worth* of jobs. Theoretical descriptions often imply that job evaluation does measure job worth, but as shown in this paper, job evaluation as practiced does not accomplish this purpose. In fact, it measures factors of jobs that are related to the wages provided in the market place. Moreover, job evaluation is not likely to be helpful in identifying worth (in any way which differs from the market) without a significant change in conceptualization and technology.

The second part of the paper addresses how job evaluation fits into the organization's total compensation process. Important to understanding this process is recognizing that organizations attempt to accomplish a variety of personnel/human resource objectives (e.g., motivating as well as retaining employees) with pay. Because these various objectives are not highly interrelated, many pay policies and procedures are developed and utilized. An employee's pay typically depends not only on job level (where job evaluation has its impact), but also on other personal and organizational characteristics as well. As a consequence, the assumption that pay differences between employees is due to job evaluation (or any other single pay procedure) is likely to be incorrect.

---

* The critical comments of Sara Rynes and the fellow authors of this volume are greatly appreciated.

I. JOB EVALUATION

Employees are typically assigned to categories within organizations called jobs. Persons performing similar tasks are said to hold the same job. The number and types of tasks to be included in a single job classification depend, however, on managerial (sometimes with union and/or employee input) discretion.

Generally, organizations differentiate between jobs for purposes of pay. Persons on two jobs may receive different amounts of pay in part as a function of job differences. Job evaluation is a measurement procedure designed to aid organizations in establishing pay differentials between jobs. Though it would be erroneous to state that there is a generally accepted job evaluation theory, there is, nevertheless, a widely shared view that job evaluation generates pay differentials by identifying the differential worth of jobs. Jobs worth more are paid more.

Worth, in turn, is assumed to be established by the degree to which jobs possess levels or degrees of *compensable factors*.[1] The latter, judgmentally derived, presumably represent dimensions of the job that the organization wishes to base pay levels upon. Figure 1 shows a simple illustrative case where two hypothetical jobs (A and B) are evaluated on four compensable factors: skill, responsibility, effort and working conditions.[2] Job A is evaluated as requiring a high degree of skill, moderate responsibility, fairly low effort, and favorable working conditions (resulting in a low factor score). Job B has a different configuration or profile of degrees on the factors. Both jobs, however, sum to eleven degree points and hence, given the tentative definition, are of comparable worth.

Comparable worth is to be contrasted with equal pay for equal work as mandated by the Equal Pay Act of 1963. The latter constitutes a special case of the former; besides equal factor score totals, equal pay for equal work further requires similar factor score profiles. The Equal Pay Act decrees that jobs of equal work be paid similarly. It does not, however, require that jobs of comparable worth be so paid. A major objection to requiring similar payments for jobs of comparable worth (as assessed by job evaluation) has to do with the possible market implications of so doing. Specifically, the rhetoric of job evaluation implies that worth has a meaning internal to the organization. This implied meaning when measured and aggregated into a

---

[1] Some forms of job evaluation utilize only one global compensable factor (e.g., ranking). However, the point system of job evaluation which is apparently the most prevalent approach used in the private sector involves multiple factors. The discussion throughout this paper assumes multiple factors unless otherwise stated. For a description of alternative job evaluation systems see any standard compensation text. For example, see David W. Belcher, *Compensation Management* (Englewood Cliffs, New Jersey: Prentice-Hall, Inc., 1974).

[2] These are the dimensions identified in the Equal Pay Act of 1963 for determining equal work.

Figure 1

COMPARABLE WORTH IN JOB EVALUATION TERMS

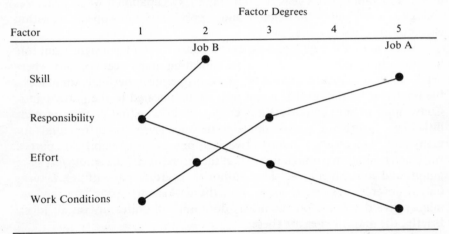

wage structure may lead to a conflict with the wage structure emanating from the labor market. If such a conflict emerges, salary decisions based exclusively on job evaluation results could lead to imbalances in labor demand and supply. An excess of employees, due to overpayment in some occupations, might coexist with shortages of underpaid employees in other occupations.

At the same time apparently, the potential variance between job evaluation results and market wages is precisely what makes it attractive to those who believe that the market wage structure has built into it the operation of discriminatory practices, especially against women and perhaps certain minority groups as well. If job evaluation validly assesses job worth, as the advocate argument goes, then would not greater reliance on job evaluation, as opposed to current wage setting practice, result in a reduction of discrimination?

This possibility is explored in the present section by an assessment of job evaluation. It begins with an examination of the need for job evaluation, particularly in the context of market forces as they also apply to wage setting processes. It next examines the promise and practice of job evaluation. Included in the latter section is a summary of research that has been performed in the job evaluation area.

II. WHY JOB EVALUATION?

Traditional economic analysis explains pay levels for jobs and resulting pay differentials (wage structures) between jobs in terms of labor markets. Pay for a particular occupation is seen as depending on the interaction of labor demand (a function of product demand and the relative efficiency of labor vis-à-vis other productive factors) and labor supply (a function of individual or family work-leisure preferences). Occupational wage structures emerge as a residual of the demand and supply interactions operating within each occupational market.

Without doubt such a process exists. Markets do play a significant role in establishing job pay rates and in allocating employees to jobs where needed. At the same time, however, markets operate imperfectly, or at least, the operation of the market is not well communicated to the participants. Constraints on both employers and employees exist so that markets provide little direct information about appropriate wage levels and differentials for many jobs. As a result, administrative decisions are also a significant part of wage determination (though not just at the discretion of the employer, since unions and government also share authority regarding pay setting). It turns out, however, that the trade-off between the market, on the one hand, and administrative decisions, on the other, does not fall uniformly on all jobs.[3] Briefly, the major issues are these:

1. Technological and administrative differences between organizations coupled with a high degree of specialization in large production units create jobs which are unique or nearly unique to particular organizations. Moreover, rapid technological or product changes result in nearly continuous modification of the content of many jobs. As a consequence, there is essentially no market for some jobs (especially production jobs), because comparable jobs in other organizations simply do not exist or are not known to exist.

2. Organizational technologies are typically structured so that demand for jobs is interdependent, e.g., as made necessary by process or assembly forms of production. Such joint demand serves to weaken the link between the wage rate for any particular job and employment decisions regarding it, including some jobs that are used widely across organizations.

3. Technological constraints on market functioning are often reinforced by many personnel/human resources policies. In effect, such policies often result in a job hierarchy where only a limited number of hiring-in ("ports-of-entry") jobs exist. Except at these entry ports, characterized by bottom level jobs whether managerial, clerical, factory, skilled craft or professional,[4] jobs are filled through internal processes involving various combinations of seniority and merit among existing employees. These procedures also serve to isolate wage change processes from employment policies.

---

[3] This point is elaborated on effectively in a paper by E. Robert Livernash, "The Internal Wage Structure," in George W. Taylor and Frank C. Pierson (eds.), *New Concepts in Wage Determination* (New York: McGraw-Hill, 1957), pp. 140–72.

[4] In all cases, ports-of-entry are characterized by jobs for which necessary training is attained outside the organization (appenticeships, public education, etc.).

Thus, organizations have, in fact, a continuum of jobs. At one extreme are *key* jobs,[5] characterized by a standardized (employed by many organizations) and stable content. Ports-of-entry jobs that satisfy these constraints are certainly key jobs. Others, however, can also be key jobs if their content is common across organizations. For such jobs a market can be thought to exist. To the extent that wages and jobs interact as predicted by economic theory, it would operate with key jobs. Thus, the range of wages for key jobs within an industry may be fairly narrow. The organization's discretion in manipulating wages is limited, though not negligible, by the traditional theoretical constraint that if the market is not met, the employer will have difficulty attracting or retaining sufficient numbers of appropriate quality personnel.[6]

At the other extreme of the continuum are jobs whose content is unique to the employing organization. For such jobs no identifiable market exists to serve as a constraint or even as a guideline for wage setting purposes. Thus, for these jobs the organization must find some methods other than the market for determining compensation.

To summarize, there are two types of jobs (arranged on a continuum), key or market and non-key.[7] Obviously, all are assigned pay, but the sensitivity to market forces varies substantially between them. In actuality wage rates at the key job end of the continuum serve as criteria for wage rates of jobs at the non-key end of the continuum. Hereafter, jobs will be referred to as key or non-key. Recognize that this distinction is one of degree and not of

---

[5] Key jobs are defined in a variety of ways in the literature. Here they will be defined only as a representative of market jobs.

[6] The market operates less efficiently even for key jobs than one might predict given a theoretical perspective. Labor market participants often have little knowledge about alternative employment opportunities. Moreover, employees weigh many factors besides wages in their decision to join, and especially their decision to leave, organizations. For an excellent review of research on labor market behavior see, Herbert S. Parnes, *Research on Labor Mobility* (New York: Social Science Research Council, 1954). For more recent surveys see, for example, Lee D. Dyer, "Job Search Success of Middle-Aged Managers and Engineers," *Industrial and Labor Relations Review* 26, no. 3 (April 1973), pp. 969–79; Thomas G. Gutteridge, "Labor Market Adaptations of Displaced Professionals," *Industrial and Labor Relations Review* 31, no. 4 (July 1978), pp. 460–73; Graham L. Reid, "Job Search and the Effectiveness of Job-Finding Methods," *Industrial and Labor Relations Review* 26, no. 4 (July 1973), pp. 479–95; Harold D. Sheppard and A. Harvey Belitsky, *The Job Hunt* (Baltimore, Maryland: The Johns Hopkins Press, 1966). As a consequence, the relationship between wage levels and employment is often tenuous. Organizations are often able to attract adequate numbers of employees at below market wages through, for example, effective recruiting practices and the manipulation of employee qualifications (George H. Hildebrand, "External Influence and the Determination of the Internal Wage Structure," in J. L. Meij [ed.], *Internal Wage Structure* [Amsterdam: North-Holland Publishing Company, 1963], p. 260). While these latter personnel/human resource practices have obvious cost implications for the organization, they represent alternative methods that the organizations may use to attract a labor force.

[7] Of course, organizations vary in the degree to which jobs serve as key jobs. A major source of variation (holding the content of the job constant) is the extent to which organizations utilize internal promotion policies as a staffing mechanism. Thus, two organizations with identical job hierarchies could vary in the number of key jobs, because one used internal promotion

kind. The process is a complex one, however, because all key job rates are typically not equally relevant for all non-key job wage rates. The main issues are as follows:[8]

1. Jobs tend to be grouped into *job clusters.* These clusters emerge as a function of technology, administrative practices (e.g., lines of promotion), geographical location, and common job content. Broad clusters typically develop around managerial, clerical and production jobs. Within the broad groupings narrower clusters may also be identified in some organizations.

2. Each cluster contains key jobs. The major source of influence on non-key job wage rates comes from the key jobs within the same or closely related clusters. Influences on key job wage rates, in turn, are both external through *wage contours* (diffusion of market forces, collective bargaining influences and governmental constraints) and internal through *wage structures* (the interconnection of key jobs within the organization).

A depiction of the influences that operate are shown by the model in Figure 2. Two clusters are shown. Within Cluster 1, for example, wages for non-key jobs (A, B, C) are most directly influenced by the key job wage rate (K_1). Key rates, in turn, are influenced by comparisons within the organization (between K_1 and K_2) and by comparisons with other organizations through the wage contour (e.g., comparisons with K_1 and K_2 type jobs in the appropriate markets).

The model is admittedly descriptive, not predictive. The relative influence of external and internal forces on key job wage rates, for example, depends on a variety of variables that vary across organizations and within organizations over time. Nevertheless, the model does show the essential variables operating on organizations as they establish wage rates for jobs. Highly important to understanding the process is the differentiation between key and non-key jobs.

Job evaluation is the major administrative procedure devised to help the organization translate the forces described above and depicted in Figure 2 when establishing pay differentials. Unfortunately, however, several common misconceptions exist regarding what job evaluation accomplishes. These misconceptions occur primarily between the way job evaluation is normatively prescribed on the one hand, and practiced on the other.

---

policies more than the other. Primary and secondary labor markets are in part differentiated along these lines (Peter Doeringer and Michael Piore, *Internal Labor Markets and Manpower Analysis* [Lexington, Massachusetts: Heath, 1975]). Primary jobs are characterized, among other things, by internal lines of promotion which are atypical for secondary jobs. Investigators (e.g., Lawrence M. Kahn, "Internal Labor Markets: San Francisco Longshoremen," *Industrial Relations* 15, no. 3 [October 1976], pp. 333–37; Christine E. Bishop, "Hospitals: From Secondary to Primary Labor Market," *Industrial Relations* 16, no. 1 [February 1977], pp. 26–34) have observed a tendency for organizations to shift from secondary to primary job hierarchies further limiting key jobs insofar as ports-of-entry are concerned.

[8] This discussion is heavily dependent on Livernash, "The Internal Wage Structure," note 3 *supra.*

Figure 2

INFLUENCES ON PAY LEVELS AND STRUCTURES

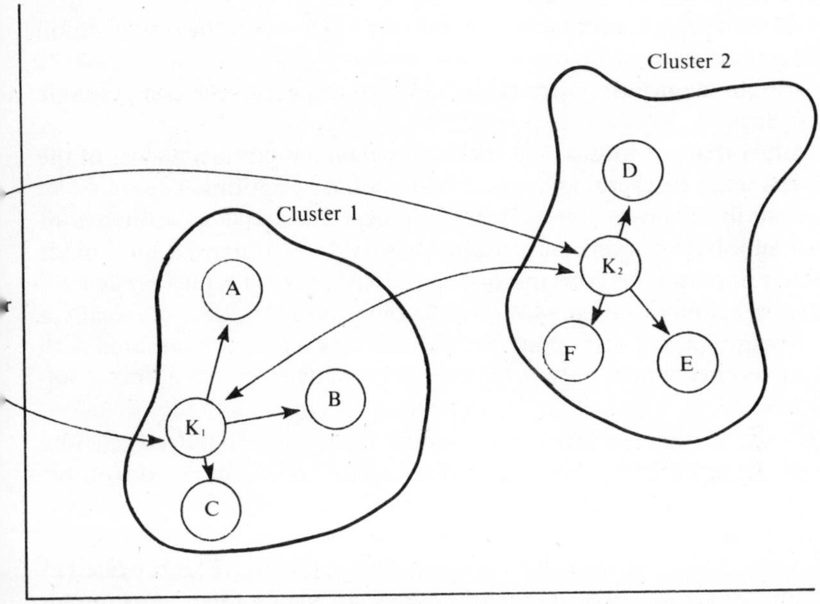

From Herbert G. Heneman III, and Donald P. Schwab, *Perspectives on Personnel/Human Resource Management* (Homewood, Ill.: Irwin, 1978), p. 209.

A. JOB EVALUATION PRESCRIPTIONS

Milkovich noted that job evaluation has been defined in a variety of ways.[9] It appears reasonable to argue, however, that a common thread exists or can readily be inferred from most of them. Specifically, job evaluation is described as a procedure that makes judgments about jobs based on content or the demands made on job incumbents. This, as noted earlier, suggests an internal as opposed to external or market orientation. Dunn and Rachel, for example, have argued that "[j]ob evaluation should consider only the inherent characteristics and duties of the job and should exclude extraneous factors such as supply and demand of labor, local wage rates, and geographic location."[10]

---

[9] See the paper by George T. Milkovich in this volume, p. 23.

[10] J. D. Dunn and Frank M. Rachel, *Wage and Salary Administration: Total Compensation Systems* (New York: McGraw-Hill, 1971), p. 168.

The steps typically discussed as achieving this perspective of job evaluation consist of:[11]

1. Job analysis is performed resulting in job descriptions of the jobs to be evaluated.

2. Compensable factors are chosen to represent what the organization wishes to reward.

3. The job descriptions are evaluated with respect to the compensable factors.

4. A hierarchy of jobs is determined based on the summed values of the compensable factors observed in the job descriptions.

As described above, job evaluation appears to arrive at estimates of worth for all jobs based on compensable factors. No differentiation is made between key and non-key jobs in this regard. Notice also that no explicit account of market pay influences is provided in this description. Typically a standard treatment suggests that job evaluation results are compared with current or market wages only *after* the above four steps have been completed.

If job evaluation were performed as described, it would indeed generate a hierarchy determined by the compensable factor scores obtained by jobs. The critical question in general, and for comparable worth in particular, would be: does the hierarchy resulting from the job evaluation procedure in fact represent the worth of the jobs evaluated? Are jobs more highly rated in job evaluations actually worth more than jobs less highly rated? Cast in this way, the major issue regarding the assessment of job evaluation is one of validity, specifically *construct validity*, which refers to the correspondence between the results of a measure (job evaluation in this case) and the underlying concept or construct (worth in this case) that the measure is designed to tap.[12]

Construct validity and the appropriate procedures to assess it are very different from empirical validity and empirical validation. In empirical validation, the correspondence between the results of two measures is assessed (independent and dependent variables, or predictor and criterion). Thus, statistical procedures such as correlation can be used to determine empirical validity. In construct validity there is no empirical indicator for the dependent variable or criterion. It is by definition a construct, that is, a mental definition of a variable.

The conceptual (nonempirical) nature of the criterion has several important implications for construct validation. Most important for the purposes

---

[11] See any standard treatment of wage administration, such as, David W. Belcher, "Wage and Salary Administration," in Dale Yoder and Herbert G. Heneman, Jr., *ASPA Handbook of Personnel and Industrial Relations* (Washington, D.C.: The Bureau of National Affairs, Inc. 1979), pp. 6; 75–122.

[12] For an overview of construct validity, see J. Nunnally, *Psychometric Theory*, 2nd ed. (New York: McGraw-Hill, 1978), pp. 94–109.

at hand is the need to carefully define the construct. What is meant by worth? The identification of appropriate empirical construct validation procedures depends heavily on how well the construct has been defined initially.[13]

Unfortunately, job worth has not been adequately defined nor has a consensus emerged as to its meaning. In fact, authors have been remarkably reticent to offer any definitions of worth at all. As a consequence, there is very little basis for accepting one set of compensable factors as better representing worth than any alternative set.

Even in the absence of adequate definitional work, there is some available evidence which has implications for the probable construct validity of job evaluation as an estimator of worth. Some of these studies have focused on job evaluation's *reliability,* while others have examined the *convergence* of alternative job evaluation techniques.

1. *Reliability*

Job evaluation involves a substantial amount of judgment in its implementation (i.e., it is a subjective procedure). Under those circumstances it is appropriate to ask whether alternative persons will arrive at the same judgments. This is a question of consistency or reliability. Reliability can be viewed as a necessary requirement for construct validity. For example, if two evaluators generate different (i.e., unreliable) worth orderings for a set of jobs, at least one ordering cannot be construct valid. Of course, both orderings may be invalid so that reliability is not sufficient for construct validity.

There are a number of points where judgments must be made in job evaluation; hence a number of reliability issues could be raised. Two in particular, however, involve judgments on the part of those who perform job evaluation. One of these involves the initial analysis and description of the job. The second consists of the evaluation of those descriptions on compensable factors.

a. Job analysis. The unit of analysis in job evaluation is the job itself. The quality of job evaluation is, thus, highly dependent on the quality of the description of the job that is provided. Traditional job analysis does not lend itself to formal reliability analysis because its output is ordinarily a narrative verbal description. It is reasonable to assume, however, that reliability is a serious problem when such a format is used due to the imprecision of language.

The standardized job analysis questionnaires developed more recently can be formally analyzed for reliability because they provide quantitative scores for dimensions of jobs. Unfortunately, the limited data generated to

---

[13] For an elaboration on this need and a discussion of empirical procedures for construct validation, see Donald P. Schwab, "Construct Validity in Organizational Behavior," in Barry Staw and L. L. Cummings (eds.), *Research in Organizational Behavior* (Vol. 2, Greenwich, Conn.: JAI Press, (1980), pp. 3–43.

date have not been too encouraging. When two or more persons analyze a set of jobs, there is usually substantial disagreement on the appropriate ordering of jobs.[14]

Presently, it is difficult to explain why such unreliability exists. The unreliability does not, for example, appear to be due to differences in the performance level of the persons performing the analysis,[15] nor does it appear to be a function of the sex of the person performing the job. It may, however, be due in part to the sex of the person conducting the analysis.[16] Other potential sources of unreliability have received very little attention.[17]

Given the unreliability obtained, it appears important to have the analysis performed independently by several persons. Results of these separate analyses should then be averaged; otherwise, the results of the final job evaluation might be biased by the idiosyncratic judgments of a single job analyst.

b. Evaluation of jobs. Once the descriptions are generated, jobs must be evaluated on the dimension(s) of the job evaluation plan. Again, reliability becomes an issue. To what extent do different raters produce similar assessments of jobs on evaluation dimensions?

As with job analysis, the results are somewhat discouraging. Disagreements on dimension evaluations can be substantial.[18] Reliability for

---

[14] For research results and citations to other research, see R. Richard Hackman and Greg R. Oldham, "Development of the Job Diagnostic Survey," *Journal of Applied Psychology* 60, no. 2 (April 1975), pp. 159–70; G. Douglas Jenkins, Jr., David A. Nadler, Edward E. Lawler III, and Cortlendt Cammann, "Standardized Observations: An Approach to Measuring the Nature of Jobs," *Journal of Applied Psychology* 60, no. 2 (April 1975), pp. 171–81; E. McCormick, P.R. Jeanneret, and R. C. Mecham, "A Study of Job Characteristics and Job Dimensions as Based on the Position Analysis Questionnaire (PAQ)," *Journal of Applied Psychology* 56, no. 4 (August 1972), pp. 347–68.

[15] Kenneth N. Wexley and Stanley B. Silverman, "An Examination of Differences Between Managerial Effectiveness and Response Patterns on a Structured Job Analysis Questionnaire," *Journal of Applied Psychology* 63, no. 5 (October 1978), pp. 646–49. See also citations in Walter W. Tornow and Patrick R. Pinto, "The Development of a Managerial Job Taxonomy: A System for Describing, Classifying, and Evaluating Executive Positions," *Journal of Applied Psychology* 61, no. 4 (August 1976), pp. 410–18.

[16] Richard D. Arvey, Emily M. Passino, and John W. Lounsbury, "Job Analysis Results as Influenced by Sex of Incumbent and Sex of Analyst," *Journal of Applied Psychology* 62, no. 4 (August 1977), pp. 411–16.

[17] McCormick, *et al.*, "A Study of Job Characteristics . . . ," compared the reliabilities of different persons (incumbents, supervisors and job analyst). Sample sizes were so small, however, that the findings may have little generality.

[18] See, for example, C. H. Lawshe, Jr. and P. C. Farbo, "Studies in Job Evaluation: 8. The Reliability of an Abbreviated Job Evaluation System," *Journal of Applied Psychology* 33 (1949), pp. 158–66; C. H. Lawshe, Jr. and R. F. Wilson, "Studies in Job Evaluation: 6. The Reliability of Two Point Rating Systems," *Journal of Applied Psychology* 31 (1947), pp. 355–65. Ash reported generally higher reliabilities, but his estimates are inflated because he correlated individual ratings with a composite which included the individual's ratings. Philip Ash, "The Reliability of Job Evaluation Rankings," *Journal of Applied Psychology* 32 (1948), pp. 313–20.

the total points (worth) generated from the dimensions is higher, but still can show substantial disagreement between any two raters.

Research has also been performed on whether some characteristics of the rater influence reliability. There is some evidence that a rater's familiarity with the job may influence assessments of the degree to which a dimension may be present in a job,[19] though there is also evidence that experience as an evaluator, per se, has little impact on reliability.[20] Moreover, there is additional evidence suggesting that the evaluator's affiliation with a union or management has little impact on the reliability of ratings.[21]

In the case of compensable factors, research has been performed on the reliability of ratings when independently arrived at judgments are averaged. Here, the evidence suggests that pooled estimates from groups of five evaluators, at least for total points, are acceptably reliable.[22]

2. Convergence

The question of appropriate compensable factors might not be so urgent if alternative job evaluation systems yielded similar results. Similarity would suggest that, empirically at least, it does not make too much difference what factors (within the range giving similar results) are included in the plan. While convergence of this sort provides little information about what is being measured in job evaluation, it at least suggests that measurement is consistent across systems.

Several studies have been performed on the convergence of alternative job evaluation or job evaluation-type plans. A summary of the results of these studies is shown in Figure 3.[23] Note that there is substantial variation in the degree to which alternative systems yield comparable results. While

---

[19] J. M. Madden, "The Effect of Varying the Degree of Rater Familiarity in Job Evaluation," *Personnel Administrator* 25 (1962), pp. 42–45; J. M. Madden, "A Further Note on the Familiarity Effect in Job Evaluation," *Personnel Administrator* 26 (1963), pp. 52–54.

[20] Scott as cited by Joseph Tiffin and Ernest J. McCormick, *Industrial Psychology* (Englewood Cliffs, New Jersey: Prentice-Hall, 1974).

[21] Management evaluators, on average, provided slightly more reliable ratings than union evaluators. Lawshe and Farbo, "Studies in Job Evaluation: 8 . . . ," *supra* note 18.

[22] Lawshe and Farbo, "Studies in Job Evaluation: 8 . . ." and Lawshe and Wilson, "Studies in Job Evaluation: 6 . . . ," *supra* note 18.

[23] T. Atchison and W. French, "Pay Systems for Scientists and Engineers," *Industrial Relations* 7 (1967), pp. 44–56; David J. Chesler, "Reliability and Comparability of Different Job Evaluation Systems," *Journal of Applied Psychology* 32 (1948), pp. 465–75; Randall B. Dunham, "Job Evaluation: Two Instruments and Sources of Pay Satisfaction" (Paper presented to the American Psychological Association, Toronto 1978); David D. Robinson and Owen W. Wahlstrom, "Comparison of Job Evaluation Methods: A 'Policy-Capturing' Approach Using the Position Analysis Questionnaire," *Journal of Applied Psychology* 59, no. 5 (October 1974), pp. 633–37.

Figure 3

CONVERGENCE OF ALTERNATIVE JOB EVALUATION PLANS

Study	No. Plans	Range of Correlation Coefficients Low	High
Atchison & French	3	.54	.82
Chesler	3[a]	.85	.97
Dunham	6	.89	.97
Robinson, et al.	5[a]	.82	.95

[a]Includes market wage survey as a "plan. "

difficult to determine given the paucity of details provided in the studies reviewed, it appears that the more divergent the evaluation methods, the more divergent the results. The Atchison and French study, for example, obtained very low convergence comparing time-span-of-discretion, as in Jaques,[24] with a maturity curve analysis. Even in other studies where more conventional evaluation prcedures were compared, however, the low end of the range suggests that alternative systems share only two-thirds to four-fifths common variance.

To summarize, job evaluation as theoretically prescribed is a mechanism for identifying worth based on job content. In fact, however, no definition of worth has been established, much less accepted. As a consequence, there currently exists no suitable basis for determining whether job evaluation measures job worth or not (i.e., whether job evaluation is construct valid). Evidence from job evaluation investigations indicates that problems of reliability where subjective judgments are at issue are substantial, though probably not unresolvable. Convergence evidence to date sugests that alternative systems do not yield highly similar results, indicating that at least some systems are not construct valid. It should be noted, however, that even if reliability and convergence problems are satisfactorily resolved, the question of what job evaluation measures in its prescribed form would still remain.

B. JOB EVALUATION PRACTICE

One might appropriately ask why a procedure is so widely used when there is so little evidence that it accomplishes what conventional descriptions suggest it does. The answer is that job evaluation does achieve an important organizational objective, although not the one prescribed (i.e., arranging jobs in a hierarchy determined by worth through job content). Specifically, as practiced, job evaluation is used by organizations to establish wage rates

---

[24] Elliot Jaques, *Equitable Payment* (New York: John Wiley and Sons, 1961); Roy Richardson, *Fair Pay and Work* (The Southern Illinois University Press, 1971).

for non-key jobs (where the market is difficult to assess) from variables (called compensable factors) that are related to key job wage rates (where market forces can be more readily determined).

The argument developed below is necessarily somewhat complicated because the actual purpose of job evaluation is seen most clearly by examining it in its most technical form. This form relies heavily on statistical techniques. A close examination of it shows that, as practiced, job evaluation identifies and differentially weights compensable factors to maximize the relationship between them and the wages for key jobs which are assumed to reflect the market. Thus, the actual criterion of job evaluation is not worth in a job content sense, but market wages. The model (compensable factors and weights) emerging from this process is then applied to non-key jobs for purposes of establishing a wage hierarchy. While it is true that job content characteristics are used in this process, they are weighted to obtain a close correspondence with existing wages of key jobs and not worth, *per se*. To what extent worth and the market might correspond cannot be known without a precise definition of worth.

As noted, there are alternative ways that job evaluation is implemented, depending in part on whether the method is a global nonquantitative process, such as ranking or classification, or a multiple factor quantitative method, such as the point system or factor comparison.[25] The following discussion focuses on the more commonly used point system.[26] It is also a formal method about which we know a substantial amount. It seems likely, however, that less formal methods operate in essentially the same way. At least, there is no reason to assume they operate differently. Figure 4 shows the steps undertaken in job evaluation as practiced.

Figure 4

JOB EVALUATION PRACTICE

Development (Performed on Key Jobs)

    Identification of compensable factors
    Specification of *a-priori* weights
    Modification of factors and weights to obtain a correspondence between
       key job wages and job evaluation results

Implementation (Performed on Non-key Jobs)

    Modified model applied to non-key jobs
    Non-key job hierarchy developed and compared with non-key job wages

---

[25] See any standard textbook on compensation for a more detailed description of these alternative systems (e.g., David W. Belcher, *Compensation Administration* (Englewood Cliffs, New Jersey: Prentice-Hall, 1974).

[26] In large part the discussion is also applicable to factor comparison and to standardized job analysis questionnaires when used for job evaluation.

1. Development

In practice a sharp distinction is drawn between the development of job evaluation which utilizes key jobs and its subsequent implementation on non-key jobs. Development typically begins with the tentative identification of compensable factors. Since there are many different job evaluation plans, there are many potentially different sets of compensable factors. In fact, relatively few factors recur time and time again. Specifically, skill, responsibility, effort, and working conditions, which were the major categories of the original National Electrical Manufacturers' Association (NEMA) plan, are common to many of the job evaluation plans that have subsequently evolved. These factors appear to conform rather closely to the components articulated in *net-advantage* discussions going back to Adam Smith's *Wealth of Nations*.[27] That is, they represent requirements that the employee must bring to the job (e.g., skill), or characteristics of the job (e.g., working conditions) that may make the job onerous or attractive. As such they seem to represent variables that are valued in the market more than factors that an employer would consider in intraorganizational decision-making.

In any event, these factors are usually assigned tentative weights based on some *a-priori* judgments about the relative importance. Specifically, differential weights are presumably established by assigning some factors more points than others. Thus, for example, total points for a skill factor may range from zero to 100 while points for working conditions (judgmentally determined as less important) may range only from zero to 50. The total points received by each key job is the simple sum of the compensable factor scores.

$$TP = \sum_{i=1}^{n} X_i \qquad (1)$$

where:

TP = total points

X_i = compensable factor scores.

It should be recognized that the intended weights (by varying the maxima) do not determine the actual significance of factors in influencing relative job standing even in this preliminary step as some might think. Actual weights depend on the variability of the distribution of factor scores, not absolute values. The influences of distributional variance is shown in Figure 5,

---

[27] See also on this point, Clark Kerr and Lloyd H. Fisher, "Effect of Environment and Administration on Job Evaluation," *Harvard Business Review* 28, no.3 (May 1950), pp. 77-96.

using the two-factor example provided above. Note that although skill has a higher maximum (and actual mean value, $\overline{X}$ = 80.00), the rank order of the jobs, which is determined by summing the two factor scores (see equation (1) above) corresponds exactly to the ranking of working conditions, whose mean value is lower, $\overline{X}$ = 24. The reason for this can be ascertained by examining the variability in the two distributions (standard deviation of working conditions—18.97, of skill—7.91).

Figure 5

**JOB WORTH AS A FUNCTION OF FACTOR VARIABILITY:
AN ILLUSTRATION**

Job	Points for Skill Factor	Points for Working Conditions Factor	Total Points or Worth
A	90	0	90
B	85	12	97
C	80	24	104
D	75	36	111
E	70	48	118
Mean	80	24	
Std. Dev.	7.91	18.97	

Key jobs are then evaluated using the factors in accordance with whatever *a priori* weighting system has been chosen. At this point the order of key jobs resulting from the preliminary job evaluation is compared to the order of the wage rates for those jobs.[28] The wage rates may be those currently paid in the organization or may represent market wages as identified through some sort of wage survey. A variety of informal "eye-ball" techniques is sometimes used to make the comparison. Frequently, however, multiple regression is employed in this step. The model is:

$$W = a + \sum_{i=1}^{n} w_i X_i \qquad (2)$$

where:

$$W = \text{wage}$$
$$a \text{ and } w_i = \text{constant unspecified weights}$$
$$X_i = \text{compensable factor scores.}$$

---

[28] See, for example, Bernard J. Fitzpatrick, "An Objective Test of Job Evaluation Validity," *Personnel Journal* 28, no. 4 (September 1949), pp. 128-32; W. M. Fox, "Purpose and Validity in Job Evaluation," *Personnel Journal* 41 (1962), pp. 432-37. Both recommend this procedure.

As noted, this model is typically fitted to only a subset of jobs where the existing wages are thought to represent adequately the market wage structure (key jobs as defined above).

The constant weights are usually estimated by regressing the wage rate on the compensable factor scores in an equation:

$$\hat{W} = a + \sum_{i=1}^{n} w_i X_i \tag{3}$$

where:

$\hat{W}$ = wage estimated by equation

a and w_i = constant derived weights

X_i = compensable factor scores.

The constants, a and w_i, are derived so that the deviation between actual wages [W in (2)] and predicted wages [$\hat{W}$ in (3)] is minimized. Note that this procedure specifies weights in terms of the factors' contributions to the prediction of wages. For any particular factor, this contribution does not depend on the *a priori* weights, nor solely on variability, but rather on the relationship between both the factor scores and wages, and the factor scores and the scores of the other factors.

Treiman reports that the regression procedure described is "standard practice" for deriving factor weights.[29] There are also a number of applications of this procedure described in the literature. The factor weights in the job evaluation system used in the steel industry were determined in this fashion.[30] More recently, wage rates for a variety of jobs have been regressed on the job dimensions of two standardized job analysis procedures, the Position Analysis Questionnaire (PAQ)[31] and the Management Position Description Questionnaire (MPDQ).[32] In some cases the wage criterion has been developed from a market survey,[33] while in others it has been wage rates within a single organization,[34] or multiple organizations.[35]

---

[29] Donald J. Trieman, "Job Evaluation: An Analytic Review" (Interim Report to the Equal Employment Opportunity Commission, Washington, D.C., National Academy of Sciences, 1979), 5, n. 2.

[30] *Ibid.* at 13.

[31] See McCormick, *et al., supra* note 14.

[32] See Tornow and Pinto, *supra* note 15.

[33] See, for example, Robinson, *et al., supra* note 23.

[34] Tornow and Pinto, *supra* note 15.

[35] Robert C. Mecham and Ernest J. McCormick, "The Use in Job Evaluation of Job Elements and Job Dimensions Based on the Position Analysis Questionnaire" (Prepared for the

It is likely that the initial choice of factors and jobs will not lead to a satisfactorily high (judgmentally determined) correspondence between job evaluation results and wage distributions. Several procedures are commonly employed to increase the correspondence. First, the sample may be changed through the addition, or more likely, deletion of key jobs. Second, factors may be added or deleted. Third, jobs may be re-evaluated and, finally, the *a priori* weighting system may be changed.

Any one or any combination of these techniques is likely to change the effective factor weights. Weights (and factors receiving weight) are especially sensitive to minor changes in the jobs which are sampled or the methods used to specify wages when the factors themselves are interrelated.[36] Moreover, the results of research suggest that the interrelatedness of factors is a serious problem in a variety of job evaluation plans.[37] Thus, modifications of the sort typically performed will generally increase the correspondence between job evaluation results and the criterion wage distribution. In so doing, however, the actual job evaluation model may be substantially altered. Thus, two job evaluation applications beginning with the same factors could lead to very different "systems," depending on the specific jobs and wages included in the regression model.

2. *Implementation*

The steps described so far are used to establish the job evaluation model. Once established, this model is then applied to non-key jobs for purposes of pay setting. Non-key jobs are evaluated on the factors surviving the developmental process. The resulting hierarchy of these jobs is in effect determined using a weighted composite of factors that correlate with wages for key jobs.[38]

C. JOB EVALUATION AND COMPARABLE WORTH

It is apparent that job evaluation as prescribed theoretically differs substantially from that accomplished in actual practice. Prescriptions focus

---

Office of Naval Research, Department of the Navy, Washington, D.C., June 1969); and E. J. McCormick, A. S. DeNisi, and L. D. Marquardt, "The Derivation of Job Compensation Index Values from the Position Analysis Questionnaire (PAQ)" (Prepared for the Personnel and Training Research Programs, Psychological Science Division, Office of Naval Research, Arlington, Virginia, September 1974) are examples.

[36] For a general discussion of the problems with, and consequences of, multicollinearity in regression, see D. E. Farrar and R. R. Glauber, "Multicollinearity in Regression Analysis: The Problem Revisited," *Review of Economics and Statistics* 49 (1970), pp. 411–25.

[37] For a review, see C. H. Lawshe, Jr. and E. J. McCormick, "What Do You Buy with the Wage or Salary Dollar?" *Personnel* 24 no. 2 (September 1947), pp. 102–06.

[38] It might be noted that the factor variability for non-key jobs probably differs from the variability obtained on the sample of key jobs. If so, the effective weights for specific factors change from the developmental to implementation models. Thus, the actual weight of various compensable factors in determining the non-key job hierarchy is typically unknown.

on job evaluation as a procedure to identify job worth. Clearly implied is the idea that worth somehow captures variance internal to the organization, or at the very least, something potentially different from the external labor market.

An examination of job evaluation as practiced, however, suggests that it may be accounting for market variables much better than either advocates or critics assume. Indeed, the developmental steps of job evaluation practice are specifically aimed at generating a correspondence between job evaluation results and wages. Samples of jobs and perhaps factors are juggled about (often statistically) until an equation is obtained which satisfactorily correlates evaluations with actual wages. The criterion is an existing wage distribution, not worth, unless it is agreed the two are synonymous.

When the resulting system is used to evaluate non-key jobs for purposes of establishing a pay hierarchy, it does so based on factors which correlate with wages of key jobs. If there is a conflict between the "worth" hierarchy for non-key jobs and the rates non-key jobs are currently being paid, it is not a conflict between the market and job evaluation results as is often assumed. Instead, it is a conflict between the variables that correlate with key job market wages and the wage structure that has emerged internally. This may indeed be a market-internal conflict, but one where the job evaluation results represent the market, not the non-key job wage structure.

While the notion of comparable worth is consistent with job evaluation, as theoretically prescribed, it is not consistent with practice. Comparable worth is based on the premise that worth can be defined and measured, something which job evaluation does not in fact do. As practiced, job evaluation chooses and weights factors to conform to a wage distribution which is assumed to be appropriate, i.e., reflects the market. Since the test of the model in the developmental stage is conformity, any factors might be appropriate so long as they result in a high correspondence with the wage distribution. Indeed, given the high degree of interrelationship among factors, a variety of models might be used which would account for about the same percentage of wage distribution variability.

Nevertheless, job evaluation serves a significant purpose. As practiced it serves the important administrative function of linking external and internal labor markets. Indeed, by using market key jobs as the actual criterion, job evaluation establishes a correspondence between the market and non-key job wage rates. No alternative procedure has been proposed that better performs this function.

At the same time, the use of job evaluation needs to be investigated more extensively. To date, research has focused almost exclusively on characteristics of compensable factors. Even here a number of questions remain. For example, it is particularly important to determine whether reliability of job analysis and evaluation of jobs can be improved.

In light of concerns about the possible discriminatory character of job evaluation, more research is needed to determine whether the demographic characteristics of either job incumbent or evaluator influence judgments about jobs or evaluations of jobs. As noted above, one job analysis study examined sex in this regard, but more research of this kind needs to be performed. Several commentators have examined research on personnel judgments in other areas to infer possible biases which might be expected to occur in job evaluation, particularly bias regarding sex.[39] If one thing is clear from research on other personnel decisions, however, it is that sex-role stereotypes operate in complex and highly specific ways.[40] Generalizations from, for example, performance appraisal research to what might be expected in job evaluation, would be risky and probably erroneous. Additional research aimed explicitly at possible sources of bias in job evaluation is still needed.[41]

Perhaps more important, however, is the need to examine the actual criterion for job evaluation practice, namely, wage distributions. The basic issue remains construct validity, but now the central question becomes: how well does the chosen wage distribution reflect the market?

One part of the answer depends on the sampling of jobs and markets. For example, which jobs are to be regarded as market jobs? This is a very difficult question because, as noted above, a continuum exists which ranges from "pure" market to totally unique jobs. Most jobs undoubtedly fall somewhere in between, so that judgment (hence subjectivity) is necessary in the choice. The problem is exacerbated in the current practice of eliminating "outliers" (unpredictable key jobs) in the developmental step as a way of increasing the correspondence between job evaluation results and wages. The market(s) to be sampled also require investigation. Appropriate markets depend not only on geographical location, but also on industry and even occupational clusters.[42] Again a substantial amount of subjectivity in choice is involved.

Another issue must be confronted if job evaluation is to be contemplated in a comparable worth sense. Specifically, to what extent does the market

---

[39] See, for example, Carol T. Schreiber, "Job Evaluation and the Minority Issue" (Paper presented at the IRC Colloquium, Atlanta, Georgia, September 14–15, 1978), pp. 47–66.

[40] As one example in the selection area see Herbert G. Heneman III, "Impact of Test Information and Applicant Sex on Applicant Evaluations in a Selection Simulation," *Journal of Applied Psychology* 62, no. 4 (August 1977), pp. 524–26.

[41] Mahoney and Blake have conducted one of the very few studies in this area. Thomas A. Mahoney and R. Hilton Blake, "Occupational Pay as a Function of Sex Stereotypes and Job Content" (Paper delivered to the National Academy of Management, Atlanta, August 1979).

[42] John T. Dunlop, "The Task of Contemporary Wage Theory," in George W. Taylor and Frank C. Pierson, *New Concepts in Wage Determination* (New York: McGraw-Hill, 1957), pp. 117–39. Indeed, one of the reasons for multiple job evaluation systems within a single organization stems from the fact that the wage distributions that serve as criteria in the developmental step are noncomparable for different job groupings.

reflect discriminatory forces and, if so, can they be separated from job evaluation results? The problems here are far from trivial as demonstrated in the papers by Milkovich and Hildebrand.[43]

III. JOB EVALUATION AND ORGANIZATIONAL PAY POLICIES

The previous section focused specifically on job evaluation. It showed that job evaluation is actually an administrative procedure for linking wages of non-key jobs (where market forces are frequently obscure) to market phenomena. This section is aimed at examining the role of job evaluation in the larger context of organizational pay administration. It is argued that organizational pay objectives are complex and, therefore, that organizational pay policies are necessarily multifaceted. Job evaluation serves as only one of several procedures that organizations use to accomplish these various objectives.

A. THE WAGE SETTING ENVIRONMENT

In the world of economic theory, payment for work serves primarily to allocate employees to jobs. Operating organizations, on the other hand, typically expect pay to aid in the achievement of many personnel and human resource objectives not just, and perhaps not even primarily, the allocation of employees to jobs. Retaining employees and motivating them to high performance levels are other behaviors that pay policies are designed to influence. Moreover, to some extent organizations view employees as being similar to customers and investors, and, as a result, employee satisfaction is frequently an objective.[44]

Empirical research has observed that these employee behaviors and attitudes are not highly related, especially in the case of the relationship between job satisfaction and behaviors such as performance[45] and turnover.[46] This, in turn, suggests that managerial policies regarding pay or other personnel/human resource practices are not likely to impact uniformly on all organizational objectives concerning employees. For example, one investiga-

---

[43] See papers in this volume by George T. Milkovich, p. 23 and George H. Hildebrand, p. 79.

[44] See also David W. Belcher, "Wage and Salary Administration."

[45] See, for example, Donald P. Schwab and L. L. Cummings, "Theories of Performance and Satisfaction: A Review," *Industrial Relations* 9 (1970), pp. 408-30.

[46] Lyman W. Porter and Richard M. Steers, "Organizational, Work, and Personal Factors in Employee Turnover and Absenteeism," *Psychological Bulletin* 80, no. 2 (August 1973), pp. 151-76.

tion found that a pay system resulting in the greatest motivation to perform at high levels was the least satisfying to employees.[47]

It is not surprising, therefore, that organizations develop and implement a variety of pay procedures to help accomplish these multiple objectives. Merit raises, fringe benefits, job evaluation, payment for seniority and wage surveys are illustrative. Some are designed to encourage participation in the organization, while others are aimed at motivating performance. Still others are expected to satisfy employees. Some have a direct impact on jobs and hence apply to all employees on those jobs; others have their major impact on individuals, independent of jobs.

These varied policies are implemented within a political as well as an economic environment. The former often attempts to modify and shape pay policies to serve other than organizational goals. Thus, state and/or federal regulation legislates minimum wages, or requires (e.g., Old Age Survivors and Disability Insurance (OASDI)) or regulates (e.g., Employee Retirement Income Security Act (ERISA)) indirect compensation, as well as reallocating direct pay through income and social security taxes. Union pressure exercised through the collective bargaining process also serves as an environmental parameter that shapes organizational pay setting processes and outcomes. Taken together, economic and other environmental factors serve as constraints that must be accounted for as compensation administrators attempt to develop pay policies.

Finally, it should be noted that pay policies do not represent the only, or even necessarily most important, means for achieving objectives concerning employees. Other personnel and human resources policies pertaining to functions such as recruitment, selection, placement, and training are also aimed at influencing the same objectives that serve as criteria for compensation policies. In some instances these latter policies may even operate to vitiate the effectiveness of pay. For example, a poorly operated recruiting process may offset the positive effects expected from high entry level salaries.[48] In other situations, alternative personnel and human resource functions may make certain pay procedures essentially unnecessary. For example, a merit pay system may not add to motivation beyond an effective policy for making promotions contingent on performance.

The major components or elements relevant to the organizational pay setting process are shown in Figure 6, which identifies major objectives that are of concern to organizations regarding their employees. Some of the pay

---

[47] Donald P. Schwab, "Conflicting Impacts of Pay on Employee Motivation and Satisfaction," *Personnel Journal* 53 (1974), pp. 196–200.

[48] Sara Rynes, Herbert G. Heneman III, and Donald P. Schwab, "Individual Reactions to Organizational Recruiting" (Paper read to the National Academy of Mangement, Atlanta, Georgia, August 1979), p. 9.

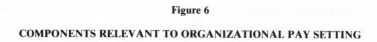

Figure 6

COMPONENTS RELEVANT TO ORGANIZATIONAL PAY SETTING

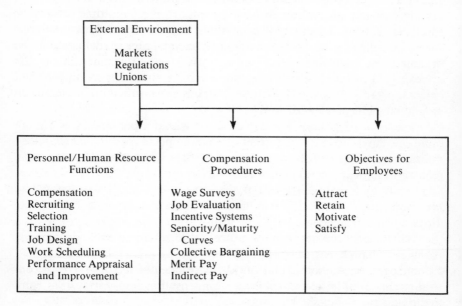

Personnel/Human Resource Functions	Compensation Procedures	Objectives for Employees
Compensation	Wage Surveys	Attract
Recruiting	Job Evaluation	Retain
Selection	Incentive Systems	Motivate
Training	Seniority/Maturity	Satisfy
Job Design	Curves	
Work Scheduling	Collective Bargaining	
Performance Appraisal	Merit Pay	
and Improvement	Indirect Pay	

procedures designed to accomplish these objectives are also shown in the center column. Other personnel and human resource functions (left column) also have procedures associated with them (not shown), which are analogous in the sense that they too are aimed at enhancing the employee objectives identified. Finally, pay setting, as well as other personnel and human resource processes, is conducted within an external environment including economic conditions, public regulation and unions.

B. PAY PRACTICES

Pay setting then is a very complex organizational process. Pay objectives are many and varied; hence, the procedures designed to accomplish them are similarly diverse. The importance of these objectives and especially the importance of the specific pay procedures—given that other personnel and human resource activities can influence the same objectives—vary between organizations and, indeed, may vary within organizations across occupational groupings of employees. In both instances, differences in objectives and procedures may be necessitated by (1) economic conditions reflected in both product and labor markets, and (2) institutional constraints such as collective bargaining or regulation, (*e.g.*, exempt-nonexempt categories of the Fair Labor Standards Act).

In administering pay, a distinction must usually be made between policies aimed at differentiating among jobs and those aimed at differentiating among individuals. Job evaluation is obviously applicable only to the former, because a single point value is assigned to each job. Such a procedure might be sufficient for pay determination if employees were homogeneous in terms of their potential for performance, as job entrants, and actual performance, as employees.

Employees are clearly not homogeneous, however. Organizations often differentially reward employees on the basis of variations in performance levels, primarily as a mechanism to motivate future performance.[49] A variety of specific methods are employed for this purpose. Among production and sales personnel, incentive systems are sometimes employed, although their use is declining.[50] In such systems the pay of the individual or work group is tied directly to the amount produced or sold. Incentive systems can distort the job wage structure dramatically, because the base (guaranteed) wage associated with the job may be a relatively small portion of total compensation.

Much more common among white collar employees are merit systems. Here, an attempt is made to tie pay increases to evaluations of past performance, usually on an individual basis. Merit systems ordinarily rely on performance appraisal as the mechanism for measuring performance. While wage structures can also be distorted by merit systems, administrative controls are ordinarily established to keep increases within the range specified for any particular job.

Also, organizations often reward longevity through seniority systems which provide increases in pay based on length of service. It is frequently assumed that employees and unions regard seniority as an equitable basis for incremental individual payment. In any event, both seniority and merit provide pay based on individual, rather than job criteria.

Most systems that provide for individual pay variation on a given job probably apply multiple criteria, often some combination of merit and seniority. In some cases the multiplicity of criteria may be explicit, as in the case where policy indicates that movement to the midpoint of the range is to

---

[49] The success of using compensation in this context has been extremely controversial among academics. Some have argued that pay is ineffective as a motivator (e.g., Frederick Herzberg, *Work and the Nature of Man* [Cleveland, Ohio: The World Publishing Company, 1968]), or that its motivating potential works at the expense of motivation from other sources (e.g., Edward L. Deci, "Notes on the Theory and Metatheory of Intrinsic Motivation," *Organizational Behavior and Human Performance* 15, no. 1 [February 1976], pp. 13–45). The evidence from both field and experimental settings, however, is fairly unambiguous in showing that pay when linked to performance can, on average, increase performance levels (e.g., Edward E. Lawler III, *Pay and Organizational Effectiveness: A Psychological View* [New York: McGraw-Hill, 1971], pp. 37–59).

[50] John Cox, "Time and Incentive Pay Practices in Urban Areas," *Monthly Labor Review* 94, no. 12 (December 1971), pp. 53–56.

be determined by seniority, while movement above that point is based on merit. In others, particularly those that purport to provide salary increases only for merit, the system becomes mixed in actuality through the use of nonperformance criteria, such as seniority, in the decision process.[51] Inflation, for example, may be accounted for through cost-of-living increases that are inappropriately labeled merit increases.

C. COMMENTS

Organizations have multiple pay objectives. Not only do they seek to attract, but also to maintain, motivate, and satisfy their work force. Since these objectives often have low interrelationships, a variety of pay policies and procedures is developed.

One set of important policies has to do with payment for the jobs themselves. Here, organizations must account for both external (market) and internal factors in developing a pay structure. When done formally, job evaluation is frequently employed to assist in this process.

Individual and indirect pay serve to complicate substantially the organizational pay structure, because the criteria for receiving them differ from the criteria used to establish job pay. Individual payments are often rationalized in policies aimed at rewarding performance and/or seniority. Because such policies obviously bear no necessary relation to policies underlying job payment, the wage structure can be substantially distorted.

This possibility is illustrated in Figure 7, which shows a portion of the planned and actual pay structure in a hypothetical organization. In the example, six labor grades are shown with overlapping wage ranges. The wage line connects the midpoint of each range. The distributions within the first, third, and fourth labor grades show the actual wages which might occur as a result of individual pay policies. In the illustration, for example, movement through the wage range might depend primarily on seniority. In the lowest labor grade turnover may be high so that the average wage falls below the midpoint. The high wages in the third labor grade illustrate the high seniority of the incumbents, which may be due to blocked promotion channels. As a result, the actual averages in grades three and four are similar despite the differences designed into the job payment system.

---

[51] Studies by Kenneth E. Foster, "Accounting for Management Pay Differentials," *Industrial Relations* 9, no. 1 (October 1969), pp. 80–87 and Edward E. Lawler, "Managers' Attitudes Toward How Their Pay Is and Should Be Determined," *Journal of Applied Psychology* 50, no. 4 (August 1966), pp. 273–79, found managerial pay levels to be related to a number of personal variables. In Lawler's study and a study by Herbert G. Heneman III, "Impact of Performance on Managerial Pay Levels and Pay Changes," *Journal of Applied Psychology* 58, no. 1 (February 1973), pp. 128–30, managerial pay levels had very low relationships with performance evaluations. Heneman even found that pay increases were only modestly related to assessments of performance.

Figure 7

PAY STRUCTURES: PLANNED AND ACTUAL

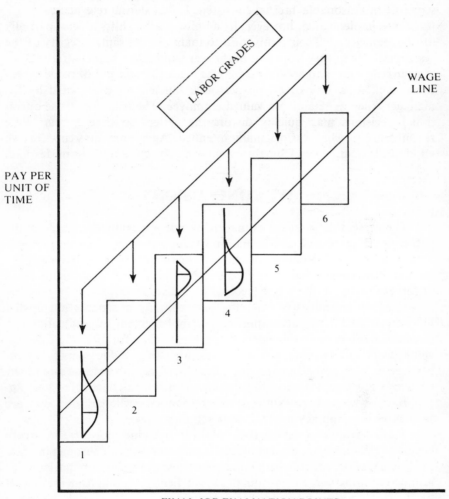

FINAL JOB EVALUATION POINTS

The issues implied by Figure 7 suggest the need for caution in attributing anything to a specific pay policy solely on the basis of the actual distribution of wages in an organization. Actual wages generally depend on a variety of policies and, hence, may say very little about any particular procedure such as job evaluation.

Another significant factor to keep in mind when evaluating pay distributions in organizations is the difference between policies as initially implemented and as the system evolves through time. The initiation of a wage structure is likely to be primarily the responsibility of wage and salary specialists using the procedures described above (and elaborated on in any standard wage and salary text). These administrators usually develop a pay structure of reasonable internal consistency and external relevance.

Once implemented, however, its administration shifts at least partially to line managers.[52] Their motivation to maintain the same integrity of the system is likely to vary from that of the wage and salary administrator. Jobs may be redefined, and arguments may be made to make out of range exceptions, etc., as a way of easing personnel difficulties confronted by the manager, such as retaining a valued employee. The results of these operational decisions may quickly distort the system so that it bears little resemblance to what was originally intended. Again, any inferences drawn about the system, *per se*, from the extant wage structure could be misleading.

IV. CONCLUSIONS

The present paper suggests that the use of job evaluation to aid in the reduction of presumed discrimination through the identification of comparable worth has two major difficulties. The first has to do with the way job evaluation establishes worth, while the second has to do with the significance of job evaluation to the wages received by individuals.

The first difficulty stems largely from a common misconception of what job evaluation actually accomplishes. As implemented, job evaluation is a managerial procedure to help develop pay hierarchies for jobs where market values are difficult to obtain, that is, for non-key jobs. It does so by first identifying correlates, called compensable factors, of key job wage rates. The latter wages are assumed to validly reflect the market. These correlates, appropriately weighted to maximize the correspondence with key job wages, are then applied to non-key jobs for wage setting purposes.

Viewed from this perspective, job evaluation does not measure worth beyond its definition in market wages; it does not estimate through internal job content variables. Job variables are only used to generate a market wage estimate for jobs where such estimates are difficult to obtain from the market itself. The choice and weighting of job content variables are based, therefore, on a criterion of wages, and not on a criterion of worth.

The notion of comparable worth, as currently articulated, implies that either the content of the job or the requirements the job places on individuals establish its worth. Jobs of equal overall content or requirements are presumed comparable. This may be so, and as a value position one might wish to argue that comparable jobs so defined be paid equally. At present, however,

---

[52] See N. Frederic Crandall, "Wage and Salary Administrative Practices and Decision Process," *Journal of Management* (Spring 1979), pp. 71–90, for a discussion of managerial responsibility for wage and salary administration.

there is no mechanism for defensibly establishing comparable worth. Certainly job evaluation does not do it.

The second major difficulty arises independently of the first. Job evaluation is only one procedure used by organizations to establish pay. Other pay mechanisms are typically used simultaneously. Organizations not only establish pay levels for jobs, but they frequently also make pay decisions about individuals. These multiple pay and decision making systems are utilized because organizations generally attempt to influence several personnel/human resource objectives with pay.

Thus, the pay obtained by any individual will ordinarily reflect not only the job he or she holds but also personal characteristics such as past performance levels and service with the organization. If individuals are aggregated into groups, such as by sex, and a difference is observed, the source of the difference could be due to job and/or individual pay variation. Consequently, attribution of the difference to only a single source may be erroneous. Moreover, to expect that the regulatory manipulation of a single pay procedure will eliminate group differences may be equally erroneous.

THE MARKET SYSTEM

By
George H. Hildebrand

Professor Hildebrand analyzes both the correlation between the external labor market and wage administration and the impact a federal comparable worth policy will have on existing internal wage structures and the economy. He begins by describing the evolution and meaning of comparable worth and the technical definition of a labor market. He demonstrates that job evaluation is essentially a wage hierarchy and a wage curve derived from the market and, thus, that the comparable worth theory cannot be harmonized with it because the theory has been formulated to exclude the external market. He asserts that a system of job evaluation must be adapted to conditions prevailing in external labor and product markets to be compatible with the survival and profitability of the firm. Professor Hildebrand concludes with a practical assessment of the economic cost to the workforce in general, and female employment in particular, of instituting a federal policy of comparable worth.

George H. Hildebrand is the Maxwell M. Upson Professor of Economics and Industrial Relations at Cornell University, where he has taught since 1960. He also is the Director of the University's Center for the Study of the American Political Economy. A graduate of the University of California in 1935, he obtained his M.A. from Harvard in 1941 and his Ph.D. in economics from Cornell in 1942. He was Deputy Under Secretary of Labor from 1969 to 1971 and is a former President of the Industrial Relations Research Association. Dr. Hildebrand has done most of his research and teaching in the field of labor economics and industrial relations and has published extensively in these areas. He is also interested in the legal aspects of the labor market and its performance and regulation. Recent publications by Dr. Hildebrand include *Manufacturing Production Functions in the United States* (Cornell, 1965); *Growth and Structure in the Economy of Modern Italy* (Harvard Press, 1965); *Poverty, Income Maintenance and the Negative Income Tax* (N.Y. State School of Industrial Relations, 1967); and *American Unionism—An Historical and Analytical Survey* (Addison-Wesley, 1979).

THE MARKET SYSTEM

This paper is concerned with the nature and significance of external labor markets as they relate to official efforts to alter particular internal wage structures to conform to the now-emerging theory of equal pay for jobs asserted to be of comparable worth.[1]

I. EVOLUTION AND MEANING OF THE THEORY OF COMPARABLE WORTH

The Equal Pay Act of 1963 prescribed the principle of "equal pay for equal work" on any job within any unit of wage administration—shop, department, plant, or entire enterprise. It also provided for exceptions to this standard, where the pay differential was the result of (1) seniority-based wage progressions; (2) merit-based increases; (3) incentive pay plans; and (4) differentials based on any other reasonable factor unrelated to sex. When Title VII was passed in 1964, it included the Bennett Amendment, which was added specifically to ensure that discrimination in compensation on account of sex did not violate Title VII unless it also violated the Equal Pay Act.[2]

The next step in the evolution of the equal pay principle has been to relax the concept of strict equality by restating it as "substantially equal" work. Today it is proposed to extend this concept still further, by reviving the principle of comparable worth, which had been rejected early in the history of the Equal Pay Act.

A. *Underlyng Premises*

In essence, this notion seems to imply three main ideas, although so far it has not been given a careful formulation. First, the idea suggests that a so-called bias-free system of job evaluation can and will be devised that can be applied to a given plant or establishment. In turn, this new system will yield a hierarchy of jobs. In the event that two or more of these occupations fall into the same evaluation level, bracket or grade, these jobs can be considered to be

---

[1] I wish to acknowledge much valuable help and criticism from my colleagues, Olivia Mitchell and Robert L. Raimon, who bear no responsibility for what follows. I also wish to express my appreciation to the Center for the Study of the American Political Economy at Cornell University for its support of this research.

[2] A more thorough examination of the relationship between these two statutes can be found in the paper by Robert E. Williams and Douglas S. McDowell in this volume, p. 197.

of "comparable worth" because they are found to be of equivalent rank under the chosen evaluation system. Accordingly, an employer would be in violation of Title VII if a job in this group contained a high proportion of women and carried a lower rate of compensation than another job in the same group with a high proportion of males. In short, what matters is that the jobs are of the same "worth" to the employer under the particular evaluation system, even if the jobs differ in required skill, responsibility, effort, or working conditions. To conform to the requirements of Title VII, then, the employer should pay the same rate on both jobs.

Second, differences in external market rates between the two jobs should not be allowed to upset this internal parity, because the structure of rates in the outside market has been twisted and distorted over the years by the influence of categorical discrimination against women, past and continuing. In short, it is assumed that most wage rates in the external market are noncompetitive in nature and, therefore, both reflect and perpetuate discrimination against female workers.

Third, the argument runs, the various systems of job evaluation now in use have been tainted by impermissible forms of discrimination under Title VII. Although existing methods of job evaluation differ in their nature, all of them contain an element of systematic bias against women and minorities, and this element of bias operates to affect the job hierarchy obtained by application of the particular method. Bias can occur through the components chosen for evaluation, such as education, effort, experience, skill or responsibility. It can also be the product of the weights assigned to any component under a complex system of evaluation. And finally, the influence of discrimination can be exerted when external market rates are introduced as the peg points for determining the final ranking of the jobs in the hierarchy as well as the wage line displayed by that hierarchy. What is needed, therefore, is a bias-free technique of evaluation that will eliminate the influence of both the external and internal factors in a wage and job structure that are adverse to women employees.[3]

Viewed as a guide to enforcement by administrative agencies, the concept of comparable worth could be used to compel a recasting of the structure of relative wage rates. The principal way in which this might be done would be through the imposition of a "value-free" system of job evaluation. Alternatively, but less likely, a defendant enterprise might be instructed to ignore market rates for jobs in which the female population is dominant, where it is believed that the external rates have somehow been biased downwards by reason of discriminatory bias forbidden by Title VII.

---

[3] It was the task of the special committee established by the National Academy of Sciences to search out the possibilities for such a bias-free technique of evaluation, and to comment upon the feasibility of such an approach. Treiman, Donald J., "Job Evaluation: An Analytic Review." Staff paper prepared for the Committee on Occupational Classification and Analysis, Assembly of the Behavioral and Social Sciences, National Research Council, National Academy of Sciences, Washington, D.C., February 1979, unpublished.

It is important to note at the outset, however, that no "value-free" system of evaluation has yet been shown to exist. To date, the notion of comparable worth involves sheer rhetoric alone; that is, it lacks operational meaning.[4] This rhetoric typically assumes that the differences in compensation, between jobs largely held by women and those mainly occupied by males, is necessarily the product of impermissible discrimination. In the usual case, jobs held predominantly by women are paid less. The comparable worth argument itself is commonly applied both at general levels, such as the whole society or entire industries or, as here, in connection with jobs involving a particular employer.

B. *The Limitations of Comparable Worth*

Underlying this rhetoric is an equally important and very old belief in the notion of "just price": namely, (1) that "fair" wages and prices have objective meaning in the real world; (2) that they can be found empirically by appropriate methods; and (3) that they should be imposed throughout the economy as an act of fundamental social justice. Needless to say, the idea of a "just price" goes back to the Middle Ages and has long since had no standing whatever in economic theory.

Two additional observations should be made. First, the contemplated extension of the principle of equal pay for substantially equal work to encompass the vague rhetoric of comparable work is directed in essence to the reconstruction and the regulation of the wage and salary structures of defendant firms and their component parts throughout the country. Potentially, the scope for this exercise has no limits beyond the personnel and administrative capacities of the government agencies that would enforce it. In short, even assuming that the full achievement of such control might take several years, the proposal leads directly to administrative wage control for the entire American economy.

The only real precedent for such an undertaking involves the National War Labor Board of World War II. There are significant differences, however, between the WLB system and the one now under contemplation. Wage control during the second World War was contemplated as a temporary measure for the control of inflation. It was put in place in a context of overwhelming national unity, and it essentially relied upon this massive moral support for its success. The system itself lasted a little more than three years, and was in the course of collapse at the time it was ultimately abandoned in early 1946.

Second, the comparable worth approach is directed at the regulation of relative wage rates internal to a unit of pay administration, as a means to enforce parities and differentials in job rates that are believed to be "fair" and "just," regardless of their degree of conflict with market rates for the

---

[4] See paper by Donald P. Schwab in this volume, p. 49.

same types of work. Apart from the principle of equal pay for the *same* work, wages as such have not been the target of anti-discrimination legislation and its enforcement. Rather, the main instrument has been Title VII of the Civil Rights Act, where the prevailing concept has been the removal of barriers to *movement,* in hiring, assignments, transfers, and promotions. As those barriers have come down, the members of formerly excluded groups increasingly have entered hitherto closed occupations and industries throughout the country. To the economist, labor flows as a whole respond to relative wage rates and, in turn, cause those rates themselves to change, in a process that is never-ending. Often these adjustments are quite slow in working themselves out, but they do have an impact.

By this point, it should be clear that introduction of the notion of comparable worth into official policy toward the American economic system is of enormous importance. It involves nothing less than an attempt to regulate wages for a vast array of specific occupations throughout the economy. The regulation is to be undertaken by government agencies, although it has not yet been shown that there exists the "bias-free" method of determining proper job rates that would be essential to the administration of such a program. Economists have already produced quantities of evidence to demonstrate how the minimum wage has deprived the young and the unskilled workers of jobs, with consequent extremely high unemployment rates. Under the comparable worth proposal, the equivalent of the minimum wage would be imposed upon all employers for all jobs in which it is decided, under an as yet non-existent standard, that rates should be raised because the proportions of women in these jobs are large. These points will be examined in greater detail at a later stage in this paper.

II. THE MEANING OF THE NOTION OF A LABOR MARKET

A. *Characteristics of Labor Markets*
There are two key characteristics of all labor markets. First, they involve people who seek or who offer employment in specific occupations. These occupations are specific in the sense that, except for unskilled jobs, they are not close substitutes for each other. For example, in this respect, a suburban dentist and a downtown dentist belong to the same occupation, because they are interchangeable. By contrast, a lathe operator does not practice dentistry and, thus, is in an occupation that is not a substitute for dentistry.

Second, all labor markets have a geographic reach that extends from the international in a few cases to the local area at the other end of the scale, depending upon the preferences of prospective employers and employees involved. For practical purposes, most American labor markets are local in extent and multi-occupational in the types of work sought and offered.

However, the variability of both the occupational and the geographic factor tends to make the whole concept of a labor market a rather fuzzy one.

Any market involves a context in which one or more buyers come(s) into effective communication with one or more seller(s). If a transaction is made, it will be composed of two basic components: a price and a commodity or service provided in exchange for the price or for a promise of payment of the price. In many situations, the price is quoted and is not normally subject to negotiation. In others, the price is fluid and constantly changing under shifts in the demand for and the supply of the commodity up for trade. Thus, we can say that markets are of two basic types: the quoted-price market and the *bourse*. In both there will be those who actually trade at the going price, and others who are only potential traders whose eventual participation depends upon changes in the ruling price.

Turning now, to the labor market, the price, of course, is the wage or salary offered to and accepted by those wishing to become employed. The demanders or buyers on the market are those employers who offer payment to obtain labor in desired amounts. Moving against the wage or salary are the services to be provided by the sellers or suppliers, that is to say, the employees. By various rules, incentives and sanctions, the employer will attempt to enforce specifications or "quality control" over the amount and character of these services.

In a free society such as our own, where slavery is illegal, the law views the bargain between employer and employee as essentially an agreement to purchase services from the employee. Thus, the correct view is that the labor market is a market for labor services, where those services are provided by free human beings who cannot be compelled to supply them for a single instant beyond their willingness to do so.

B. *Wage or Salary and the Nature of the Commodity*

All of the above analysis, of course, involves the grossest of over-simplifications, which only in part can be made more realistic in this particular paper. Consider first, the wage or salary. Usually it is thought of as a pure nominal or money rate per hour, week or month, as with simple time rates. Many rates, however, are put on an incentive or bonus basis, in which measured results in output become decisive and are backed up by a minimum guarantee of payment per unit of time. Beyond time and incentive pay systems, there are fringe benefits which now account for one-third or more of total pay, and which further complicate the concept of the price of labor. In short, is the true price of labor services the gross price that includes all fringe benefits and incentive earnings, if any, or is it simply the basic pure wage rate that is paid typically per unit of time? Clearly, where regulation by government is contemplated, all of these variations and still others unmentioned will be serious complications to any such program.

A second difficulty concerns the nature of the commodity that is paid for in the exchange. Is it the mere presence of the employee in the shop, as some have argued? Although simple time-wage systems would suggest this, obviously no rational employer is merely buying companionship for himself. In other words, the buyer is hiring a certain type of potential working capacity. It may range from the simplest types of effort, such as putting groceries on shelves or sweeping the floor, to an intricate bundle made of skill, experience, knowledge of complex equipment, ability to assume responsibility in various ways, or a willingness to work under difficult, dangerous, or unpleasant conditions. In these latter cases, the purchaser of labor services has in mind a complex group of jobs specifications, such as would be required of a surgical nurse or a mining engineer, for example. In between these highly skilled occupations, neither of which is a close substitute for another, is a large range of semiskilled jobs. These rank above undifferentiated unskilled labor at the bottom of the scale, but in their own requirements as regards skill, training, and experience, they are relatively unimportant. These jobs are usually filled by promotion from below or transfer from another line of promotion, and their incumbents, therefore, usually are not recruited from the outside market. The wage they receive thus depends upon the vacancy into which they happen to be placed.[5]

C. *Supply and Demand*

Clearly, potential working capacity is not the homogeneous labor jelly that Karl Marx spoke of as "abstract socially necessary labor time." Speaking more generally, we can say at this point that both jobs and people are highly differentiated in their respective natures. People differ in their capacities for potential service. They vary in skill and experience, in their willingness to take risks, in their strength and their willingness to put forth physical effort, and in their tastes for various kinds of jobs. In a free society, these differences, which find expression through labor supply, become one of the main sources for wage structure or for relative wages. The other source, of course, is demand.

For those who believe that systematic discrimination is rampant in American society, it will also be argued that this wage structure is further distorted, in a major way, by barriers to the occupational movement of the groups discriminated against. Allegedly, they are locked into the poorest and lowest-paid jobs, because they have no means of advancement to better opportunities. Wage rates are low in these occupations, because there is an oversupply of candidates for jobs and there is little mobility for the candidates as regards moving to alternative means of employment. Such jobs thus can

---

[5] Oaxaca, Ronald L., *Theory and Measurement in the Economics of Discrimination*, Industrial Relations Research Association Series, 1977, pp. 181–82.

become identified as "female jobs" or as "laborer jobs" dominated by blacks and other minority groups.

This view of the matter is by no means free of challenge. In economic theory two main theoretical explanations have been advanced for these low-paying female and minority jobs. One is that the local labor market is usually dominated by a single employer or by a few employers acting in collusion to hold down wages by agreement—the so-called "monopsony" case. The other explanation does not consider monopsony in the labor market, but instead contends that even with fully effective competition, the wages of certain occupations will be depressed because their incumbents are women or are members of minority groups. The underlying reason given is that these groups always have been barred from certain jobs in the past, and to some extent still are. As a result, they crowd into those occupations that are open to them, and this increases the labor supply relative to demand in these occupations, with depressed wages as the result.

Although these theoretical matters must be explored more fully at a later point, a few brief comments are essential here. The most important observation which can be made about the monopsony explanation for low wages in this category of jobs in local labor markets is that the evidence for it has never been either extensive or convincing. On the contrary, it has been so slight as to be negligible, as is indicated by one of the very few efforts to study the question empirically.[6]

By contrast, the case for the occupational barriers theory is much stronger, particularly in respect to the past. But the occupational barriers argument has a weakness of its own, which is that it rests upon emphasis of a single causal factor as the explanation for low-wage occupations where females or members of minorities predominate. This neglects the very important additional consideration that competition itself creates low-wage jobs, and will continue to create such jobs, because these are the occupations in which skill requirements are low or even non-existent and therefore the number of candidates on the supply side is very large. Another consideration, however, is that the line of causation may well run in a reverse direction: namely, that most "female" jobs are low-wage jobs not because they are dominated by females but because their requirements are easy enough to permit large numbers to seek entry into them. But as Title VII becomes increasingly effective, labor mobility among different occupations also will continue to increase. In turn this will permit many women to compete effectively for better jobs and, thus, reduce the pressure of excess supply, thereby improving wages in the present so-called "female" jobs. Nonetheless, limited occupational mobility is only one factor in the explanation for low wages in the jobs

---

[6] Bunting, Robert L., *Employer Concentration in Labor Markets*, Chapel Hill, N.C. University of North Carolina Press, 1962, pp. 101, 112; Bunting, Robert L., "A Note on Larger Firms and Labor Concentration," *Journal of Political Economy*, LXXIV:4 (August 1966) pp. 404–05.

under discussion, and its gradual removal as a factor is not likely by itself to cause a substantial improvement in the wages for these particular occupations.

III. COMPARABLE WORTH, JOB EVALUATION, AND THE EXTERNAL LABOR MARKET

Every business enterprise has a job structure, although in very small firms it may be no more than an informal and pragmatic assignment of tasks to people. In addition, every business enterprise has a system of compensation, consisting of wage rates and fringe benefits, that is associated with these jobs. It is this correlated job and pay structure that is the real target of the advocates of the theory of comparable worth. In essence, their goal is to raise the pay rates on jobs in which female employees are dominant. Comparable worth is an intended rationale for such action.

The notion of comparable worth itself is essentially internal to the job structure of a firm or plant. It is not a market-based concept. Although increased compensation—and back pay as well—for the female jobs in the structure are the ultimate goal, the new rates of pay thus established would introduce a new collateral structure of pecuniary worth to go with the job structure as a whole in the given production unit. The primary factor, however, is the revised ranking of jobs in the job hierarchy. More importantly, the outside labor market would not determine the pecuniary worth of those jobs coming under the proposed criteria of comparable worth.

What role would job evaluation play in the proposal? Strictly viewed, job evaluation rests upon two components that in practice are inseparable. One of these is the internal rank order or hierarchy of the jobs as yielded by the chosen method of evaluation—simple point weighting, weighted-components with variable points for each, or other systems now in vogue.

The other essential component of job evaluation in any form is the associated wage curve that is derived from the external market rates for those key jobs in the structure that possess sufficient inter-firm comparability to acquire external standing as to base pay and fringe benefits. Typically, these are the key jobs that serve as peg points for fixing the position of the wage curve as a whole. A wage curve can be obtained by simple ranking of the market-based pecuniary worth of the key jobs, with slotting or interpolating to fix the compensation value for the remaining jobs; also, as Donald Schwab points out, a prediction equation can be devised from the components of the key jobs, first to determine the relative influence of these elements upon the rank order of the key jobs in the compensation scale. Then the equation can be applied to the measured components[7] of the "non-key" jobs to obtain an

---

[7] Standard components would include effort, dexterity, skill, experience, responsibility, and working conditions.

imputed or predicted pecuniary worth for them as well. Short of this rather technical approach, the wage curve might also be derived by simple least squares fitting as applied to the job peg points obtained by survey.

What requires strong emphasis at this point is some elaboration of the fundamental distinction between the two basic elements of job evaluation: the job structure or hierarchy and the wage curve however obtained. The hierarchy yielded by job evaluation is simply an internal rank order of occupations that reflects *ordinal* characteristics that produce the hierarchy, but the ordinal factor says nothing about money values. In fact, this is the central weakness of the principle of comparable worth. It makes no allowance for a wage curve because it deliberately has been formulated to exclude the external market. As a result, for jobs claimed to be of comparable worth, a compensation rate must be arbitrarily inserted. By contrast, the wage curve does rest upon the external market. In this way it provides a means to assign pecuniary values to each job in the hierarchy. In other words, it represents the *cardinal* aspect of job evaluation, because it yields absolute dollar values to go with the internal rank order of the jobs involved.

Accordingly, it should be obvious now that the comparative worth approach to job pricing is only half a loaf. Because it purposely excludes the external market in setting pecuniary values for certain jobs, it is not job evaluation at all, but simply arbitrary intervention into the internal wage structure for other purposes. By contrast, the purpose of job evaluation is to produce an acceptable and efficient system of wage differentials for a given unit of wage or salary administration.

Acceptable and efficient in what sense? First, the wage or salary structure, including fringes, ultimately should produce a consensus among the employees that the system is "fair." Second, the compensation rates established through evaluation should enable the employer to obtain workers who are acceptable to the employer, and to retain them to a degree adequate to hold labor turnover to tolerable amounts. Finally, the rates paid under the system should be congruent enough with the external market to avoid inflation of internal labor costs and the competitive disadvantage that it entails.

IV. KEY JOBS AND THE EXTERNAL MARKET FOR LABOR

A. *Types of Labor Markets*

One of Clark Kerr's lasting contributions to labor economics is a very useful classification of labor markets according to type.[8] One type is the "neo-classical market," in which competition is effective enough to establish

---

[8] Kerr, Clark, "Labor Markets: Their Character and Consequences," *American Economic Review*, Papers and Proceedings, XL:2 (May 1950) pp. 278–91.

uniform market-clearing rates for well-defined occupations, and there are no unions.[9] A second type is what he called the "natural market." Here, too, there are no unions, but competition is weak, occupations are poorly defined, and rates of compensation show much dispersion, even for comparable work.

In addition, Kerr's classification has two other categories. One is the "institutionalized market," in which collective bargaining prevails; institutional rules set job limits and labor flows; institutional relationships rather than labor flows produce interrelations among labor markets; and policies of unions, employers and government largely replace market forces in the making of wage movements. Finally, there is the "managed market," by which Kerr referred to schemes for rationalizing existing labor markets. Under one variant—"compulsory individualism"—unions would be abolished in the service of fully competitive labor markets. Under the other, which he called "collective determination" of wages, the government would set wages and the unions would either be limited to a single firm or abolished. Thus, the comparative worth notion also belongs in the "managed market" category.

Kerr's typology is very helpful in understanding labor markets as such and the different ways in which economists think about them. More light can be shed on the concept of comparable worth, however, if we employ Kerr's classification as background and undertake to categorize occupations instead. Like Kerr, we shall treat the "typical" labor market as local both for reasons of costs of movement and limited job information available to the participants.

B. *Types of Occupations—Key Jobs*

When the emphasis shifts to occupations, the convention has been to assume "that workers are hired on an occupational basis," as Robert Raimon once put it.[10] The model, here, is that of the craftsman, who brings with him a clear-cut group of skills. This is one category of worker who, either through effective competition or effective unionism, brings to the employer a specific service at a specific price. What we have, then, is a skilled key job whose explicit compensation rate serves as a link between the internal and the external wage structure; hence, it serves as a peg point for a wage curve under job evaluation.

Note two other considerations in this connection. First, skilled craft jobs of this type are entry points that give position and stability to the wage structure in a given firm. Second, some jobs involving non-manual skills, such as, legal secretary, also are occupationally standardized, carry a definite rate, and are "ports of entry" (Kerr) for the newly hired.

---

[9] Schultz, George P., "A Nonunion Market with White Collar Labor," in National Bureau of Economic Research, *Aspects of Labor Economics*, Princeton, N.J.: Princeton University Press (1962) pp. 107–46.

[10] Raimon, Robert L., "The Indeterminateness of Wages of Semiskilled Workers," *Industrial and Labor Relations Review* (January 1953) p. 181.

Consider, next, the usual notion of an entry-level job: that of unskilled labor. Here, too, the market provides a going rate, but in this instance no specific skills are offered—only energy and the capacity to learn. Common labor also can be considered a key job, because it involves a point of entry and, therefore, a source of personnel to fill the bottom rungs of the job ladder in industries that operate on the concept of permanent engagements, with internal markets, vertical job structures, and promotion mainly from within. On the clerical side, Filing Clerk B to some extent is a counterpart.[11]

The point should now be clear. Certain jobs are standardized, usually due to technology, across many firms in a given local labor market; in fact, they may reach across several industries as well. For example, on the blue collar side, there are machinists and millwrights, or computer programmers, secretaries, and accountants on the clerical side. These jobs provide the basis upon which the wage curve can be built, precisely because they tie the external and internal markets together. For these reasons, they are called key jobs.[12]

Three types of key jobs are of particular interest here. Because most key jobs are standardized as to content, minimum qualifications and the going wage including regular fringe benefits, they can be termed *market-oriented* key jobs. These must get the going rate or the employer will obtain inferior candidates and suffer the added expense of high turnover.

Every internal wage structure is likely to have some of these market-oriented jobs, at the entry level and above the entry level as well. The point to be emphasized is that firms that are not unionized, that depend upon local markets, and that compete with others that require the same types of job skills are likely to have numerous market-oriented jobs. Thus, if they also have a job evaluation system, the rates for these jobs will become what Livernash calls "peg points" for the entire internal wage structure.

The second type of key job can be termed *union-oriented*.[13] Here, because of the presence of collective bargaining, there exists a special kind of external influence, deriving from the interests of the union itself. For craft jobs such as electrician or die caster, the union will usually impose a standard rate for the key job, to which rates for helpers and apprentices will be tied in a definite manner. When the employer requires an electrician, he calls the craft hiring hall and pays the going rate. This, then, is one way that unionism can impose peg points affecting portions of the internal pay and job structure.

Another kind of union-oriented job structure emerges when the union represents a large fraction of the workforce in the shop, store, warehouse or

---

[11] *Id.*

[12] In some cases, an occupation can be a key job even though it may have no rate in the outside market. Cases such as these may reflect technology or leadership of a work crew or other specialized status.

[13] Hildebrand, George H., "External Influences and the Determination of the Internal Wage Structure," in J. L. Meij, ed., *Internal Wage Structure*, Amsterdam: North Holland Publishing Company, 1963, pp. 282-90.

plant. Considerable diversity is possible in these cases, although some principles of a universal kind do emerge. In one situation, the internal unit is relatively unique in the local labor market. Here, the union will negotiate a structure that must respond to what the members consider to be key jobs, clusters, and progressions within the plant. In their thinking the key jobs link through standard differentials to related jobs of lesser importance. If some jobs must be staffed from the outside, then in these cases the union will have to respect market forces. In any event, the use of job evaluation in these situations will clearly have to accommodate both the equity factors reinforced by unionism and the competitive factors imposed by the market in matters of recruitment and retention.

Finally, there are those union-oriented job structures typical of national industries with multiplant employers. The cases to be cited are familiar, but they remain instructive. In basic steel, automobiles, and other national-market industries, some forty years of collective bargaining have produced a highly standardized job and wage structure; indeed, in steel the system was created and is still regulated by a joint system of job evaluation. The central point is that in such a context the particular plant is isolated from virtually any competitive influences from the local labor market. The reason? The nationally negotiated wage structure is so high relative to the local market for all jobs involved that recruitment and retention simply are not problems in any of the given plants. In this special sense, all of the jobs are union-oriented; hence, the pay structure tends largely to reflect membership notions of equity. At the same time, key jobs, clusters, ladders and their linkages will dominate the pattern of internal relationships.

So far we have identified market-oriented and union-oriented key jobs. There remains a third class that can be called *cost-oriented*.[14] These occupations can also be market- or union-oriented as well. Such jobs are vital because they account for a substantial portion of total labor costs. Hence, any price set for them carries important implications for the employer's unit labor costs and profit margins. Examples are bench and line assemblers in the automobile industry, miners in underground or development and extraction work, and operators and mechanics on public transit systems.

For present purposes, cost-oriented jobs serve as a third type of conveyor belt by which outside influences are transmitted to the internal pay and job structure. The pay rate in these cases does not gain its external importance from the outside labor market, nor from external union considerations. Rather, it is derived from the product market, through the relationship between price and cost which determines profit. That is to say, where a number of employers compete in the same product market, their relative costs become vital. Because product similarity will enforce a common technology, a standardized inter-firm job structure will emerge. Within this structure,

---

[14] *Id.*, pp. 278–82.

certain occupations will be cost-oriented for the reasons just cited and they too become part of the external market whose influence will be felt within a given unit of wage or salary administration.

C. *Function of Key Jobs*

In most work situations, key jobs serve as the center of a cluster of related jobs involved in the same particular function. If collective bargaining prevails without job evaluation, negotiations will center upon the rates for key jobs, while the satellite jobs in the cluster will get traditional (institutionalized) differentials linking them to the key job from below. If, instead, bargaining includes a joint job evaluation system, then the sequence of wage classes derived from the wage curve will provide the ties between subordinate occupations and the key jobs.

Alternatively, if the plant or firm is non-union, job evaluation still will play the same role in filling out the internal wage structure. Finally, if the firm is non-union and does not use job evaluation, then the external market will provide part of the internal wage structure through key jobs at various levels ranging from points of entry on up the hierarchy, while the non-key (dependent or isolated) occupations will be assigned arbitrary rates on a unilateral and pragmatic basis.

Before we leave this topic, it is appropriate at this point to call attention to Raimon's important distinction between occupational and non-occupational hiring.[15] In the usual case, a key job is a job with an external market rate. By contrast, many jobs, particularly at the semi-skilled level, do not involve hiring on an occupational basis. What counts are not experience and skill, but adaptability, speed and dexterity. Such jobs are not normally filled from the external market. Instead, they are filled from within, by persons already in employee status, by means of promotions or transfers. By contrast, employees in most skilled occupations as well as workers completely lacking in skill are hired from the outside. Thus, these latter groups are the ones that supply the link between the internal wage structure and the labor market.

Because of this dichotomy in hiring, the internal wage structure typically involves lots of jobs for which rates must be contrived. Job evaluation is one way to do this. Straight collective bargaining is another, while arbitrary slotting is a third. Consequently, for jobs in which hiring by occupation is not involved, there is likely to be more variance in inter-firm rates of compensation than for the key jobs whose positions in the external markets are well-established.

---

[15] Raimon, Robert L., "The Indeterminateness of Semiskilled Workers," *Industrial and Labor Relations Review* (January 1953), pp. 180–94.

V. WHAT IS THE "WORTH" OF A JOB?

The notion of comparable worth poses the serious semantic issue of what one means by "worth." To address this issue, we must recall the distinction between the ordinal and cardinal phases of all methods of job evaluation. That is to say, the initial procedure of ranking jobs in an ascending *order* according to those components that management considers compensable, and the next step, which calls for the assignment of absolute pecuniary values (total compensation including fringes), to those jobs according to their positions in the hierarchy. Comparable worth, which is not in fact an evaluation procedure, is directed solely to the desirability of the arbitrary placement of certain jobs (female or minority dominated) at certain points on the pecuniary scale.

The simplest notion of the "worth" of a given job is the "price" assigned to it—through collective bargaining, by management acting alone, or by the outside market in cases in which competition is strongly effective. The first complication we encounter is the "price" itself. Is it the straight-time hourly rate; the overall hourly rate inclusive of incentive, shift and other bonuses; or the aggregate annual cost of employing a worker full time, inclusive of all fringe benefits, such as health insurance, pensions, paid holidays and vacations, and employer-paid Social Security taxes? There is no unequivocal answer to the question. It depends entirely upon the reasons the question is asked. Normally, however, fringes are included in job evaluation, because any system of evaluation must take prevailing fringes as well as going rates into account if it is to recruit and retain an acceptable workforce.

Moreover, job price is not the only dimension of job worth. As with the emerging doctrine of comparable worth itself, job worth can mean the internally measured value of the occupation yielded by a system of job evaluation employed to obtain a ranking of a group of jobs within an administrative unit. Whatever the system and whatever its component elements, the outcome is an index of ordinal ranking by which the jobs involved can be put in sequential order from lowest to highest. In some cases, the index value of two or more jobs in the hierarchy either will be identical or the differences so trivial as to warrant the judgment that they are entirely comparable in point values or membership in a given class or group of occupations. In fact, this is what "comparable worth" is really about.

What must be emphasized here, however, is that the comparability and the rank order obtained are purely statistical artifacts: both depend upon the evaluation method chosen. Under a different method, the ordering could be different and some of the comparability could well vanish. To illustrate, if the primary components of the method were, say, skill and undesirable working conditions, the results might differ sharply from those obtained by a method that emphasized degree of formal education and prior job experience.

Although the internal ordinal sequence of jobs must correlate with the external cardinal or pecuniary sequence at least for the key job in the evaluation, the correlation will fall well short of perfect. One important source of divergence is the influence of collective bargaining, where it is present. Another is that external market supply and demand for certain key jobs, as compared with jobs of "comparable worth" in the internal ranking order can thrust such key jobs and their associated clusters well above the "comparable worth" jobs in the pecuniary order obtained from the evaluation.[16]

Next, it should be recognized that a job or a specific occupation is in fact an administrative abstraction, selected both for convenience in assigning tasks and responsibilities, and for encouraging the development of skill, dexterity, and experience. All of these contribute both to personal productivity, and, in the great majority of cases, to the promotability of incumbents to higher levels in the job structure. Finally, through the careful designation of job content, management also can establish indicators of the success or failure of incumbents. Before leaving this topic, the point must be reiterated that the internal index obtained by job evaluation cannot be self-sufficient for the determination of an internal wage structure, although the ranking and comparabilities so obtained for occupations can often improve employee morale, by providing a structure that generally comports with employee notions of equity and fairness.

Nonetheless, in the end it is the pecuniary order obtained from the wage curve yielded by the external market that is the most significant, even if collective bargaining is present. First, the total compensation rates for the occupations in the internal system must be sufficient to recruit new employees of acceptable qualifications or potential, and to retain others with the same traits. Second, if certain key jobs are significantly cost-oriented, their compensation must line up quite closely with the contour rates being paid by competing employers in the same product market. If a given employer's rates are excessive for these jobs, they will function well for recruiting and retention, but at the same time will squeeze his profit margins through higher unit labor costs.

To conclude, then, no system of job evaluation can be compatible with the survival and profitability of a private enterprise if the wage structure derived from it is not closely adapted to conditions prevailing in the external labor and product markets. At the same time, the structure must change with these conditions as well.

---

[16] Two qualifications are needed: (1) Supply and demand on the external market may reflect discrimination and segregation in some cases; and (2) some internal jobs may have no external counterparts, but instead are interpolated within the internal structure.

VI. SOME LEGAL AND ECONOMIC ASPECTS OF THE DOCTRINE OF COMPARABLE WORTH

A. Judicial Treatment of Comparable Worth

The principle of comparable worth is not new. It has always been implicit to all systems of job evaluation. Moreover, as far back as 1962 it was proposed in Congress that "comparable work" rather than "equal work" should be the standard to be applied to claims alleging pay discrimination based upon sex. However, in the upshot "equal work," together with the four affirmative defenses allowed by the Bennett Amendment, were adopted in the final version of the statute. As the Federal District Court observed in *IUE* v. *Westinghouse*,[17] the reason that Congress avoided the far more elastic notion of "comparable work" was to limit "the job reevaluation necessary by the Secretary of Labor and subsequently the Courts." Or as the Fourth Circuit held earlier in *Brennan* v. *Prince William Hospital Corporation*,[18] "Congress realized that the majority of job differentiations are made for genuine economic reasons unrelated to sex. It did not authorize the Secretary or the Courts to engage in wholesale reevaluations of any employer's pay structure in order to enforce their own conceptions of economic worth." In short, in the view of the appellate court, economic worth is determined by competition in the external marketplace.[19]

At the outset, the EEOC framed its guidelines to make them consistent with the statutory principle of equal work. By 1972, however, the Commission substituted a new formulation that, in the opinion of the Federal District Court in another *IUE* v. *Westinghouse* case[20] decided early in 1979, employed language that apparently adopted "the plaintiffs' view of the statute." Their view was expressed by a claim that the company at its Trenton plant had violated Section 703(a) of Title VII by (a) paying female employees less than males "performing the same or substantially the same work;" and (b) paying female workers lower rates than would be paid if their "skill, effort and responsibility were evaluated on the same basis as is used in evaluating work performed by males. . . ." In addition, the plaintiffs claimed that Westinghouse was also in violation for paying women lower rates than men "whose jobs have been evaluated by the Defendant Westinghouse as having *the same number of evaluation points based on education, experience, aptitude, effort, responsibility, and working conditions required for the job*" (emphasis supplied). In sustaining the employer's motion for dismissal, the

---

[17] *IUE* v. *Westinghouse Electric Corp.*, 17 FEP Cases 16 (N.D.W.Va. 1977).

[18] *Brennan* v. *Prince William Hospital Corp.*, 503 F.2d 282, 9 FEP Cases 979 (4th Cir. 1974), *cert. denied*, 420 U.S. 972, 11 FEP Cases 576 (1975).

[19] For a more complete discussion of the legal issues involved in this discussion, see the Williams and McDowell paper, beginning on p. 197.

[20] *IUE* v. *Westinghouse Electric Corp.*, 19 FEP Cases 450, 455 (D.N.J. 1979). This decision has been appealed by the plaintiffs (3rd Cir., Nos. 79-1893/1894).

Court found that the complaint of unequal pay for "unequal, but comparable, work" provides no claim upon which relief can be granted under Title VII of the Civil Rights Act of 1964.

The U.S. Court of Appeals for the Eighth Circuit, faced a similar issue in the Christensen case.[21] The University of Northern Iowa had introduced the "Hayes" system of job evaluation. All jobs were evaluated and assigned to grades worth the points assigned. Jobs with the same evaluation points were placed in the same grade regardless of differences in job content. Each grade was then given a pay range based upon market rates for similar jobs. It was found that the starting rates assigned for physical plant jobs were below the outside market, and, hence, had to be adjusted upward for recruitment and retention purposes. The clerical jobs in the same grade, which were held by females, were not increased, which produced the claim that work "of equal value" to the employer was given unequal pay. Obviously the strategy of the appellants was to rest a claim for equal pay upon the comparable evaluated worth of the jobs in the same grade, irrespective of differences in their content or in their external market rates. In short, as the appeals court noted, they were claiming that equal ordinal value of jobs to an employer constitutes grounds for equal pay.

In its view of the matter, the district court had ruled that the work was not substantially similar and that no sex discrimination was involved, because the employer was merely responding to the market rate and had applied the new rate to both males and females in the physical plant group. In the higher court, the appellants argued that since the lower paid clerical jobs were traditionally "female jobs," the introduction of the adverse differential within the same pay grade simply perpetuated the effects of past discrimination against women workers. In short, their market rate was lower because they had been excluded so long from the better paid occupations.

In its decision, the court of appeals rejected this argument, holding that the real purpose of Title VII was to break down the barriers to equality of opportunity in employment. It stated that the Act does not require the employer to ignore the external market, nor confine itself solely to comparative internal evaluation points in working out its internal pay structure. Since the female employees were not "locked into" clerical jobs, no judicially cognizable claim remained to be decided in the case.

B. *Categorical Discrimination Against Women*

The effort to stretch the concept of equal work to encompass work that is substantially or entirely different in job content, although identical or almost so, and, therefore, *comparable* under a system of internal job evaluation, has an obvious ultimate purpose: to extend the concept of equal pay to comparable as well as equal work. To achieve this ultimate objective,

---

[21] *Christensen v. Iowa*, 563 F.2d 353, 16 FEP Cases 232 (1977).

however, it is necessary to eliminate, if not entirely then at least for those specific occupations dominated by female incumbents, any influence of the external labor market upon the determination of internal wage structure—a proposition with truly sweeping implications that will be considered further in the closing section of this paper. In any event, the justification for the exclusion of market forces is a belief that the wages prevailing for "female" occupations are generally low because of categorical discrimination against women. To gain a better understanding of the doctrine of comparable worth, it is necessary to undertake first a brief excursion into discrimination theory.

As used here, "discrimination" refers to the systematic disadvantageous treatment of certain categories of workers, such as women and minority groups, because all members of the category share a common identifiable trait—sex, color, or ethnicity. In turn, this systematic disadvantage has found expression in lower wages and exclusion from employment in better occupations. As a technical matter, however, it has proved extremely difficult to isolate the factor of categorical discrimination as such from other influences that give rise to wage differentials and that affect the distribution of workers among occupations.[22] Accordingly, there is some tendency to attribute all gross differences in wages or employment distributions to categorical discrimination and to leave the question at that. In other words, in this rather simplistic view of the matter, the workers involved are presumed to have the same skills and abilities, but nonetheless get different wages in the same market.[23]

In any event, two major facts have been established about women workers in the United States. One is that they have long been highly concentrated in relatively few occupations, while the other is that generally women earn less than men.[24]

1. *"Neo-classical"* or *"Taste"* Theory. To address these facts, Gary Becker developed a so-called "neo-classical" line of explanation that attributes discriminatory differentials to the operation of a "taste for discrim-

---

[22] Friedman, Milton, *Price Theory: A Provisional Text,* Chicago: Aldine Publishing Company (1962), pp. 211–25. The book is a thorough discussion of the many factors that determine the occupational wage structure and its changes. Among these influences are barriers to occupational movement arising from discrimination; variations in the relative attractiveness of jobs apart from wage rates; transitional differences because adjustments of wages to changes in labor demand and supply are slow; geographic immobility of workers; and differences in ability among workers.

[23] Oaxaca, Ronald L., *Theory and Measurement in the Economics of Discrimination,* Industrial Relations Research Association Series (1977), p. 20.

[24] Treiman, Donald J. and Terrell, Kermit, "Women, Work and Wages—Trends in the Female Occupational Structure," in Kenneth C. Land and Seymour Spilerman, eds., *Social Indicator Models,* New York: Russell Sage Foundation (1975), pp. 159–71; Stevenson, Mary J., "Relative Wages and Sex Segregation by Occupation" in Cynthia B. Lloyd, ed., *Sex, Discrimination and the Division of Labor,* New York: Columbia University Press (1975) pp. 188–94; Fuchs, Victor, "Differences in Hourly Earnings Between Men and Women," Monthly Labor Review, 94 (May 1971) pp. 9–15.

ination" against females by many males in industry.[25] This discriminatory preference may be the employer's own, or it may emerge from his male employees. It might even be derived from his customers.[26] If the employer is the source, he will expect extra compensation from hiring women, and this will find expression in an adverse wage differential for women employees—in short, their wages will fall below their economic productivity. Alternatively, if the male employees are the principal source, then they will demand a wage premium for working with women. The employer can avoid this, however, by segregating women in separate occupations or not hiring them at all if the male supply of labor is sufficient. More accurately, employers legally could segregate or exclude women before passage of Title VII. Today, this is no longer lawful.

As Professor Madden notes, indulgence of either form of discrimination adds to the employer's costs. Thus competition should favor the non-discriminating employers in the industry or trade, which should gradually wipe out the differentials and the segregation—an inference so far not borne out by the evidence. In point of fact, even Title VII has not accomplished these results, although it has been in force for 15 years.

2. *Monopsony Theory.* The second main type of discrimination theory substitutes market power and institutionalized rules and practices for the rather individualistic and subjective notion of tastes and preferences. The power theory goes by various names—monopsony theory,[27] occupational "crowding,"[28] and group behavior as a manifestation of male power.[29]

Suppose, first, that a concentration of women in a relatively few occupations is primarily either (1) the product of systematic exclusion from other jobs—exclusion that could arise from refusal of employment, rejection from union membership, or segregation in special jobs; or (2) the result, if not always the intent, of originally benign protective legislation, discriminatory job specifications and qualifications, or even a social tradition that encourages women themselves to confine themselves to particular occupations.[30] On these suppositions, the supply of female workers to a given employer will be very low in average elasticity; in technical language, the

[25] Becker, Gary, *The Economics of Discrimination*, 2d ed., Chicago: University of Chicago Press (1971) pp. 13-17.

[26] Madden, Janice Fanning, "Discrimination—A Manifestation of Male Market Power?" in Cynthia B. Lloyd, ed., *Sex, Discrimination and the Division of Labor*, New York: Columbia University Press (1975) p. 150.

[27] Robinson, Joan, *The Economics of Imperfect Competition*, London: MacMillan and Co., Ltd. (1933) pp. 292-304.

[28] Bergmann, Barbara R., "The Effect on White Incomes of Discrimination in Employment," *Journal of Political Economy*, 79 (March–April 1971), pp. 294-313.

[29] Madden, Janice Fanning, "Discrimination—A Manifestation of Male Market Power?" in Cynthia B. Lloyd, ed., *Sex, Discrimination and the Division of Labor*, New York: Columbia University Press (1975).

[30] *Id.*, pp. 136-58.

supply curve will be positive but quite steep, and the marginal wage cost curve still steeper. Together the two curves allow the employer to choose the wage he will pay. Since the corresponding curves for male workers usually will lie outside and to the right in the plane diagram because men enjoy greater occupational mobility, the employer will pay women less in order to maximize profits.[31]

Regarding this explanation, it is reasonable to assume that if monopsony is present in a given labor market, there ought to be visible a collateral concentration of employment as well. To illustrate, the largest firm might employ one-third to one-half of all employees in the locality; the four largest employers could employ similar or even larger proportions; or the ten largest in the area may account for the great majority. As the number of these employers increases, collusion must develop among them to depress wages, and collusion is both difficult, expensive, and unstable as numbers increase.

Surprisingly, little sustained research has been done on this problem. Working with 1948 county data, Robert L. Bunting studied 1774 different labor market areas, finding that the extent of concentration among firms in the unskilled sectors of local labor markets was "low."[32] Based on additional work involving the 25 largest American firms in 99 of the original areas for which all of the reporting units of each firm could be consolidated, Bunting found that firms with concentration ratios of .2000 and more accounted for only 12.3 percent of total employment in these areas.[33] If we accept geographic concentration of employment as a reasonable test of monopsony, then it follows that not much monopsony actually prevails. Accordingly, the monopsony explanation at the least is put in grave doubt.

3. *Statistical Theory.* Both the "taste" and the "market power" models show that categorical discrimination can be a logical outcome under the conditions established for either model. In addition, other models have been developed that are termed "statistical" by Dennis Aigner and Glen Cain.[34] In their judgment, there is a need for a model that can account for the substantial and persistent wage and earnings differentials as for example between men and women with the same productivity. The general principle of this class of models is that employers wish to avert high-risk employees; hence, they rely upon various quantitative indicators of job success in select-

---

[31] An employer will set total employment where its labor demand equals the marginal wage cost (MWC) of all labor; males will be hired to the point where MWC_M = demand, and their wage will be the male supply price for that quantity. Because the MWC_F curve is much steeper as well as inside MWC_M less women will be wanted, and their average pay rate will also be less. See Madden, *Id.*, p. 153.

[32] Bunting, Robert L., *Employer Concentration in Local Labor Markets*, Chapel Hill, N.C.: University of North Carolina Press (1962) pp. 101–12.

[33] Bunting, Robert L., "A Note on Large Firms and Labor Concentration," *Journal of Political Economy*, LXXIV:4 (August 1966) p. 405.

[34] Aigner, Dennis J. and Cain, Glen G., "Statistical Theories of Discrimination in Labor Markets," *Industrial and Labor Relations Review*, 30 (January 1977) p. 175.

ing among candidates. Even if two groups of men and women were identically distributed in their personal productivities, however, the cautious employer will assume that the indicator he uses, like years of formal schooling or test scores, will be less reliable for women, and in consequence will offer them lower wage rates.[35] Furthermore, if the risk-averse employer continues to assign women of equivalent productivity to lower-rated jobs, the very fact of such assignment would yield a self-fulfilling prophecy, since the jobs in question do dictate lesser standards of performance.[36]

4. *Isolating Measures of Discrimination.* A more serious problem with all of these models is their practicability for isolating precise measures of discrimination in, for example, wages and earnings. Obviously, this point is crucial if any attempt were made to redesign internal relative wage structures so that comparable worth would yield equal pay as between two jobs, because to do so would be to attribute all wage differentials reflected from the external market as arising from wage discrimination. This, indeed, is the very basis offered for excluding outside market rates from consideration.

Clearly, this basis is both narrow and inadequate. Competitive forces themselves make for wage differentials. For example, they reflect non-pecuniary differences in the attractiveness of jobs (location, prestige, interest); the stability or instability of earnings expected from different jobs; differences in the actuarial returns after allowance for seasonal and cyclical factors, or the average length of working life.[37] Indeed, under fully competitive conditions, an inter-firm comparison of rates and earnings for a particular job will show dispersion rather than a single mode. Since differences in job content will occur among firms, these too will produce dispersion.

Thus, even for well-standardized jobs, there will be wage differences that cannot be attributed to categorical discrimination. However, the existence of such discrimination is not to be denied, for today or in the past. It is embedded in some wage differentials; the problem is to detect it, and for practical purposes, to measure it separately from the other factors influencing wages. But even here the problem is difficult. As Friedman has noted, segregated ("non-competing") groups can arise from deliberate restrictions on entry (licensure, high union entry rates) or discriminatory barriers to movement. Some of these restrictions involve sex or color, while others are probably attributable to natural differences in human ability or the surviving effects of socio-economic stratification.[38]

---

[35] *Id.*, p. 186; Oaxaca, Ronald L., *Theory and Measurement in the Economics of Discrimination*, Industrial Relations Research Association Series (1977), p. 21.

[36] Oaxaca, *supra* note 35, p. 22.

[37] Friedman, Milton, *Price Theory: A Provisional Text*, Chicago: Aldine Publishing Company, (1962), pp. 211–25.

[38] Bunting, Robert L., note 6 *supra*, pp. 222–25.

To summarize the argument at this point, the fact that categorical discrimination continues to influence certain occupational rates can be accepted. The problem is to find a reliable way to identify and measure the discrimination component with precision. We already possess a plethora of models for discrimination. What is lacking is a convincing statistical showing, which is based upon actual tests of these models. The solution certainly does not lie in the gross major occupational groupings gathered by the Census Bureau and the Bureau of Labor Statistics. The chances for accuracy are somewhat better if Professor Mary Stevenson's approach is followed. Her model standardizes narrowly defined occupations in groups according to similarity of education and training required on the jobs. The groups, which she designates "occlevels," can then be ranked according to this measure.

What really matters, however, are the wage differentials among the jobs in an "occlevel." Presumably, one could expect that women in a job group would earn less on the average, would have more formal education, would be congested in a few jobs, and would suffer from adverse pay differentials.[39] Of course, one can challenge these presumptions. Given the data used, comparative job content would vary across firms and variations in tastes, job disutilities, and degrees of responsibility for personnel, equipment, and product also would contribute to the sex differentials within each "occlevel." All of this simply re-emphasizes, however, the practical difficulties implicit in any government program designed to bring about a major reconstruction of relative occupational wages in the United States.

VII. SOME POTENTIAL ECONOMIC AND POLITICAL IMPACTS

Comparative worth looks like a simple principle, surely reasonable on its face, and not deserving of much attention and concern, but appearances are deceiving. What the principle calls for is federal intervention into the occupational wage and salary structure on a very large, and possibly even massive, scale.

A. *Regulatory Problems*

Initially, comparative worth requires some form of job evaluation merely to identify the jobs that qualify, and it is well accepted that no workable method for accomplishing this has been put forward so far. Nonetheless, it will be worthwhile merely to examine the nature and scope of the regulatory problem.

---

[39] Stevenson finds these expectations to be borne out in her study. Stevenson, Mary J., "Relative Wages and Sex Segregation by Occupation," in Cynthia B. Lloyd, ed., *Sex, Discrimination and the Division of Labor*, New York: Columbia University Press (1975) pp. 175–98.

Today, there are approximately 14 million private firms in the country, employing a labor force of roughly 85 million, and there is no way to estimate with any precision how women are distributed among these many firms. Employment data prepared by the BLS for 1976 indicate that there were 30.7 million female employees on nonagricultural payrolls, of which 24.0 million were in the private sector. For 1976, the female labor-force participation rate stood at 47.3 percent, which warrants the inference that by 1979 it had finally passed the half-way point.[40] By occupation, those in which the number of female employees exceeded one-half million in 1976 (public and private sectors) were as follows: registered nurses, 0.965 million; teachers, except college and university, 2.19 million; bookkeepers, 1.52 million; cashiers, 1.1 million; office machine operators, 0.535 million; and secretaries-typists, 4.3 million. In broader occupational categories, 12.2 million women were in clerical occupations; 1.94 million in managerial-administrative; and 5.6 million in professional-technical. By contrast, only 6.7 percent of women employees were in sales jobs; 1.6 percent in working crafts; 1.1 percent in non-farm labor; 3.1 percent in private household work; and 1.3 percent in farm work.[41]

Looking, then, at the statistical aspects of the wage regulation problem, as of today it would embrace up to 24 million female employees in the private sector, who work for over 13.9 million firms as of 1975. Unfortunately, for the intercensal years the data are poor as regards the industrial distribution of working women, but as of January, 1974, some of the key private industries were banking (780,000 female employees), credit agencies (225,000), insurance carriers (603,000), personal services (554,000), miscellaneous business services (642,000), medical and other health services (3,071,000), and educational services (610,000).[42]

Consider, next, the administrative dimensions and implications of a program to introduce the principle of comparative worth into the American occupational wage structure. First, given the occupational and industrial patterns of the female workforce, the regulatory task will embrace nearly 12 million proprietorships and partnerships. Furthermore, with service activities of various kinds employing over five million women in January, 1974, of which approximately 3.2 million firms were proprietorships and partnerships, it follows that the EEOC would be dealing with a great number of very small enterprises. Within this large segment, formal notions of job and wage structure are often quite unknown, let alone the idea of job evaluation. By contrast, however, finance, insurance, and real estate also draw heavily on

---

[40] U.S. Department of Labor, Bureau of Labor Statistics, *U.S. Working Women: A Databook*, Bulletin 1977, Washington, D.C.: GPO (1977) pp. 5, 7.

[41] *Id.*, pp 8–9. Certain occupations, e.g., craft labor, are available in percentages. It also should be noted that 4.8% of female employees in 1976 were classed as operatives (factory and transport).

[42] Data are for January, 1974, provided by BLS.

the female labor market (2.2 million women employees in January, 1974), and here both extremes would be encountered: 1.2 million unincorporated firms, and 436,000 corporations.[43]

Given the enormous scope of the universe of enterprises that would become subject to this wage regulation, the responsible federal agency would confront an uncomfortable administrative choice: either attempt a vast expansion of staff to cover the entire field, or adopt a highly selective strategy of concentrating upon a relatively few big corporations so that the publicity gained from victories through concessions or through the courts would aid in a subsequent broadening of the initial program. This latter alternative seems more likely.

The second administrative consideration posing great difficulties concerns the regulatory principles themselves. How is comparable worth to be defined and measured, particularly in small firms? Is application to be confined solely to jobs in which women are the exclusive incumbents or the majority of them? Is the external wage structure simply to be ignored when the internal one is redesigned to meet the regulatory standards to be imposed? Is compensation for past "losses" to be awarded those who win pay increases? Does there exist, or can there even be devised, a system of internal evaluation that could be applied consistently to the whole variety of firms in the universe?

Turning to the broader issues, what we actually face, as a latent and so far unrecognized element in this new proposal for wage regulation, is yet another large-scale regulatory intervention into the private sector. Given that the costs of regulation already have passed $100 billion yearly and that for over a decade the business sector has been assaulted with a seemingly endless assortment of regulations, it is now proposed that there be detailed federal management of the wage structure. Except for the very special case of the "inequities" program of the War Labor Board 35 years ago, nothing comparable has ever been seriously proposed in peacetime.[44] Already there is a growing concern over the diversions of capital and executive energy spent on compliance with this mass of regulations. In addition, it has at last begun to be recognized that the overall productivity of labor and capital has been slowing in its annual gains for over a decade, and now, ominously, has turned negative. Unless this tendency can be turned around quickly and strongly,

---

[43] U.S. Department of Labor, Bureau of Labor Statistics, *U.S. Working Women: A Databook*, Bulletin 1977, Washington, D.C.: GPO (1977), pp. 561–62. As of 1974, almost 11 million of a total of 11.9 million unincorporated businesses had annual receipts of less than $100,000. See U.S. Department of Commerce, Bureau of the Census, *Statistical Abstract of the United States, 1978*, 99th Annual Edition, Washington, D.C.: GPO (1978), p. 562.

[44] It should be noted that in 1951 the distinguished economist, A. P. Lerner, did propose a regulation of the occupational wage structure to cause it to provide full employment without inflation, but his program was aimed at producing market-clearing pay rates for all occupations, by a set of guidelines that would add no unemployment. Lerner, Abba P., *Economics of Employment,* New York: McGraw-Hill (1951) pp. 20–241.

there can be no hope for the continued broad improvements in real per capita incomes, including real wages, that we have enjoyed for so long. In the presence of this very real threat to national well-being, therefore, productivity rather than controversial notions of wage justice should dominate our attention.

B. *Economic Ramifications*

At this juncture, we have reached the point where it is essential to meet the issues of a policy of comparable worth head on. Suppose, first, that in a full burst of passion for what its proponents would call social justice, the wage differentials between "male" and "female" jobs are slashed so that female jobs are increased even as much as 50 percent relative to "comparable" male occupations. What should we expect in an economic system where 80 percent of gross national product originates with private firms operating under the profit and loss system, and in which labor costs account for 75 percent of total costs? A substantial portion of so-called female jobs are in the low-wage category. To inject a series of substantial increases in their compensation rates in the service of the comparable worth notion would involve the same predictable results that are already obvious in the plight of those of limited abilities or who are vocationally unprepared, or inexperienced workers. What are these results and what is their cause?

For those under 25 years in particular, who compose an important share of this entire group, unemployment rates have gradually reached astronomical levels, particularly for blacks and members of other minorities, where they usually exceed 25 percent. Even worse, almost half of total overt unemployment involves those under 25 years of age. Keeping in mind that the two basic reasons for these excessive rates of pay are the federal minimum wage and the very high entry rates imposed through collective bargaining upon new and unskilled workers, the principal explanation for the plight of these workers is that their personal productivity is too low to qualify them for employment at present rates of pay.

In the language of the economist, there is a persistent and substantial excess supply of low-productivity workers in the United States, because the price for such labor has been made so high by legislation and collective bargaining. Intervention of this kind has priced several millions of these workers out of the market.

Now it is being argued that the government should extend the minimum wage principle much further, by imposing a policy of comparable worth. We already know enough about the consequences of the policy to be able to predict that it will increase unemployment still further, having the greatest effect on low-productivity workers. In fact, because of the cumulative consequences of discrimination in the past, many of those who are displaced will be women who are black or from other minority groups whose earnings already place them at the poverty line or near to it.

There are three ways by which a comparable worth policy will increase unemployment, and along with it, poverty and welfare dependency. First, as with the minimum wage it will raise the price of low-productivity workers without improving their productivity. In consequence, employers will be induced to lay part of the group off to hold down the enforced rise in their costs. Unlike the minimum wage, comparable worth would affect many more workers because it is intended to reach much further into the labor market. Second, for the low-paid women working in the numerous small or even tiny firms, the imposed rise in labor costs will bring about either much bankruptcy or voluntary closure. Disemployment of these workers will follow. Third, in larger firms the imposed increase in labor costs will create an incentive to substitute capital and to revise plant or shop organization to replace low-paid women or alternatively, to raise hiring standards so that fewer workers of either sex who are more productive can replace them.

In summary, economic theory tells us that if comparable worth is put into effect (1) unemployment rates for females will rise, (2) unemployment of females also will rise, (3) the major victims will be the poorest female workers, (4) welfare dependency will grow, (5) female youngsters will be large losers of job opportunities, and (6) there will be some withdrawal of discouraged women workers from the labor force, precisely because official policy, in the purported service of a peculiar concept of social justice, will have destroyed their jobs for them, despite their own efforts to be productive and self-supporting citizens.

Beyond these socially destructive results, theory also tells us that the policy will extend the downward rigidity of wages and prices, while at the same time directly inflating wage costs by adding to the present upward pressures deriving from collective bargaining and other inflationary actions of government. I do not suggest by this that inflation "begins with the payroll," as Schumpeter used to contend, but surely the policy will accelerate it further.

Finally, the irony of the notion of comparable worth is two-fold: it is supposed to help women workers when in fact it will make them worse off, especially the poorest ones, because it proposes to ignore the external wage rates of the labor market. Yet, at the same time, Title VII already provides a constructive and effective means of improving the economic positions of all female workers, by opening up a great array of occupations for them. Under this policy women are obtaining better jobs, opportunities for employment never before available, and a pay structure that, because it is the result of this steadily increasing mobility, will yield higher real incomes with no accompanying enforced unemployment. Why, then, attempt to impose wage structures by administrative and judicial fiat?[45]

---

[45] An excellent demonstration in the small of what government management of relative wages and salaries can bring about in adverse results for the economy and the public can be found in the Davis-Bacon Act of 1931, 40 U.S.C. §§276a to 276a-5.

WAGE SETTING AND COLLECTIVE BARGAINING

by

Herbert R. Northrup

Professor Northrup contends that the purpose of job evaluation and other wage classification systems is not to provide for compensation but for a systematic wage schedule and for the orderly training and upgrading of employees. He demonstrates that these systems have proved to be constructive tools in the management of human resources and have contributed to the peaceful negotiation of new collective bargaining agreements and the resolution of disputes arising out of contract administration and interpretation. He then asserts that comparable worth is not grounded in market realities or upon an acceptable relationship of jobs. Instead, its adoption would open all jobs to a reclassification process that, unlike job evaluation, would not reward employees for relative skills nor would it encourage training and upgrading. Professor Northrup concludes that the underlying purpose of comparable worth is compensation parity, i.e. to raise substantially the compensation rates of female and minority employees regardless of the positions in which they work.

Herbert R. Northrup is a Professor of Industry at the Wharton School of the University of Pennsylvania. He is also Director of the School's Industrial Research Unit and is Chairman of its Labor Relations Council. A graduate of Duke University, Professor Northrup received his M.A. and Ph.D. in economics from Harvard University. Before beginning his teaching career in 1961, he served as an economist and Senior Hearing Officer at the National War Labor Board and in the industrial relations departments of both Penn Texas Corporation and the General Electric Company. Dr. Northrup is well known for his writings on a wide variety of subjects in the field of labor relations, especially his work in the Industrial Research Unit's series on the social policies of American industry and studies on black employment. He is the author of several books including *Compulsory Arbitration* and *Government Intervention in Labor Disputes*, (Labor Policy Association, 1966); *The Impact of OSHA*, (Industrial Research Unit, 1978); and with Gordon F. Bloom he co-authored *The Economics of Labor Relations*, which is now in its eighth edition.

WAGE SETTING AND COLLECTIVE BARGAINING

Collective bargaining requires that conditions of employment be determined by a set of rules—"a system of industrial jurisprudence," as the late Professor Sumner H. Slichter termed it.[1] Wage structure relationships are at the center of these rules, fundamental both to wage setting and administration and to the orderly establishment and handling of almost all other terms and conditions of employment. Job evaluation or other wage classification schemes not only determine the relationships of tasks and therefore wage differentials, but they also provide a means of orderly job progression and transfer. As a result, the methods for determining such relationships are inextricably intertwined with seniority, promotions, layoffs, training, and all other aspects of intraplant mobility. Unless the relationship of jobs is agreed upon, any orderly disposition of labor-management issues, both in negotiating new contracts and in administering existing ones, becomes extremely difficult. Moreover, once agreed upon, job relationships change as technology improves, methods are perfected, or products or tasks are altered. Thus, a satisfactory relationship of jobs and compensation requires that the parties to a collective agreement design a system to settle disputes between the contract's effective dates.

I. EVOLUTION OF JOB EVALUATION AND WAGE CLASSIFICATION METHODS IN BARGAINING

Before the advent of unions, companies were forced to design systems to determine job relationships in order to determine not only how to compensate personnel but, equally important, to devise on-the-job training systems. For example, in paper mills, "everyone knew and understood . . . that an employee started on the bottom job on a paper machine and learned his way up to the top job. The same understanding prevailed in the woodyard, the

---

[1] This is the term used by the late Professor Slichter in his famous book, *Union Policies and Industrial Management* (Washington: The Brookings Institution, 1941). The book was later revised, just before his death, with James J. Healy and E. Robert Livernash as his coauthors: *The Impact of Collective Bargaining on Management* (Washington: The Brookings Institution, 1960). Chapter 19, "Evaluated Rate Structures," is an excellent summary of the role of job evaluation in collective bargaining.

pulp mill and so on. . . ."[2] Under this system, one filled in for the person in the next position up when the latter was absent and, by this and observation, learned that job; as one progressed, it was also understood that one would instruct the person below.

In such situations, there were often no formal job evaluation systems but a slotting of jobs based upon the natural job progression—that is, the increasing complexity of jobs from the lowest skilled, requiring the least knowledge, to the highest skilled, commanding the greatest knowledge obtained from years of experience in operations involved in direct work in a department or organization. Wage differentials were established which recognized that, as one progressed up the job hierarchy, one's compensation should reflect that progress.

Two problems, however, arose. One was that the relationship of jobs and wages among different sectors of a plant or plant complex was often crude at best. This caused fewer problems in an industry like paper manufacturing where competence or knowledge of one operation, for example, the paper mill, did not provide the skills necessary to work in another, for example, the pulp mill, woodyard, or power house. In other industries, however, where skills throughout an operation were similar, the failure to evaluate jobs and to pay wages on a consistent plant or plant complex basis resulted in serious personnel problems and contributed naturally to the upsurge of industrial unionism. As one former paper mill executive noted:

> One of the things that the union demanded from the beginning was a meaningful seniority system at our plant. The employees wanted to have contractual rights in advance, and job security based upon seniority. They wanted to formalize, in effect, what had been our practice. So lines of progression were put into our contract, setting forth how a man progressed from one job to the next higher one.[3]

The second problem was the lack of certainty for employees that an informal procedure would be adhered to, and of course, sometimes it was not. This led to demands that management policies in regard to promotion and pay be set down in writing and that management be bound by these rules.

Essentially, therefore, on-the-job training programs by which persons progressed up the occupational hierarchy were incorporated into collective bargaining agreements, modified, and institutionalized. At the same time, unions forced companies to negotiate plant-wide rate structures, enabling employees in different sectors of the operations to receive wages that were comparable. Similar to their insistence on a contractual system of job pro-

---

[2] Comment of a retired paper industry executive, quoted in Herbert R. Northrup and Richard L. Rowan, *Negro Employment in Southern Industry*, Studies of Negro Employment, Vol. IV (Philadelphia: Industrial Research Unit, The Wharton School, University of Pennsylvania, 1970), Part One, p. 39.

[3] *Ibid.*

gression, employees, through their unions, also desired an orderly wage system. They felt it would ensure that they were receiving compensation that had a consistent and understandable relationship to the compensation of their fellow employees and, in addition, reflected market realities. The advent of unionism forced companies to review their internal wage structures and to join with unions in establishing methods of internal wage reviews that did not interfere with plant operations or inhibit peaceful and orderly collective bargaining.

In this paper, the development of the role of evaluation and classification systems in collective bargaining is examined, emphasizing the significant role of the National War Labor Board of World War II, management initiatives and union acceptance over time, the issues which arise under job evaluation and wage classification schemes in collective bargaining, and the problems which would be caused by imposing an ill-defined theory of comparable worth on the existing collective bargaining system. The paper concludes with the assessment that establishing federal agencies as the final arbiters of wage rates, ill equipped as they are for this purpose, would be unnecessarily costly in terms of inflation, loss of jobs, and industrial strife.

II. WAR LABOR BOARD IMPACT

The National War Labor Board (WLB) of World War II gave job evaluation and related internal wage classification systems in collective bargaining a tremendous boost. The WLB was faced with the enormous task of stabilizing wages and settling labor disputes throughout the country. Moreover, many of the bargaining relationships were new, the bargaining participants inexperienced, and the wage systems more chaotic than rationalized. To complicate the problem further, many companies had converted from their regular peacetime operations to the production of war materials. This necessarily involved new processes that required different levels of knowledge, effort, and skills and, consequently, different wage levels and relationships. Finally, of course, thousands of workers were not only new to their jobs but had never before worked in an industrial plant.

The task of determining wage levels and of settling disputes involving new contracts was enough to overwhelm the administrative capability of the WLB. To this was added the complication of numerous internal disputes concerning alleged wage inequities. The author, for example, who served as a WLB hearing officer in the Detroit and New York regions, vividly remembers numerous cases involving fifty or more issues, all of which concerned wage rate differentials or relationships of wages for one job to others. Such cases were by no means atypical. Understandably, the WLB turned to job evaluation and related wage classification programs as a necessary tool both to control intraplant wage rates and to settle disputes over alleged intraplant inequities.

A. *Southern California Aircraft Industry*

Prior to the existence of the War Labor Board, the Southern California aircraft industry had reached the conclusion that its future would be impaired unless the companies in the region achieved a rational wage structure. Although the United States had not yet entered the war, the industry was expanding rapidly due to its overseas trade and its participation in the preparation of this country's defense. Some of the seven companies were unionized, but it was the company presidents who agreed formally on the need for a rational wage structure for the group. A working committee established a structure for five of the companies, and Lockheed and Vega (later merged) established a similar one with the International Association of Machinists (IAM).[4] The primary purpose, of course, was not only to establish a reasonable internal wage structure, but also to reduce expensive labor turnover induced by job hopping from one company to another because of wage disparities among the companies.

The Southern California Aircraft Industry (SCAI) plan had considerable success both in overcoming inconsistencies, which "can appear very quickly in a new and expanding industry,"[5] and in deterring job hopping and labor piracy. In addition, acceptance of formal job evaluation was made easier by the plan's implementation. There were problems, however. The Southern California plan developed decided weaknesses as unions became stronger and more competitive. For example, the United Automobile Workers organized North American and Douglas, and the IAM expanded its strength to Consolidated and Vultee. When the UAW refused to support either the general plan or the Lockheed version, the WLB ordered that the plan be put into effect and set up a tripartite committee to supervise it and to adjudicate disputes arising under it.[6]

. . . [T]he IAM and UAW quickly found two areas in which the plan could be manipulated to the unions' advantage. One weakness of the plan was the lack of precision in job descriptions. This opened

---

[4] Robert D. Gray, *Systematic Wage Administration in the Southern California Aircraft Industry*, Industrial Relations Monograph No. 7 (New York: Industrial Relations Counselors, Inc., 1945). This monograph recites how the program was developed and its immediate results. The companies involved included North American (now a division of Rockwell International), Lockheed, Vega (since merged into Lockheed), Consolidated, Vultee (later merged, and now the Convair Division of General Dynamics), Douglas (now part of McDonnell Douglas), Northrop, and Ryan.

[5] *Ibid.*, p. 35.

[6] Arthur P. Allen and Betty V. H. Schneider, *Industrial Relations in the California Aircraft Industry*, West Coast Collective Bargaining Systems Monographs, No. 8 (Berkeley, Cal.: Institute of Industrial Relations, University of California, Berkeley, 1956), p. 22.

the door for individual classification grievances and requests for upgrading. Success in key cases led to the reclassification upward of hundreds of workers assigned to similar work. Another attack was directed at the evaluation placed on certain classifications. Early re-evaluation of the welder classifications, for example, provided a plausible basis for further efforts of the same kind in other categories.

The result was that the SCAI plan in practice became a permanently open contract under which constant negotiation took place around problems of classification, upgrading, merit rating, etc. So, although the War Labor Board rejected demands for a general wage increase, this stand was largely nullified by approval of the SCAI plan. The revision of the plan by such means as piecemeal re-evaluation of jobs allowed the whole wage scale to be jacked up gradually to higher levels. It is estimated that the operation of the plan in Southern California resulted in an average wage increase of more than 15 cents an hour between July 1943 and June 1945.

Early in 1944, the War Labor Board ruled that arbitration of individual grievances by the tri-partite Committee, as well as wholesale re-evaluation of jobs, should cease. The Board ordered that a Re-Study Committee, composed of union and management representatives, attempt an overall revision of the plan. The study was carried on for more than 18 months and was completed by the industry members of the Committee when, in the postwar period, the union representatives withdrew. Recommendations of the Re-Study Committee, many of which were adopted when the committee was still bi-partite, became the basis for postwar job evaluation schemes at all companies except Ryan, which continued to follow the original SCAI plan.[7]

The wartime experience with job evaluation of labor and management in the Southern California aircraft industry led to an appreciation and understanding of the system which has since minimized disputes over intraplant wage relationships. Although subsequent labor relations in the industry have been both stormy and stable, job evaluation and its use in the classification of jobs do not seem to have been matters of serious contention.[8] Professor Harold M. Levinson noted in 1966:

With minor modifications, the labor grades and the wage levels applicable to each of them have been substantially the same during the

---

[7] *Ibid.*, pp. 22–23.

[8] *Ibid.*, p. 24; and Harold M. Levinson, *Determining Forces in Collective Wage Bargaining* (New York: John Wiley & Sons, 1966), chapter 2.

entire postwar period for all the major airframe companies in Southern California.[9]

He also noted, however, that some companies followed a more liberal policy in evaluating and classifying jobs, thus permitting higher effective rates in some companies rather than others[10]–a process which can, of course, seriously affect wage relationships among concerns.

B. *WLB's General Policies*

The apparent success of the use of job evaluation to resolve disputes in the Southern California aircraft industry and the fact that "a significant number of wage matters before the National War Labor Board involve a change in the relationship between the rates paid for different jobs by the same company"[11] led the WLB to favor the correction of "intra-plant gross inequities" by means of evaluation plans. The Board did not "inquire into the method used to rank jobs as long as it is objective."[12] Instead, it provided general rules limiting the amount of wage increases which could be generated by correcting inequities, and it pressed hard to have job evaluation plans adopted. Thus, as late in the war period as April 1945, the Board's then chairman, the late Dr. George W. Taylor, admonished industry as follows:

> One of the most striking impressions I have of American wage rate structures, is a failure of a large part of industry to develop properly aligned wage schedules in the plants—with jobs defined, rates standard for those classifications and rates for particular jobs compensating with reasonable accuracy for the skill involved. Too many wage scales have what I call "random rates" based not on the job but on the individual. I think a great task before a large part of American industry—certainly the mass production industries—is to work out rational wage structures which provide a definite rate structure for definite jobs.[13]

The WLB's interest in job evaluation and related wage classification programs was, as already noted, prompted by its mandate to preserve industrial peace and its need to devise systems that would reduce its tremendous case burden. To encourage employers and unions to settle internal wage classification and job relationship disputes, the WLB not only ordered them to develop systems of their own to resolve these issues, but also permitted a

---

[9] Levinson, note 8 *supra*, p. 42.

[10] *Ibid.*, p. 43.

[11] Opinion of Dr. George W. Taylor, *Matter of Thirty Michigan and Northern Wisconsin Lumber Companies*, Case Nos. 11–31–C et al.; quoted in *The Termination Report of the National War Labor Board* (Washington: Government Printing Office, 1946), Vol. 1, p. 240.

[12] *Termination Report*, Vol. I, p. 241, note 2.

[13] Quoted in *Termination Report*, Vol. I, p. 243.

five cents per hour average increase (then a substantial sum) to settle "intraplant inequities" arising from the installation of a job evaluation or other wage classification system.

As a result, unions were under pressure from their membership to agree to a classification or evaluation system. In addition to the five cent carrot, union officials began to understand that such systems not only relieved them from a considerable case load of their own, but also enabled them to avoid the politically difficult task of supporting positions that would increase wages of some jobs and not others.

Management's interest in supporting the WLB position that systems for resolving internal wage and classification disputes be developed was at least equally strong. The establishment of an orderly method of relating wages reduced production-upsetting disputes and had the potential of curtailing turnover at a time of zero unemployment and persistent labor shortages.

Given these attitudes, it is not surprising that the WLB became a major force for the installation of job evaluation and other wage classification plans. In cases involving the basic steel industry, the iron ore industry, cotton textile, other textiles, West Coast lumber, shipbuilding, and other industries, and in numerous individual company cases, the WLB ordered the parties to develop and to implement a job evaluation program.[14] Of these cases, the one with the most far-reaching impact was the basic steel case decided by the WLB on November 25, 1944.

III. THE BASIC STEEL PROGRAM

In determining that the steel industry's wage structure must be rationalized, the National War Labor Board laid down certain methodologies and criteria for evolving a job evaluation plan under collective bargaining that have had a lasting impact. The Board's directive included the following points:

(c) The company and the union shall negotiate the elimination of existing intra-plant wage rate inequities and reduction in the number of job classifications in accordance with the following steps:

(1) Describe simply and concisely the content of each job.
(2) Place the jobs in their proper relationship.
(3) Reduce the job classifications to the smallest practical number by grouping those jobs having substantially equivalent content.
(4) Establish wage rates for the job classifications in accordance with the provisions of Par. (d) below.

---

[14] *Termination Report*, Vol. I, pp. 253–58.

(d) The following guide-posts are established for collective bargaining:

(1) The extent of wage adjustments required to eliminate intra-plant wage rate inequities will vary between the companies. From the record, it appears that little or no increase to eliminate intra-plant wage rate inequities will be needed in some plants where wage rates are now in a sound relationship. The largest increase in payroll costs may be expected where little or nothing has been done in the past to correct wage rate inequities.

(2) The maximum increase for any one company shall not exceed an amount equivalent to an average of five cents per hour for all its employees covered by this directive order.

(3) The wage rate adjustments which may be made are to be solely for that purpose of eliminating intra-plant wage rate inequities. They cannot be general across-the-board wage increases, and any such general increases will be disapproved.

(4) As an aid to determining the correct rate relationship between the jobs in the particular plant, the company and the union may take into account the wage rate relationships existing in comparable plants in the industry. The contention that wage rate relationships in other plants in the industry have no significance for this purpose is rejected.

(5) The reduction of an out-of-line wage rate shall not be effective to reduce the wages of present incumbents. . . .[15]

This directive insured the United Steelworkers a co-equal role in the development and administration of the proposed plan, despite the fact that the labor members of the WLB dissented from the directive. It ordered job descriptions and a reduced number of classifications, limited the amount of wage increases which could result from reclassifications incident to the job evaluation plan, endorsed the consideration of wages in comparable plants when establishing the wage structure under the plan, and "red circled" all incumbents by proscribing individual wage reductions as a result of the adoption of the proposed plan. These principles have governed not only the basic steel job evaluation program but nearly all collectively bargained plans, as well as many of those installed by management.

A. *Development of the Steel Program*

The basic steel case of 1944 involved eighty-six companies which then employed approximately 400,000 workers. Initially, twelve of the largest formed a group to examine the relationship of jobs and wages. This study

---

[15] Quoted in *Termination Report*, Vol. I, pp. 252–53.

group has been institutionalized as the Cooperative Wage Bureau and is now composed of seventy companies. It provides information to participants concerning the application of job description and classification procedures.

The development of the program has been succinctly stated by Herbert L. Sherman, Jr.:

> To implement the Board's Directive, United States Steel Corporation proceeded first since it would have been awkward for all eighty-six companies to negotiate simultaneously with the Union. A Joint Wage Rate Inequity Committee was formed for United States Steel Corporation's steel producing subsidiaries. . . . Meeting for the first time in February, 1945, the Joint Committee proceeded with its consideration of methods for describing and classifying jobs. The union undertook joint responsibility with Management for the Development of an acceptable and practical Manual.
>
> Following mutually approved uniform procedures, the parties at top level then tested the Manual which they had developed by describing and classifying Benchmark and Specimen Example jobs. Almost 2,500 such jobs were eventually described and classified. The next step was to describe and classify the jobs at each plant. This was done by local Management and Union representatives who were guided by the Benchmark and Specimen Example job descriptions and classifications. If the local plant committees could not reach agreement, the dispute was referred to the Joint Wage Rate Inequity Committee. In the steel producing operations of the United States Steel Corporation about 25,000 jobs were described and classified at this time.
>
> Craft and assigned maintenance jobs were given special treatment, and special conventions were developed for testing and inspection, spell hand, and groupleader jobs. The description and classification of hourly rated clerical and technical jobs, and instructor and learner jobs, about 10 percent of the total, were held for later consideration. Classification of these jobs was completed in 1948 and 1949.
>
> As previously planned, in late 1946, the parties proceeded with the problem of negotiating a standard hourly wage scale. Such a wage scale, progressing upward from job class to job class in uniform increments, was put into effect in February, 1947. All rates in effect lower than the Standard Hourly Wage Rates were raised. Wage rates in effect higher than the Standard Hourly Wage Rates were red-circled (personal out-of-line differentials were created, identified and applied to the individual employees while they remained on those jobs). Starting in May, 1947, all of the jobs described and classified were also reviewed for error under the guidance of the Joint Wage Rate Inequity Committee.

Since April 22, 1947, the Basic Labor Agreements between the United States Steel Corporation and the United Steelworkers of America have provided that no grievance alleging a wage rate inequity may be filed or processed. However, provision has been made for the handling of grievances which may result from disputes in the description and classification of new or changed jobs. And each new Basic Labor Agreement negotiated has included consideration of the standard hourly wage scale of rates, since such a scale is the basis for the actual earnings of each employee represented by the Union.

In January, 1953 the various inequity agreements developed over the years by the Union and the United States Steel Corporation were condensed and incorporated without change in substance into one document, the January 1, 1953 Job Description and Classification Manual for Hourly Rated Production, Maintenance and Non-Confidential Clerical Jobs.

All of the large basic steel companies except Inland Steel have adopted the Cooperative Wage Bureau's job description and classification Manual and its related procedures. In fact, this Manual has been applied to cover the description and classification of nearly 180,000 jobs covering some 600,000 employees in many different companies.[16]

Over the years, the parties have made a number of changes in their system. Both in 1963 and 1971, the number of master job descriptions was reduced so that, after 1971, there were 662, as compared with 9,826 in 1953.

As significant as the steel industry's job evaluation program has been, it still is a system that is derived fundamentally from the structure of the industry and its collective bargaining relationships, and it is not easily transferred or duplicated elsewhere. The industry has a common technology and job structure, both of which are reasonably mature. The industry deals with one union that has a history of strong central administration and an influential professional staff. Management and the union have done unusually careful and detailed work in defining jobs and assigning weights, with responsibility a key factor. With different and varying technologies, more dynamic change and less maturity, different and several unions, even within the metal trades, and other variations, it is not likely that the steel program can easily be emulated in most other industrial situations. Moreover, even disregarding technological and institutional factors, unless such a system emanates from the parties and has their uninhibited support, its success would be doubtful if it were copied or imposed.

---

[16] Herbert L. Sherman, Jr., *Arbitration of the Steel Wage Structure* (Pittsburgh: University of Pittsburgh Press, 1961). For a more complete history of this program, see Jack Stieber, *The Steel Industry Wage Structure*, Wertheim Publications in Industrial Relations (Cambridge, Mass.: Harvard University Press, 1959).

IV. MANAGEMENT INITIATIVES AND
UNION ACCEPTANCE

Although the directives of the National War Labor Board gave a strong stimulus not only to the use and extension of job evaluation as such but also to union participation in the development and administration of such programs, most job evaluation plans, both before and after World War II, have been installed and administered by management. Thus, according to the outstanding work on the subject:

> Various industry groups were particularly important in influencing the adoption and spread of job evaluation. Groups such as the American Management Association and Industrial Relations Counselors early saw the significance of job evaluation as a device both to improve company wage structures and wage administration and to maintain management control of the wage structure under collective bargaining. Industry associations, most notably the National Metal Trades Association, took the lead in directing the introduction of job evaluation.
>
> Just as all personnel activities were directly and indirectly stimulated by the expanding union movement, job evaluation was used by management partly to deter or prevent unionization, partly to rationalize its wage scales prior to unionization and establish principles and practices for future wage administration, and partly to stabilize the wage structure and eliminate continuous bargaining over particular rates after unionization.[17]

Even when management selects or develops the plan, "unions influence the timing, the method, and the character of the introduction. . . . Unions have usually achieved a significant degree of formal or informal participation in the introduction and administration of plans, which, no doubt modified the particular placement of jobs."[18] In short, the collective bargaining process encompasses the job evaluation plan, process, and administration, as it does less formal classification methods. Moreover, whether the plan is jointly or unilaterally developed, individual grievances can be raised which question the positioning of jobs, the evaluation of tasks which have changed over time, etc. Thus in a collective bargaining context, the union can seek redress for any challengeable management action.

Not surprisingly, a key for union acceptance is that, whatever the system of wage classification, it must be clearly understood, and the union officials and employees must be convinced of both its equity and the fairness and reasonableness of its administration. Because of the need for such acceptance,

---

[17] Slichter, Healy, and Livernash, note 1 *supra*, p. 561.

[18] *Ibid.*, p. 560.

there seems to be a definite trend away from complicated point and rating systems toward job slotting after the designation and rating of benchmark jobs. Such companies as General Electric and DuPont now generally slot jobs without the benefit of an elaborate point system. The automobile industry, with its relatively simple and flat wage structure, utilizes classification slotting schemes. Different industries have different approaches which derive from their technology, job structure, employee relations history, the nature of the collective bargaining relationship, and union structure and history. Moreover, multiplant companies with varied product lines often issue manuals which set forth the principles of the classification or job evaluation program and emphasize its importance to the running of the business but, at the same time, give operations management considerable latitude in the design and structuring of the plan. The National Labor Relations Board and the courts have supported a broad right of union information for all aspects of a company job evaluation plan and its administration.[19]

Writing in 1960, Slichter, Livernash, and Healy remarked: "The outstanding aspect of the establishment and modification of wage rates for particular jobs is the extent to which controversy has been eliminated and considerable agreement achieved on policies of wage administration. Wage administration procedure has also been definitely improved."[20] There is no change in this conclusion today.[21] Indeed, so accepted has job evaluation become in the collective bargaining process that, since 1960, no thorough general analysis of the relation of job evaluation and collective bargaining has appeared in the industrial relations literature.[22] The reasons for this development are found in the key role which job evaluation plays in employment, deployment, upgrading, and compensation of employees.

A. *Employment, Deployment, and Upgrading*

In order to employ persons with requisite skills, management must have adequate job specifications of what skills and attributes it requires, and these, in turn, must be based upon the job descriptions which not only reflect the immediate job opening but also the jobs to which the newly employed person can expect to be upgraded over time. Thus, as noted earlier, any job

---

[19] See *NLRB v. Acme Industrial Co.*, 385 U.S. 432 (1967); *Procter & Gamble Mfg. Co. v. NLRB*, 603 F.2d 1310 (8th Cir. 1979).

[20] Slichter, Healy, and Livernash, note 1 *supra*, p. 558.

[21] Professor Harold S. Jones, using a questionnaire survey, found that there appeared "to be a modest trend toward the acceptance of job evaluation in the 1970s" by union officials. "Union Views on Job Evaluation: 1971 vs. 1978," *Personnel Journal*, Volume 58 [February 1979], pp. 80–85. In practice, this acceptance is, in our experience, far greater than union officials found it expedient to admit in reply to written questionnaires to which an affirmative reply would appear to be an endorsement of what is conceived of as a management tool.

[22] One recent textbook on job evaluation has a chapter on union attitudes and union control. See Richard J. Henderson, *Compensation Management: Rewarding Performance in the Modern Organization* (Reston, Va.: Reston Publishing Company, 1976), chapter 14.

evaluation or wage classification plan must both reflect and provide for an orderly job progression. Jobs must be rated so that employees are rewarded when they are upgraded and hence desire to be promoted. Moreover, the rating system must be consistent with the operating structure of the facility so that employees can be deployed as widely or as narrowly as required for efficient operations. Essentially, this means that jobs may be narrowly or broadly described and rated depending upon production processes, extent of market, size of output, and a host of related factors that permit the system to fulfill the need for orderly and efficient labor utilization. Finally, the system must be consistent with the natural progression of job skills in order for employees to receive the amount of on-the-job training which is necessary to prepare them for upgrading.

B. *Compensation*

Job evaluation and related systems do not provide for compensation but for an orderly system of compensation. Wages have to be set at market levels, but internally they must also reflect the differences among jobs. Evaluation of jobs provides for consistent and meaningful differentials among jobs so that the wage structure encourages training and upgrading and discourages disputes over whether persons are properly compensated in relation to their peers. Since production processes and methods constantly change and, thus, so does job content, job evaluation also provides a means to accommodate change:

> Both stability and orderly change have been achieved by job evaluation. An evaluated wage structure agreed to by a union holds rate relationships constant unless job content changes. With changes in job content, a frame of reference has been set up for use in the grievance procedure and arbitration. Job evaluation thus leads to better administrative practices as well as to a more equitable wage structure.[23]

V. JOB EVALUATION AND COLLECTIVE BARGAINING

Without a job classification system, managements and unions faced potential strife over each and every wage rate in the bargaining unit. Managements' interest in job evaluation to simplify and to solve such problems has been well summarized by R. Conrad Cooper, former Executive Vice-President of Industrial Relations at United States Steel Corporation:

---

[23] Slichter, Healy, and Livernash, note 1 *supra*, p. 561.

... the principal ingredients of the [pre-evaluation] wage rate situation . . . were: a body of specific rates emerging from differing backgrounds in various localities; a new union striving for position; employees' possession of a new device by which to explore real or imaginary wage rate grievances; no fixed wage scale in the agreements; a specified right to challenge the equity of any particular rate; no agreed yardstick by which to judge the equity of a rate once challenged; and no termination point for the settlement of such differences.[24]

The fact that union problems of administration can be equally difficult is well illustrated by the following excerpts from documents sent by two former Steelworker officials to some of their staff:

... Remember those thousands . . . of inequity grievances which you had arise? They were driving you insane. . . . Our people were at one another's throats . . . at this business of inequities. One machinist would say, "Look at Joe over there. He is getting a buck and a half and I am getting $1.40." There was veritable hell going on.

* * *

... we urged the people to give rise to these grievances on wages and inequalities and later created a problem for ourselves that was almost impossible of solution . . . we got everybody of the opinion that all they had to do to get a raise was to join the union. . . .[25]

A. *Negotiating New Contracts*

In short, the bargaining process breaks down without stable wage relationships. Negotiators for new contracts find themselves unable to deal adequately with the major issues, because their time and energies are consumed by attempting to settle a myriad of almost individual disputes concerning whether employees are compensated fairly in relation to their peers and whether certain jobs are properly classified in relation to others. Moreover, the settlement of one issue is as likely to trigger additional disputes as it is to bring peace. Job relationship disputes involve not only compensation but social and peer prestige as well. If the multiple spindle grinder operator was being paid the same wage rate as the shaper operator, and then the latter's rate is raised, the former is likely to become quite upset. He is now lower rated in money and, from his perspective, perhaps in social standing as well. Without criteria upon which to rely, the union is forced to process a huge volume of grievances, and the company is faced both with potential labor

---

[24] Quoted in Slichter, Healy and Livernash, note 1 *supra*, p. 565.
[25] Quoted by Stieber, note 16 *supra*, p. 7.

disputes, or a constantly rising wage bill, or both. The results can be chaos, declining market share, lost jobs, or even business failure. The larger the facility, of course, the more difficult and expensive are the problems that arise.

Clearly, it follows that strike incidence is certain to be higher if there is no coherent mutually acceptable system. With individual wage disputes clogging the calendar, it can become politically impossible for union officials to agree to general settlement terms until such individual disputes are also resolved. From management's perspective, solution of such disputes without the criteria provided by a job evaluation system can result only in higher labor costs, still more disputes, and a continued upward spiral of the same. Consequently, management, literally to maintain the viability of the company, must stop giving. Unless the parties can agree to a reasoned system of job classification, the strikes that result can be long and bitter and the basic problem left unresolved.

B. *Administering the Contract*

Collective bargaining does not cease with contract negotiations and agreement. The agreement must be administered during its life as well. Over 90 percent of all collective agreements provide for grievance machinery, terminated by recourse to arbitration by a third party for disputes which arise over the interpretation of contracts. Union officials are just as alert to the possibility of obtaining additional benefits for their membership during the life of the contract as they are in negotiations. Moreover, various lower union officials in the shop may try to expand their followings by attempting to gain through pressure or clever grievance handling what the top officials failed to achieve in bargaining for a new contract. If a rival for the union leadership can make gains in this manner, he might win election to a higher union post in the future.

Management personnel may also do more than rest upon the contractual status quo. Plant managers and supervisors, anxious to maintain and improve their cost and profit positions, sometimes attempt to shade or to water down the agreement by various practices. The negotiated contract, in a very real sense, is only a temporary resting place in the relations of the parties.[26]

Given these facts, it is not difficult to understand why both management and union officials literally require a type of wage classification system to determine wage rate disputes during the life of a contract. Without the criteria provided by a job evaluation or other wage classification program, the upward whipsawing of wages could continue during the contract. This would not only raise wages substantially and, therefore, endanger a firm's competitive position and the jobs of its employees, but also probably would clog up the grievance machinery or cause it to break down. Basic problems

---

[26] For an interesting analysis of how management and employee groups use the contract as a bargaining tool, see James W. Kuhn, *Bargaining in Grievance Settlement* (New York: Columbia University Press, 1961).

would then remain unsolved, and relations would likely deteriorate. Again, the prospects for industrial peace would be lessened.

Another result of the failure to have the job structure governed by a jointly acceptable plan is excessive recourse to arbitration, a development which has several shortcomings. It is, first of all, quite expensive. Second, the procedure can be quite lengthy, and settlements lag while unrest and dissatisfaction continue. Third, to the detriment of good relationships and industrial peace, excessive resort to arbitration again clogs the machinery and prevents cases from being heard and expeditiously determined. Fourth, it means that a third party establishes the job relationships and rates of pay. Some companies, including General Motors and General Electric, feel so strongly about this issue that they permit unions to strike over such matters during the life of the contract rather than submit them to arbitration or have wages set or jobs evaluated or slotted by third parties. In most companies, however, the arbitrator would become the final determiner of the rates paid and the jobs' position in the structure.

This last shortcoming is, perhaps, the most serious aspect of excessive arbitral decision making, because it turns the decision making function over to a third party, who, however expert and judicious, is not required to live with the results. There is, moreover, no reason to expect an arbitrator, whose knowledge of production needs is certain to be less than that of the parties, to accomplish what they have failed to do. Hence, excessive resort to arbitration not only creates serious inherent problems for the parties but in addition may yield quite unsatisfactory results, because the root cause is not addressed—the lack of a coherent, acceptable, job evaluation or similar system.

C. *Incentive Impact*

Once the system is introduced and accepted, problems can arise in bargaining which affect it. While such problems can be caused by factors outside the system, they still can damage the system unless carefully rectified.

Job evaluation and other classification plans are, for example, frequently seriously affected by wage incentive plans. The problem usually arises in regard to the relations of earnings of maintenance craftsmen and production operatives. Under incentives, the latter, who are the less skilled and therefore, rated lower in an evaluation plan, can sometimes earn more than maintenance personnel, who are generally paid on an hourly or time, rather than incentive, basis. In the basic steel industry, this has occurred even though maintenance personnel, as well as production personnel, are paid on an incentive basis. The steel companies and the United Steelworkers found that the problem was so serious that skilled craftsmen were transferring into less skilled production jobs in order to earn higher wages. The problem was "solved" by tinkering with the wage structure: maintenance machinists were left at evaluation grade 16, where the cooperative evaluation program had pegged them, but then compensation was adjusted so that they would be paid as if they were in grade 18.[27] According to a knowledgeable source: "While the language [of the labor agreement] indicates that the adjustment was required because of the technological changes, it was frankly a reaction to the difference of pay being received by trade and craft employees as compared with production employees, with the latter receiving lucrative incentive pay."[28]

The action of the steel industry and the Steelworkers in adjusting the compensation of maintenance machinists, while maintaining their evaluation at the same grade, illustrates the need to avoid tinkering with a job evaluation program when the problem is skewed earnings, not improper evaluation. The problem in the steel industry undoubtedly is that the incentive plan is more an earnings bonus than a reward for productivity. This creates earnings inequities that require correction; to utilize the evaluation program to make such a correction would create more problems than it would solve. If the level of machinists were changed from grade 16 to 18, others in grade 16 could demand a change, too, and the whole structure could be affected. Hence, the solution was to upgrade wages, not grade levels, in order to minimize ripples in the evaluation program.

D. *"Red Circle" Rates*

When job evaluation is introduced, some jobs inevitably are found to have been undervalued and others overvalued. An almost universal practice is to increase the rates of those persons who have been undervalued so that they conform to the evaluation system but leave undisturbed the wages of those whose rates exceed the rate or rate range established for their jobs by the evaluation. New employees or those promoted into the classification where "red circle" rates exist are paid pursuant to the job evaluation classification structure.

The policy of red circling rates was adopted by the National War Labor Board and subsequently has been almost universally followed. Unions certainly would not agree to any system which reduced rates, and most managements feel that the unhappiness and dissatisfaction that result from reducing rates without any job change is certainly not worth any savings engendered.

Nevertheless, red circling can cause severe problems. It perpetuates an inequity. Moreover, whether it is determined to deny all or portions of wage increases to those red circled or to permit them to receive the increases, the dissatisfaction continues from some group or another. Paying red circled employees lump sums of cash to give up their above classification rates is a

---

[27] See *Agreement between United States Steel Corporation and United Steelworkers of America, Production and Maintenance Employees*, Pittsburgh, Pa., September 1, 1965, pp. 36–38, especially item 8, which increases the craft rating by two full job classes; and the *Agreement* of August 1, 1968, p. 41, in which the parties made permanent the adjustment as a basic part of the classification system. All basic steel companies have similar contracts.

[28] Letter to author, September 18, 1979.

method some companies have used, but of course, this causes resentment from those who receive no such bonus.

Two possible solutions exist, yet they are rarely practical. One is to transfer or promote red circle rate employees to other jobs within the classified structure. Of course, such employees will not accept such transfers if it means a wage reduction. It is not at all unusual for red circle rates to exceed the rates for the next higher or even the next two higher grades, especially if the job evaluation is introduced into a hitherto chaotic structure. A second solution is to grant a general increase when an evaluation is introduced so that the entire wage structure is raised and can encompass some out-of-line high individual rates. This could be expensive, and can also be insufficient to avoid some red circling. If neither transfers nor general increases can avoid red circling, the above job rates will remain a point of agitation to be endured until the recipients either retire or otherwise leave the scene.

E. Settling Disputes

Although job evaluation as such is no longer a controversial matter between unions and management, this does not mean that grievances do not arise concerning evaluated jobs. Quite the contrary is true. Disputes over the slotting of particular jobs usually vie with questions of seniority and rights to overtime as the items that comprise the largest share of the grievance load. This is what one would expect as changing product, technology, and methods alter job content. What job evaluation does, as we have noted throughout this chapter, is to provide criteria for the settlement of these disputes and, by its existence and acceptance, preclude many other disputes from arising. This is its great contribution in collective bargaining.

F. Salaried v. Hourly Plans

There is no agreement in industry about the advisability of whether to include all jobs under a single plan or to have separate plans for hourly and salaried employees, or even three plans—one for hourly, one for nonexempt salaried, and one for exempt salaried. Many companies have separate hourly and salaried plans, because they desire to maintain complete separation of wage and salary administration between their unionized hourly employees and their nonunion salaried groups. Nevertheless, there are many firms whose salaried employees are nonunion that operate under one plan.

A basic difficulty of placing all employees within one plan is that conditions of work are radically different in the office as compared with many plants. For example, while most offices are air conditioned, free of dirt and grime, and operate without safety hazards, the very opposite may be the case in plants. It is, thus, quite difficult to rate work in offices and plants by the same criteria and provide a fair evaluation to all concerned. It can, however, be accomplished, but the factors used must be sufficiently flexible to avoid unfair comparisons. Otherwise, the job categories of the lower salaried group in particular are likely to be adversely affected.

Where salaried employees are part of the same system, they can also find that hourly incentive systems result in skewed earnings for equally rated job classifications. This happened in the steel industry, where a significant proportion of clerical and technical employees are nonunionized. In 1971, the steel companies and the United Steelworkers negotiated a "service bonus plan" designed to accomplish two objectives: 1) reduce absenteeism and 2) increase compensation for the clerical and technical employees who are not covered by incentives.[29]

VI. JOB EVALUATION AND DISCRIMINATION

Like any other tool, job evaluation can be, and has been, misapplied. This is why some evaluated wage structures become chaotic and demoralized and others fail to perform the function for which they were created.

Like any other instrument, a job evaluation or wage classification system can be perverted and therefore biased. It is, thus, quite possible that jobs with large numbers of women or minorities may have been, or even presently are, classified unfairly or discriminatorily. Since the enactment of the Civil Rights Act, many major companies have either reevaluated their wage classification plans or had them audited by consulting firms specializing in this field in order to determine whether discrimination can be inferred as a factor in the evaluation or slotting of jobs. Some have made changes as a result.

Discussions with civil rights advocates, including both those within and outside the government, give the firm impression that they want the Equal Employment Opportunity Commission and other civil rights enforcement agencies to require that a single job evaluation or other wage classification plan be adopted by companies for their entire work force—in other words, that salaried and hourly employees be included within the same plan. As we have already explained, however, a one-plan program could be quite discriminatory for office employees, a large portion of whom are women. It would, therefore, appear that such an approach is simplistic and not responsive to any problems of discrimination that may exist. Civil rights advocates also may believe, however, that forcing companies to adopt a single company or plant-office complex plan may make it easier for government civil rights investigators and compliance personnel, most of whom are not schooled in compensation practices, to enforce regulations.

Actually, discrimination in most instances is probably not the result of wage classification but rather of inequitable treatment in employment,

---

[29] *Agreement between United States Steel Corporation and the United Steelworkers of America, Salaried Employees*, Pittsburgh, Pa., August 1, 1971, pp. 157–58.

promotion, and related activities. The concentration of blacks in blast furnaces in the steel industry, in woodyards in the paper industry, and in lower echelons of work in general[30] could not have been corrected by attacking job evaluation or related problems. Rather, EEOC properly has moved against the practices which have instituted, encouraged, and institutionalized discrimination in employment and upgrading. In so doing, however, it has often sought solutions which ignore basic operational and industrial relations factors that are not discriminatory *per se,* but that may require modification to avoid institutionalizing past discrimination.

For example, the EEOC strongly advocates plant seniority rather than occupational or departmental seniority. Neither of the latter two is discriminatory *per se,* and as the author has pointed out in another context, they work differently for the underprivileged or minorities under different economic conditions:

> In general, management prefers the smallest possible seniority districts, with no provisions for workers to hold seniority in more than one district. Under such regulations, layoffs and rehiring do not involve much dislocation in the plant and hence do not interfere materially with the efficient organization of personnel.
>
> Union and employee preference as to the size of seniority districts varies considerably. In general, in times of unemployment, skilled workers prefer wide seniority districts and unskilled workers narrow ones. This is because skilled workers can replace unskilled ones, but not vice versa. Hence the wider the seniority district in times of layoffs, the greater the chance for the skilled worker to find a spot by exercising seniority, and the greater the chance that the unskilled worker will be pushed out of a job. In times of prosperity the opposite is likely to be true because expanding employment gives unskilled workers the opportunity to advance in the occupational hierarchy, and this they like to do without sacrificing their seniority in their former jobs. On the other hand, skilled workers see in expanding employment more competition for jobs when times become depressed. Hence they favor narrow seniority districts during prosperous periods.[31]

The solution is, therefore, the elimination of practices which make seniority discriminatory, not the elimination of occupational or departmental seniority. Similarly, discrimination will not be corrected by requiring that

---

[30] For background on these practices, see Herbert R. Northrup et al., *Negro Employment in Basic Industry*, Studies of Negro Employment, Vol. I (Philadelphia: Industrial Research Unit, The Wharton School, University of Pennsylvania, 1970); and Northrup and Rowan, *Negro Employment in Southern Industry*, note 2 *supra.*

[31] Gordon F. Bloom and Herbert R. Northrup, *Economics of Labor Relations*, 8th ed. (Homewood, Ill.: Richard D. Irwin, Inc. 1977), p. 187.

a single plan cover both salaried and hourly employees. It will be eliminated by ending or modifying any practices which discriminate in the administration of job evaluation, regardless of whether salary and hourly personnel are found in the same plan.

VII. PARITY EMPLOYMENT AND COMPARABLE WORTH

As this paper has made clear, job evaluation and related classification systems have proved useful and constructive tools in the management of human resources and have contributed to the peaceful resolution of industrial disputes, both in the negotiation of new collective agreements and in the determination of disputes arising out of contract administration and interpretation. Nevertheless, judging by a rash of articles and newspaper stories on the subject,[32] the EEOC and other civil rights organizations appear determined to alter traditional and current wage classification concepts as a means of seeking fundamental changes in methods of wage determination. The balance of this paper examines this goal, which is seen as an aspect of the drive for parity, rather than nondiscriminatory employment, or a means of achieving "parity compensation" in lieu of parity employment.

A. *Parity v. Nondiscriminatory Employment*

Essentially, the EEOC and other EEO-enforcement agencies liken the employment process to one of random selection. Their model implies that, absent discrimination, the breakdown of a company's labor force should resemble that of the population. In other words, the proportion by race and sex of craftsmen, managers, professionals, and technical workers in plants should approximate the proportion of these occupational groups by race and sex in the labor market.[33]

Such assumptions clearly are unrealistic. First, differences encountered among race and sex groups as to the quality and type of education and experience can be substantial in determining qualifications. Also, there are

---

[32] See, e.g., Ruth G. Blumrosen, "Wage Discrimination, Job Segregation, and Title VII of the Civil Rights Act of 1964," 12 *U. Mich. J. L. Ref.* 399 (1979). See also "Equal Pay for Comparable Work Offers New Approach to Issue of Sex Discrimination," *Daily Labor Report* (No. 211), October 30, 1979, pp. A-2-3; Owen Ullman, "Equal pay for work of 'comparable value' urged," *Philadelphia Inquirer*, October 28, 1979, p. 14–A; Leslie Bennetts, "The Equal Pay Issue: Focusing on 'Comparable Worth,'" *New York Times*, October 26, 1979, p. A20.

[33] The EEOC's theory of random selection has been enunciated and supported by Professor Barbara Bergmann. See, e.g., Barbara R. Bergmann and Jill Gordon King, "Diagnosing Discrimination," in Phyllis Wallace (ed.), *Equal Opportunity and the AT&T Case* (Cambridge, Mass.: MIT Press, 1976), pp. 49–110; and B. R. Bergmann and William Krause, "Evaluating and Forecasting Progress in Racial Integration of Employment," *Industrial and Labor Relations Review*, Vol. 25 (April 1972), pp. 399–409.

differences among ethnic groups in regional mobility preferences and in attitudes toward different occupations. Third, location within a labor market is significant. If, for example, blacks are concentrated on the south side of a city and a plant is on the north side, commuting difficulty could effectively exclude many blacks from the company's real labor market; intervening opportunities between the homes of the prospective employees and the plant probably would reduce any attempts to seek jobs at the farther distance.

Moreover, the labor pool of a plant is also constantly changing. For example, there has been a sharp jump in labor force participation of females in recent years. Increased hiring or layoffs at other plants in an area also would quickly change the labor pool, as would decisions of high school students to seek work or to attend college, or of older persons to retire or to keep working. Random selection assumes a stationary pool of prospective workers, not one that is constantly undergoing change.

Finally, employers attempt to select employees with much more care than a random casting. Experience and selection tools are utilized to attempt to obtain workers who will be the most productive. In addition, legal constraints involving race, color, creed, sex, the handicapped, older workers, and veterans all play a role. Thus, both legitimate employment and legislative goals cast serious doubt on the applicability of a random selection process in employee selection.[34]

Random selection clearly is something quite different from non-discriminatory employment. The latter assumes that the best qualified person will be chosen and that no form of discrimination will cloud the selection process. This does not necessarily lead, however, to parity employment—that is, employment of various race, sex, and other protected groups in proportion to their representation in the labor market. The AT&T experience, summarized below, is illustrative of the difficulties of achieving parity employment even when such a concept is supported by stringent quotas.

B. Quotas—The AT&T Experience

In January 1973, the American Telephone and Telegraph Company (AT&T) signed a consent decree with the EEOC and other government agencies[35] which, in effect, obligated the company to meet race and sex goals for each occupational group in the system. In a concurrent study, this author has examined the AT&T experience over the five years of the decree's incum-

---

[34] These arguments are taken from Herbert R. Northrup and John A. Larson, *The Impact of the AT&T-EEO Consent Decree*, Labor Relations and Public Policy Series, No. 20 (Philadelphia: Industrial Research Unit, The Wharton School, University of Pennsylvania, 1979), chapter VII.

[35] *Equal Employment Opportunity Commission v. American Telephone & Telegraph Co.*, 419 F. Supp. 1022 (E.D. Pa. 1976), *aff'd*, 556 F.2d 167 (3rd Cir. 1977), *cert. denied*, 438 U.S. 915 (1978).

bency.[36] It is very clear from this record that the goals that had to be met were in fact quotas and that the result of their implementation was that the proportion of minorities and women in AT&T's upper ranks increased substantially. On the other hand, the adherence to quotas also resulted in the introduction of white males as operators and clericals and, therefore, a decline in opportunities for such positions for the non-college educated females. Moreover, the large numbers of excellently educated and highly qualified females—the ones who profited most from the decree—have created more competition for minorities for the better jobs.

The decree also resulted in a substantial increase in the number of jobs held by females in inside crafts[37] and outside crafts. Unfortunately, in the latter category the increase was at the expense of a huge turnover and female accident rate which was almost three times that of males, despite enormous expenses by AT&T on redesigned safety and training measures in order to meet these unscientifically and artificially contrived quotas.

The AT&T consent decree pushed America's largest company toward parity employment, but it did not achieve it. White females were the principal gainers, expecially those who were well-educated. Most women continue, however, to prefer clerical to craft work, both at AT&T and throughout the economy and, despite quotas for male clericals at AT&T, continue to be the primary source for that classification at the company and elsewhere. Likewise, men are predominant in the crafts, and craftsmen continue to receive higher remuneration than secretaries. It is clear that parity at AT&T was not achieved by the quota system.

C. *Comparable Worth and Parity Employment*

Given the difficulty, if not the impossibility, of achieving parity employment, even with the use of very stringent quotas and the limitations imposed by the laws and the courts on the power of government enforcement agencies to impose additional quotas,[38] it now seems apparent that civil rights advocates and enforcement agencies are seeking an additional, or corollary, tool to accomplish their objective. A recasting of pay practices which ignores the labor market in setting wages could possibly equalize wages by sex or race regardless of duties. If parity employment cannot be achieved, then, according to this approach, at least parity pay or even income might be approximated. "Comparable worth" has apparently been seized upon as the tool that could be utilized to move toward this goal.

The key aspect of comparable worth is that it would require compensation based upon the "worth" of the job in comparison with other jobs.

---

[36] See Northrup and Larson, note 34 *supra*.

[37] For details, see *ibid.*, particularly pp. 60–64.

[38] See *United Steelworkers v. Weber*, 443 U.S. 193, 99 S.Ct. 2721 (1979), *rev'g* 563 F.2d 216 (5th Cir. 1978); and *University of California Regents v. Bakke*, 438 U.S. 265 (1978).

Stripped of its verbiage, this seems to imply that the criteria now utilized in wage classification procedures discriminate against minorities and women and, therefore, that different and not clear criteria should be utilized. For example, if secretaries are paid less than crafstmen but are "worth" as much to the business as craftsmen, the two positions should have an equal evaluation and thus, equal compensation, regardless of market values.

It is apparent that the theory of comparable worth, as used by civil rights activists, actually is derived from the same mold as random selection and parity employment beliefs. It is based on the premise that women and minorities are concentrated in positions that pay lower salaries, and while the EEOC and other civil rights organizations undoubtedly have reduced these concentrations, they have not been eliminated even when quotas are enforced, as at AT&T. A theory of comparable worth would, according to this thinking, compensate those now "discriminatorily" paid lower wages, thereby encouraging a better racial and sex distribution of work by restructuring pay.

The problems with this approach are many. In the first place, what a job or person is "worth" is not subject to a very real sense of objective determination. There is really no such thing as a "fair wage." What is fair is a matter of opinion. In our economy, job pay rates are established either by collective bargaining or by the employer's determination. In either case, if the rates are set below the market rate, the employer will find it difficult to recruit labor; if they are established at too high a level, the resultant costs will put the organization's products at a price disadvantage and, therefore, will cause a decline in sales and loss of jobs. Although the market often moves slowly, even the strongest unions have discovered that excessive wage costs sooner or later impact directly upon the employment of their members.[39]

Job evaluation and wage classification systems do not set wages. They are merely a means of establishing an orderly wage structure and of facilitating and encouraging an orderly job progression. Thus, rates must be established which induce personnel to accept and to take training so that they will be rewarded for so doing and thus, aspire to more important and responsible positions. Moreover, the job classification system must be accepted by employees and employer alike as fair if it is to accomplish these objectives and, very importantly, if it is to serve as a vehicle for the peaceful resolution of disputes over job classifications and wage rates. It has already been

---

[39] The policies of the building trades are a case in point. The excessive wage costs of union construction have resulted in nonunion companies' winning a major share of the business. See Herbert R. Northrup and Howard G. Foster, *Open Shop Construction*, Major Study No. 54 (Philadelphia: Industrial Research Unit, The Wharton School, University of Pennsylvania, 1975).

emphasized that, without an acceptable job evaluation program, individual employee wage disputes clog, or even overpower, the collective bargaining process and preclude the orderly settlement of other issues both in contract negotiations and in contract administration.

The comparable worth doctrine proposes a job evaluation or wage classification system and wage structure that is not related to the internal labor market of the firm. Jobs under such a procedure would not necessarily be rated in accordance with an orderly progression system, and thus such a system might not encourage training and promotion. Productivity could be decreased and costs increased. The net effect would certainly be a loss of sales and jobs for minorities and women as well as for white males.

It is also clear that the comparable worth theory would greatly raise the wage level. Jobs re-evaluated down—if any—by the comparable worth criteria would at most be red circled, with the attendant problems already discussed. Jobs re-evaluated up would be raised. This would not only cause an increase in costs in itself, but would surely trigger demands from related groups who did not receive increases for upward adjustments or from union officials ready to whipsaw the wage system upward. In turn, this would mean not only additional costs but considerably more labor strife as managements and unions attempt to settle difficult problems without the benefits of agreed-upon job criteria or a jointly settled plan.

Perhaps the most pernicious aspect of the comparable worth theory is that it would establish a government agency as the final arbiter of wages. The National War Labor Board of World War II found itself overburdened by individual wage disputes and gave job evaluation enormous impetus as a means of returning the task to the parties, who the Board's public, industry, and labor members believed were best qualified to handle it. The wisdom of the WLB's policies has become apparent, because job evaluation as such is no longer a contentious union-management issue. Moreover, experience has demonstrated that settlement by the parties of such issues is far better in terms of lasting results than determination by third parties. This is true even if the arbitrator is the clear choice of the parties because only the parties must live with and make work the determination that results.

Neither the EEOC nor any other government civil rights agency has ever demonstrated expertise in industrial relations or wage compensation, nor would they be acceptable arbiters to unions and managements. To have the EEOC or, for that matter, any government agency as the self-appointed determiner of job evaluation or wage levels, is certain to result in extensive controversy, litigations, and concomitant industrial strife. Moreover, the courts are not better suited in terms of expertise and are hardly more acceptable to the parties. What is being considered has the potential of drastically altering our system of collective bargaining, substantially increasing labor strife, dramatically raising labor costs, adding greatly to inflation, and worsening America's international competitive position.

D. *Back Pay and Equal Worth*

Ever since the AT&T consent decree, government EEO agencies have concentrated on gaining back pay awards in litigation or conciliation settlements. The purpose of back pay is twofold; it builds up support for the enforcement agency among protected groups, and it serves notice on potential violators, or even litigants, that failure to expand employment opportunities can be costly. The second point is obvious; the first is equally significant to the agency involved and to its bureaucracy.

The comparable worth theory has the potential of generating billions of dollars worth of back pay by altering the basis for evaluated pay structures. If that occurs, the EEOC would undoubtedly be the recipient of considerable gratitude on the part of those who benefit. The cost, employment, and inflationary impact, the transfer of work abroad, and therefore, the net results could well be far less salutary.

E. *AFL-CIO Resolution*

In the final day of its 1979 convention, the AFL-CIO passed a resolution calling on the AFL-CIO leadership to "encourage all efforts to reevaluate women's jobs according to their 'real worth' without regard to sex so that wage rates paid will truly reflect skill, effort, responsibility and working conditions." The resolution further urges the AFL-CIO to "treat job inequities resulting from sex and race discrimination like all other inequities which must be corrected, and adopt the concept of equal pay for work of comparable value as an organizing and negotiating strategy."[40]

On its face, the resolution seems both to support the comparable worth theory and to oppose it. Thus, jobs are to be reevaluated according to an undefinable standard "real worth," but job inequities involving race and sex are to be treated "like all other inequities which must be corrected," which can be interpreted clearly as the way they are now, and should be, handled. Perhaps the key to this puzzle lies in the embarrassment of AFL-CIO leadership with their own problem—a thirty-five member, all male Executive Council and their desire to interest potential female members to offset a shrinking membership—and the typically shrewd AFL-CIO capability of supporting all political pressure groups (minorities, women, senior citizens, etc.) in order to gain support for organized labor's political objectives.

Reports emanating from the AFL-CIO convention indicate that the resolution was approved only after bitter behind-the-scenes wrangling, and after a threat was made to embarrass the AFL-CIO all-male hierarchy with a floor fight over the issue. The view of the opponents of the resolution is well

---

[40] "AFL-CIO Names Panel to Explore Ways to Increase Female and Minority Membership," *Daily Labor Report* (No. 225), November 20, 1979, p. A–8.

summed up by the statement attributed to Sol Chaikin, president of the International Ladies' Garment Workers' Union, the membership of which is approximately 85 percent female:

> I'll be damned if I know a way to get the women more money. . . .
> The value of their work isn't set by theoretical principles but on the
> value of the work in the marketplace, and in the face of competition
> from overseas, where garment workers make 30¢ an hour. . . . Just
> to pass a resolution grounded on pie-in-the-sky, to be on the side of
> the angels, doesn't mean a thing.[41]

VIII. CONCLUDING REMARKS

,A fundamental problem with government regulation of business is the fragmentary character of government enforcement. Each law has spawned an agency which is concerned with the correction of a single problem area and gives little or no heed to others. Thus, antitrust regulations preclude an American company from expanding, but a foreign company moves in and captures the new business (and employment). The National Labor Relations Board certifies a union as exclusive bargaining agent, although the union's officers may be denying rights guaranteed to employees by the Landrum-Griffin Act. The Environmental Protection Agency prohibits the burning of coal by utilities, forcing them to import oil at higher prices, or puts coke ovens out of business, reducing employment and encouraging imports of coal and the transfer of jobs abroad. The costs, as well as the benefits, are too little considered, and the costs are often broad social ones as well as those involving individual employers and employees.

Often, too, actions of regulatory agencies are based upon limited information, theory, and ideology rather than understanding of the direct consequences of their actions. Thus, the EEOC and other government agencies "negotiated" a 19 percent female quota with AT&T for outside craft workers. This quota was based on nothing more than the fact that it was one-half of the then labor force participation ratio of women. AT&T made the quota by excessive training, enormous turnover, and at the expense of an accident ratio for women that, at the end of five years' experience, was 26.73 per thousand as compared with 9.76 per thousand for men.[42] Obviously, the EEOC did not consider the accident implication nor the public policy expressed in the Occupational Safety and Health Act in its "bargain" for a 19 percent female "parity" in AT&T's outside craft work.

Similarly, the EEOC's apparent desire to advance the comparable worth theory demonstrates little or no concern with its impact upon labor costs,

---

[41] "The new pay push for Women," *Business Week*, December 17, 1979, p. 69.

[42] Northrup and Larson, note 34 *supra*, p. 64.

employment, inflation, peaceful industrial relations, or the international competitive position of the United States. Yet the instigation of such a program, if successful, could well have considerable adverse effects upon all these aspects of the economy's well-being to the detriment of all members of the labor force. If discrimination exists in the development or administration of a job evaluation plan, it should be dealt with and corrected. To advocate the destruction of a system that has served the economy well on the basis of a highly questionable theory of wage determination, and to proceed on that basis without regard for the economic, employment, and industrial relations consequences, seems a prime example of administrative irresponsibility.

A FOREIGN PERSPECTIVE

by
Janice R. Bellace

Professor Bellace's analysis of the experience of the European Community, Sweden, Canada, Australia and New Zealand in trying to achieve the principle of equal pay demonstrates that none of the countries can be confidently categorized as applying a comparable worth approach to equal pay matters, although several clearly subscribe to it in theory. She begins with a discussion of the International Labour Organisation's Convention No. 100, Equal Pay Remuneration between Men and Women, and Article 119 of the Treaty of Rome, which mandates equal pay in the European Community. She then reviews the methods the thirteen countries have adopted to conform to these guarantees. She contends that there is no common foreign definition of comparable worth, nor is there uniformity as to the definition of "equal value," a term commonly used in European and international agreements. Moreover, there is little similarity in the methods the countries use to resolve equal pay matters. Professor Bellace also notes that in the four countries which come closest to adopting the comparable worth theory, there is a history of widespread job evaluation and the trade unions there have sanctioned the relative equalization of all wage rates in the belief that the existing wage range is too great and should be compressed.

Janice Bellace is an Assistant Professor of legal studies and management at the Wharton School of the University of Pennsylvania. She is also a senior faculty research associate at the Wharton School's Industrial Research Unit, specializing in multinational studies. After receiving her bachelor's and law degrees from the University of Pennsylvania, Professor Bellace attended the London School of Economics on a Thouron Fellowship, and earned her master's degree in industrial relations there in 1975. While in London, Professor Bellace also worked as a labor law journalist. A member of several professional societies, such as the American Bar Association and the International Industrial Research Association, Professor Bellace is the author of a number of Industrial Research Unit publications including "Co-determination in Germany, The Netherlands and Luxembourg," (1976); "Disadvantaged Upgrading and Legal Consideration," in the *The Objective Selection of Supervisors* (1978); and she co-authored with Alan Berkowitz, *The Landrum-Griffin Act: Twenty Years of Federal Protection of Union Members' Rights*, (1979). She is currently preparing an article on union decertification under the National Labor Relations Act.

A FOREIGN PERSPECTIVE

In the last twenty years, every major Western industrialized country has witnessed a sharp increase in its female labor force participation rate. Factors such as declining birth rates, increasing life expectancy, the attainment of higher educational levels, and the introduction of more laborsaving devices into the home have propelled increasing numbers of women into the labor market. In the same period, all advanced industrial societies have experienced a growth in white-collar employment at the expense of blue-collar employment. This has generated a demand for workers to fill office and service jobs which have been viewed as particularly suitable for women. These factors, common to all industrialized countries, have produced a generation of working women who have become increasingly dissatisfied with traditional sex-based wage differentials.

This paper analyzes the methods that industrialized countries have adopted to achieve the principle of equal pay, with a special emphasis on the criteria used to determine when women are entitled to equal pay and on the relative success of the methods. The analysis will begin with a view of two well-known guarantees of equal pay, the International Labour Organisation's (ILO) Convention No. 100 and Article 119 of the Treaty of Rome, and will conclude with an examination of the application of these guarantees in the European Community, Sweden, Canada, Australia and New Zealand.

First, however, some commonly used terminology needs explanation. The discussion of the different equal pay formulations will proceed on the assumption that the phrase 'equal pay for equal work' encompasses equal pay for work that is substantially similar, both in terms of job content and working conditions. When it is noted that a country subscribes to the "comparable worth theory," it is meant that the guarantee of equal pay extends to jobs which are not similar, either because the jobs are performed under different working conditions or because the content of the two jobs is dissimilar, yet the positions are deemed to be of equal worth under some system which evaluates a job's compensable factors.[1]

In the contemporary debate on equal pay, when the term "comparable worth theory" is used, Americans comprehend that a formulation broader

---

[1] See the paper by Donald P. Schwab in this volume, p. 49, for an explanation of job evaluation and the meaning of comparable worth.

than "equal pay for equal work" is meant. It should be emphasized that the conceptual difference between these two pay formulations often is not readily apparent in foreign legislation because the commonly-used phrase, "equal pay for work of equal value" can arguably be interpreted as guaranteeing "equal pay for equal work" or "equal pay for jobs of comparable worth." To avoid confusion, this paper attempts to define precisely what a particular formulation is interpreted as meaning in a given country. In addition, deviations between meaning and practice will be noted so that the impact of incorporating a comparable worth theory into the equal pay guarantee can be gauged.

I. CROSS-CULTURAL INFLUENCES

In confronting a common problem under somewhat similar circumstances, national governments have tended to examine carefully the experience other countries have had with equal pay. Since the United States was one of the first countries to take legislative action to implement the principle of equal pay, its 1963 statute frequently has provided the starting point for deliberations of other countries seeking to establish the principle of equal pay. Likewise, the British experience with equal pay has been closely monitored, especially by other countries in the Commonwealth whose laws and traditions are based on Britain's. This cross-fertilization of ideas has not been limited, however, to national developments. Two supranational instruments have greatly influenced the debate over equal pay. One is Article 119 of the Treaty of Rome, which mandates equal pay in the European Community, discussed later in this chapter. The other is Convention No. 100, Equal Remuneration between Men and Women, of the International Labour Organisation.

Drafted in 1951, ILO Convention No. 100 states that signatory nations[2] shall "ensure the application to all workers of the principle of equal remuneration for men and women workers for work of equal value." The Convention does not define what is meant by "work of equal value;" Article 3 does state, however, that differential base wage rates which are not sex-based but which correspond "to differences, as determined by such objective appraisal, in the

---

[2] At the annual meeting of the International Labour Conference, decisions in the form of conventions, recommendations or resolutions may be taken. Two-thirds of the delegates present and voting must support a proposed convention for it to be adopted. Once a convention has been adopted, all member governments are required to submit the convention within one year to the national legislative body for the enactment of national legislation or other appropriate action. If the legislature consents to the ratification of the convention, the nation's formal ratification of the convention is communicated to the Director-General of the ILO. Signatory nations are under an obligation to ensure that national law and practice comply with the provisions of the ratified convention. It should be emphasized that the ILO has no enforcement mechanism whereby it can compel signatory nations to implement a convention. The ILO limits itself to reporting on conditions within countries. The information for these reports is usually supplied by the member nations.

work to be performed" do not contravene the Convention. Of the thirteen countries discussed in this chapter, all except New Zealand have ratified ILO Convention No. 100.[3]

The question whether the ILO's adoption in 1951 of the formulation equal pay "for work of equal value" was designed to incorporate the comparable worth theory cannot be definitely answered. The origins of the phrase can be traced back to the 1919 Peace Treaty ending World War I and setting up the ILO. It has been noted that the use of the phrase equal pay "for work of equal value" rather than the more generally used slogan, "equal pay for equal work," can be attributed to Lord Balfour who preferred a more precise statement of the guarantee.[4] There is nothing to suggest that Lord Balfour intended this formulation to extend beyond equal pay for substantially similar work and, prior to World War II, it certainly was not interpreted as having a broader meaning.

After the ILO became a specialized agency of the United Nations in 1946, several conventions dealing with employment practices and industrial relations were proposed, among them Convention No. 100. Although it is possible to discern among the presentations made during the highly politicized 1951 session some statements which might be characterized as supporting the comparable worth theory of equal pay, it seems clear that many of the delegates approved the use of the familiar 1919 wording as an acceptable method of expressing what we today understand by "equal pay for equal work."[5] It should be noted, however, that officially, the ILO perceives its equal pay formulation as being broader and more flexible than equal pay for substantially similar work.[6]

II. THE EUROPEAN COMMUNITY

In 1957, six nations in Western Europe signed the Treaty of Rome, establishing the European Economic Community (EEC). At that time, Germany, Belgium, France and Italy had signed Convention No. 100 of the ILO which guarantees equal pay for work of equal value. Article 119 of the Treaty of Rome sets out the Community's equal pay guarantee. In the official English translation,[7] Article 119 states: "Each Member State shall during the

---

[3] The United States has not ratified Convention No. 100 but it should be noted that the United States has ratified very few ILO conventions.

[4] G. A. Johnston, *The International Labour Organisation* (London: Europa Publications Ltd., 1970), pp. 160–61.

[5] For the draft of the convention with the final report, see ILO: Report VII (Part II), International Labour Conference, 34th Session, Geneva, 1951.

[6] For a discussion of the equal pay guarantee, see ILO: Report III (Part 4B), *Equal Remuneration*, International Labour Conference, 60th Session, Geneva, 1975, p. 55–57.

[7] *Treaties Establishing the European Communities*, Office for the Official Publications of the European Communities (Luxembourg, 1973), p. 272.

first stage ensure and subsequently maintain the application of the principle that men and women should receive equal pay for equal work.''

Since the original treaty was not drafted in English, it is of some importance to know what were the exact words used in the original texts. The French, Italian and Dutch texts used *même travail, stesso lavoro,* and *gelijke arbeid,* respectively, thereby clearly indicating that women shall receive equal remuneration with men for the ''same'' work. The German text is less precise, using *gleicher arbeit,* a term which could encompass ''similar'' work in addition to the ''same'' work.

When the European Commission (the secretariat of the EEC) began to monitor the implementation of Article 119, it immediately encountered difficulty in determining what the formulation of the equal pay guarantee meant in actual practice. In July 1960, the president of the Commission publicly expressed his view that the concept of equal pay for work of equal value, as embodied in ILO Convention No. 100, was not incorporated in Article 119 which merely required equal pay for the same work.[8] In their responses to a European Commission questionnaire distributed a year later, all six member states proclaimed that the principle of equal pay had been implemented but in a report on the application of the principle, the social affairs commission of the EEC observed that the differences between men's and women's wages throughout the Community was so great as to cast serious doubts on the accuracy of the governments' responses.[9] The social affairs commission noted, however, that it was reluctant to reach any conclusion since it could not state with any precision what the guarantee of equal pay meant, let alone comment on whether it had been implemented.[10] As a result, the social affairs commission asked that two special working groups, one composed of lawyers and the other of statisticians, be established to study the correct application of Article 119.

Various deadlines for the implementation of Article 119 were missed and, throughout the 1960s, successive reports of the European Commission on the progress of the member states' implementation of the equal pay guarantee indicated that very little progress had been made. In its later reports, the Commission's appreciation of the magnitude of the problem became increasingly refined. For instance, in its report on the progress of implementation of equal pay as of December 31, 1968, the social affairs commission singled out persistent indirect discrimination as the factor accounting for much of the disparity between male and female wages. This

---

[8] Excerpt from the cover letter of Walter Hallstein, dated July 28, 1960, to the foreign ministers of the member states, reported in European Parliament, Document 68, ''Rapport interimaire fait au nom de la commission sociale sur l'égalisation des salaires masculins et féminins,'' October 20, 1961, p. 3.

[9] See comments of Bertrand Motte, European Parliament, Débats Compte Rendu in Extenso des Séances, October 20, 1961, p. 258-60.

[10] Document 68, *supra* note 8, p. 10.

discrimination, it found, was based on the general undervaluing of duties deemed to be predominantly female, the classifying of predominantly female work as "easy work," and the overvaluing in job evaluation plans of such factors as physical force compared to dexterity and attention.[11] In its conclusion to this report, the commission commented that it was difficult to interpret the notions of *equal work* and *equal pay* without a better understanding of what constituted *equal work,* an understanding which would require further study and the agreement of interested parties.[12]

Shortly after the United Kingdom, Ireland and Denmark acceded to the European Community in 1973, the European Commission announced its intention of taking action to compel the implementation of the principle of equal pay.[13] In November 1973, it submitted to the Council of the European Communities a proposed directive on the approximation of the member states' laws on the application of the principle of equal pay, a directive which would be given priority under the Commission's social action program. On February 10, 1975, the Council adopted the proposed directive.[14]

The equal pay directive[15] contains ten articles. Article 1 declares that the principle of equal pay set out in Article 119 of the Treaty of Rome means equal pay "for the same work or for work to which equal value is attributed." Article 1 further states: "In particular, where a job classification system is used for determining pay, it must be based on the same criteria for both men and women and so drawn up as to exclude any discrimination on grounds of sex." The equal pay directive does not contain a definition of what amounts to work of equal value.

The remaining articles of the equal pay directive specify what measures the member states must take to implement equal pay, such as enacting legislation, providing enforcement mechanisms, publicizing the existence of the

---

[11] European Parliament, Document 21/71, "Rapport sur l'état d'application au 31 décembre 1968 du principe de l'égalité des rémunérations entre les travailleurs masculins et féminins," April 19, 1971, p. 3-4.

[12] Ibid., p. 13.

[13] Article 100 of the Treaty of Rome promotes the harmonization of conditions within the member states with the aim of creating a unified community. One method of harmonizing conditions is by requiring the member states to approximate their legislative and administrative rules to each other's. Harmonization is achieved under Article 100 by means of directives, issued by the Council of the European Communities acting unanimously on a proposal by the European Commission.

[14] Both the Commission and the Council proceeded on the assumption that Article 119 required implementation by the member states and was not directly applicable without the member states' taking some action. In *Defrenne v. Sabena,* (Case No. 149/77, June 15, 1978), the European Court of Justice held that Article 119 was directly applicable. The court held that this did not, however, preempt the Commission from acting in this area.

[15] Council Directive of February 10, 1975 on the approximation of the laws of the Member States relating to the application of the principle of equal pay for men and women, 75/117/EEC. Printed in the *Official Journal of the European Communities,* No. L45, February 19, 1975, p. 19. Hereinafter referred to as the "equal pay directive."

right to equal pay and taking action to abolish sex-based differentials in collective agreements and wage scales.

The member states were originally given one year in which to comply with the equal pay directive but, at the urging of several countries, notably West Germany, the deadline was pushed back until August, 1978. The setting of a deadline did precipitate, however, a spurt of legislative activity within the member states of the European Community, although some countries, especially Ireland, were clearly reluctant to take prompt action.

The 1975 equal pay directive required that the European Commission report by 1979 concerning the status of equal pay in the Community, a deadline which the Commission met. In its report,[16] the European Commission reviewed mere technical compliance with the equal pay directive's requirements and was highly critical of the progress made in this limited area. On March 22, 1979, the European Commission announced that it would initiate infringement proceedings against seven member states for failure to comply fully with the equal pay directive. The United Kingdom, Denmark and Germany were considered to be prime targets of this proceeding, because their lack of compliance was of a patently substantive nature. The failure to name Ireland and Italy as respondents in the infringement proceedings caused some surprise in the Community, until the Commission pointed out that it had reviewed each country's technical compliance with the equal pay directive and found that recently both had passed statutes which complied literally with the directive's requirements.

The European Commission has indicated that these infringement proceedings are only the first stage in a campaign to ensure that the member states implement equal pay. Within the past few months, it has become evident that the named countries, once threatened with legal action, have moved to meet the Commission's complaint. Even Germany, which had long and adamantly claimed its legal provisions were sufficient, has backed down and introduced a bill designed to comply with the equal pay directive.

In the next stage of its campaign to ensure that equal pay is implemented, the European Commission will review conditions within the member states to determine if the guarantee of equal pay is actually being enforced. Any future report of the European Commission, however, will probably confront the broader question of the status of working women in the Community since two other directives aimed at achieving equality for working women have been adopted since 1975. The adoption of directives on equal opportunity in employment and equal treatment in working life reveal the Commission's awareness that unequal pay is only one manifestation of discrimination against working women.

---

[16] Commission of the European Communities, "Report of the Commission to the Council on the Application as at February 12, 1978 of the Principle of Equal Pay for Men and Women," COM (78)711 final of January 16, 1979.

Although it is arguable that Article 119 of the Treaty of Rome incorporated a comparable worth theory and even though the 1975 equal pay directive does not define what is meant by equal pay for work of equal value, it is clear from the Commission's 1979 report that it views the equal pay directive as mandating equal pay for work of comparable worth. In its conclusions, the Commission states that a narrow interpretation of the directive's equal pay guarantee "would completely negate" the directive, "the aim of which on the contrary is to broaden the concept of 'same work' to that of 'work of equal value.' "[17] The Commission's objections to the Danish and British legislation and its praise of the Dutch legislation underscore its view on the current interpretation of the equal pay guarantee.

Developments in the nine member states of the European Community will be briefly noted by referring to the member state's compliance with the equal pay directive. As will become evident, most equal pay statutes have been in force less than five years and their impact is just beginning to be felt. In this review, greater attention will be paid to those countries in which job evaluation is common. The United Kingdom will be a focus of this discussion because several British cases have explored what constitutes "like" work, highlighting the problems of incorporating a comparable worth theory in the application of the equal pay guarantee.

A. *United Kingdom*

Great Britain[18] is the only country in the European Community which enacted legislation on equal pay before it was formally required to do so, either by ratifying Convention No. 100 of the ILO or by signing the Treaty of Rome. Since its statute predates the equal pay directive, the British formulation of the equal pay guarantee was based on a detailed consideration of what were the feasible limits in Britain of legislation implementing equal pay. In 1979, the European Community initiated infringement proceedings against the United Kingdom, claiming that the country's legislation did not guarantee equal pay for work of equal value in all work situations as required by the equal pay directive; and it is not clear if or when the statute will be amended to meet the Commission's objectives. The discussion will refer to the statute as it now stands, because its equal pay formulation raises several interesting issues relating to the theory of comparable worth.

Although the Trades Union Congress (TUC) first called for equal pay for women in 1888, it was not until the Second World War that the

---

[17] Ibid., p. 139.

[18] In the past decade, statutes enacted by the British Parliament sitting at Westminister cover, in most cases, only Great Britain. Orders can extend a modified form of the statute to Northern Ireland. The Equal Pay Act of December 17, 1970 applies to Northern Ireland. This statute was amended by the Sex Discrimination (Northern Ireland) Order of 2 July 1976. The European Commission report refers to the United Kingdom because the United Kingdom, as a nation, is a member of the European Community. The legislation referred to in this section is the British act of May 29, 1970.

government appointed a Royal Commission to consider the issue of equal pay. In its 1946 report,[19] the members of the Commission failed to agree on why women were not receiving equal pay with men and on what would be the cost of implementing equal pay. The members of the Commission did agree, however, that if the principle of equal pay were to be implemented, it should be confined to the non-industrial government sector where the difficulties of implementation would be less marked. In 1955, the government acted on this recommendation of the Commission.

In its election manifesto in 1964, the Labour party committed itself to supporting the principle of equal pay. When it took office, the Labour government set up a working group, composed of representatives from employers' groups and unions, to study the feasibility of implementing equal pay. Although the committee members were not unanimous in their recommendations, the government decided to introduce a bill on equal pay in 1970, after further consultation with the TUC and the Confederation of British Industry. In May 1970, the Equal Pay Act was enacted with the stipulation that it not take effect until December 29, 1975, in order to give employers sufficient time in which to make the necessary adjustments required by this new statutory obligation.

The Equal Pay Act of 1970, as amended by the Sex Discrimination Act of 1974, contains a rather complex definition of the equal pay guarantee because the statute specifically considers whether the woman's job is covered by a job evaluation scheme. Under section 1(2), a woman is entitled to equal pay if she is employed on "like" work with a man or if her work has been "rated as equivalent" to that of a man in the same employment.

Section 1(4) defines "like" work as work "of the same or broadly similar nature," with any differences between the woman's work and the man's work "not of practical importance." If "like" work is found to exist, the woman is still not entitled to equal pay if the variation in pay is "genuinely due to a material difference" other than the difference of sex. Moreover, under section 1(5) a woman's job can be considered to have an equivalent rating to that of a man's only if both are covered by the same job evaluation plan. This section is intentionally drafted in such a way to make it clear that only analytic job evaluation plans using the factor comparison or points rating method can be cited. That is, schemes in which grades are first defined and then jobs, based on their descriptions, are slotted into the grades, do not qualify as job evaluation plans under the section. Section 1(5) does incorporate the traditional approach of job evaluation techniques by noting that a woman is entitled to equal pay only if her job has been given "an equal value, in terms of the demand made on the worker under various headings (for instance, effort, skill, decision). . . ." Besides indicating that physical effort is

---

[19] Great Britain, Office of Manpower Economics, First Report on the Implementation of the Equal Pay Act 1970, *Equal Pay* (1972), p. 4.

an acceptable factor to rate, this section also implicitly accepts the traditional method of job evaluation where an objective assessment of a job's demands on the worker is made.[20]

From a mere examination of the statutory provisions, some points quickly become evident. First, a woman is not entitled to equal pay under the 1970 statute if she performs work which would have been rated equivalent to a man's job in her workplace if an evaluation plan had been introduced, but her work is not broadly similar to his. In this regard, the European Commission's objection, noted above, is well taken, because the British statute does not guarantee equal pay for work of equal value in all circumstances. Second, the statutory approach to job evaluation does not take into account the possibility that a job evaluation plan could make a subjective assessment of the effects a job imparts on a worker, as the German professors Rohmert and Rutenfranz advocate. The statute, therefore, seems to sanction the type of job evaluation which has been attacked as undervaluing women's work. Third, the statute requires that there be a comparable man if the woman is attempting to claim equal pay under the "like" work section. Since the majority of women do not work in positions which men also occupy, the statute has limited utility. As mentioned later in this chapter, the New Zealand parliament considered the British experience when it enacted its own equal pay statute which creates a notional man when there is no comparable man employed at the same firm. At the 1979 conference of the Trades Union Congress, female delegates urged that the Equal Pay Act be amended to allow for a hypothetical comparable man.

Even with these alleged shortcomings, the British statute has generated great interest. Although fewer cases than were expected have arisen, Britain by far has recorded the highest number of equal pay cases of any country in the European Community. The litigation process normally involves a woman filing a complaint with an industrial tribunal, a body composed of a law-trained chairman and two laymen. Hearings before the tribunals are conducted informally and decisions are reached on the basis of common sense as dictated by reason and experience. Appeals may be taken to the specialized Employment Appeal Tribunal. In a very small number of cases, a further appeal may be taken to the Court of Appeal. In addition to this enforcement mechanism, a union may file a complaint with the government's Central Arbitration Committee (CAC) alleging that the wage scales in a collective agreement are discriminatory. The CAC is empowered, after a hearing, to order an employer to modify his wage scales to implement the guarantee of equal pay.

The theory of comparable worth as it relates to job evaluation weightings has arisen as a direct issue in only a few cases. More often, the

---

[20] In the late 1960s, job evaluation plans became increasingly popular in Britain as a means of restructuring chaotic wage grades. The National Board for Prices and Incomes encouraged the implementation of such plans. See National Board for Prices and Incomes, Report No. 83, *Job Evaluation* (1968).

woman complainant challenges the entire job evaluation exercise undertaken at her workplace. Since many firms have only recently introduced job evaluation,[21] there has been some question as to the thoroughness and impartiality of the exercise. The Employment Appeal Tribunal has held that an industrial tribunal must consider the results of a validly conducted job evaluation exercise; the tribunal is not free to disregard the results unless the woman can show that the evaluation is invalid.[22]

In two cases, the points allocated to specific factors were challenged. *Gardner* v. *Dunlop Ltd.*[23] involved a "highly sophisticated" job evaluation system which rated the alleged comparable man's job six points higher than the woman's, a difference which placed the man into the next higher job grade. All six points related to a lifting requirement in the job. The industrial tribunal refused to disturb the findings of the evaluation or to re-grade the woman's job. In *Aubertin* v. *Edwards High Vacuum*,[24] female light assemblers sought equal pay with male pump assemblers. The men's job had been rated considerably higher in a job evaluation study on the basis of several factors, including physical effort. The industrial tribunal agreed with the employer that a difference in points "fairly accurately" represented the difference between the two jobs.

The "like" work formulation in the equal pay statute has required industrial tribunals to consider even more arcane differences between men's and women's jobs than those confronted in the job evaluation cases.[25] In general, tribunals have found that physical effort does merit higher pay.[26] The difficulties tribunals have experienced in attempting to scrutinize the employer's conclusions about the relative dirtiness encountered or skill required for specific jobs has led them, for the most part, to accept the employer's wage structure unless it is demonstrated that the employer is relying on sham factors. As such, some women have become disillusioned with the prospects of gaining equal pay by pursuing an equal pay claim through the tribunals.

---

[21] Many employers seized on job evaluation in the 1970s as a means of curing sex-based wage anomalies and of rationalizing the job ranking order prior to restructuring the wage scales. See P. Glucklich, M. Povall, M. W. Snell and A. Zell, "Equal Pay and Opportunity," *Department of Employment Gazette*, (July 1978), pp. 777–80.

[22] *Green v. Broxtowe District Council*, Employment Appeal Tribunal, 431/76, (October 10, 1976); *Eaton Ltd. v. Nuttall*, Employment Appeal Tribunal, 416/76 (January 21, 1977).

[23] Birmingham tribunal (Central Office of Industrial Tribunals 563/92) January 14, 1977.

[24] Brighton tribunal, (Central Office of Industrial Tribunals 428/34) February 23, 1976.

[25] For instance, there have been several cases which required tribunals to decide whether male janitors were employed on "like work" with cleaning ladies. Accordingly, the tribunals were required to determine what items were cleaned, what was their condition prior to cleaning, and in what manner were they cleaned. In a few cases, tribunals were asked to decide whether janitors cleaning men's toilets could be paid more than women cleaning ladies' toilets on the grounds that men's toilets are generally dirtier.

[26] See, e.g., *IDS Brief*, No. 102 (1977), pp. 10–16; *IDS Brief*, No. 123 (1977), pp. 15–18.

If Britain amends its statute to guarantee equal pay for work of equal value regardless of whether a job evaluation exercise has taken place, and fails to amend its enforcement scheme, industrial tribunals will be confronted with the necessity of making even more subjective determinations of a job's value vis à vis other jobs at the woman's workplace with, at best, only incomplete information on which to base their conclusions. In this connection, Baroness Seear, one of Britain's leading equal pay advocates, recently observed, "there is really only one solution: the extension of the use of job evaluation."[27] Baroness Seear recognized, however, that it would not be feasible to place upon the employers the legal obligation of introducing job evaluation. Hence, she concluded that rather than have untrained industrial tribunal members make the valuation judgment, outside experts should be called in, either as court-appointed consultants or as a standing "Comparability Board." If such a system were to arise, it would seem likely that many employers would introduce their own job evaluation plan rather than face the prospect of government-appointed outsiders revamping their job grading system.

Even though an equal pay study conducted by the London School of Economics found that in the companies studied, the greatest progress towards equal pay had been made where job evaluation was used,[28] there has recently been some concern with the fairness of such plans. In July 1978, Britain's Employment Opportunities Commission appointed a working party to formulate guidelines on the application of job evaluation plans. This working group has yet to make its recommendations.[29]

B. *Italy*

Article 37 of the 1948 Italian constitution provides that women are entitled to equal pay for equal work. Although Italy was one of the founding member states of the European Community, it took no action to fulfill its obligations under Article 119 of the Treaty of Rome until compelled to do so by the 1975 equal pay directive. It delayed so long in responding to the 1975 directive that the two other equality directives had already been announced before Italy took legislative action to implement the equal pay guarantee. As a result, Italy passed one statute, the Law of December 9, 1977, which is a comprehensive equality statute designed to comply with all three equality directives of the European Community. The language of this statute complies literally with the equal pay directive.

Article 2 of the 1977 act states that women shall receive equal pay for work of equal value and further provides that common criteria for men and

---

[27] Baroness Seear, " 'Where do we go from here?' Equal Pay and Equal Opportunity," *Department of Employment Gazette*, September 1979, p. 864.

[28] Ibid.

[29] Great Britain, Equal Opportunities Commission, *Third Annual Report*, (1979), p. 14.

women must be adopted in formulating grading and salary structures. Prior to 1972, collective bargaining agreements in Italy tended to divide jobs into only three categories; white-collar, blue-collar and intermediate (services). Since that time, there has been a movement to slot jobs into a greater number of classifications, usually seven or ten by means of a non-analytic job grading method and not an analytic factor comparison or points rating method.

In Italy's submission to the European Commission,[30] the government, employer federations and trade unions all agreed that women, for the most part, are predominantly found in a few low-paying occupational classifications. The trade unions claimed that this concentration is one reason that traditionally female work was undervalued, an assertion that the government and the employer federations disputed. In view of the simplistic method of job evaluation now being used in Italy, this claim of undervaluing does not represent an allegation that disproportionate weightings are being attached to characteristics traditionally found in male jobs. Instead, it represents a claim that simple, light, repetitive work requiring little skill or training is usually in the lowest job grades by definition. Unless the number of grades was reduced, rather than increased as is now being done, it is difficult to see how traditionally female jobs could be upgraded. In essence, then, the trade unions' claim can be seen as one of higher pay for women rather than equal pay for work of equal value.

Since Italy's equal pay statute has been on the books less than two years, it is not surprising that no case proceeding on a comparable worth theory has been brought. Whether this issue will be brought before the courts is doubtful, because in Italy's highly politicized labor relations scene, trade unions are more likely to resort to industrial action rather than litigation to achieve their goals.

C. *Ireland*

Ireland is perhaps the country which has experienced the most difficulty in complying with the equal pay directive. This is not surprising when it is recalled that, prior to 1975, not only sex-based wage differentials but also wage differentials based on marital status were common in Ireland. In addition, since women were often required to resign their job upon marriage, traditionally female jobs were usually held by young women with little seniority.

To comply with the equal pay directive, the Irish parliament enacted the Anti-Discrimination (Pay) Act of 1974, which was to take effect from December 31, 1975. Prior to this date, however, the government introduced a bill in parliament to postpone the effective date of the act in certain sectors

---

[30] In gathering material for its Report of January 16, 1979, the European Commission solicited the views of the governments, employers' federations and trade unions in the member states. The submissions of these bodies to the Commission are specifically noted at various points in the Report.

of the economy on the grounds that employers in these industries would be financially unable to implement equal pay fully by the required date. The Irish government applied to the European Commission for a temporary derogation from the equal pay directive.[31] After considering the opposition of the Irish Confederation of Trade Unions to the government's request, the Commission rejected the application in March 1975, whereupon the government withdrew the bill.[32]

The 1974 statute, as amended by the Employment Equality Act of 1977, states that women are entitled to equal pay for "like" work which is defined as the same or similar work, or work of equal value. Section 3(b) of the 1974 Act defines this category as follows: ". . . work performed by one is equal in value to that performed by the other in terms of the demands it makes in relation to such matters as skill, physical or mental effort, responsibility and working conditions."

As previously noted, the European Commission is of the opinion that the Irish statute is in technical compliance with the equal pay directive. Although the Irish formulation is similar to that found in the British statute, the European Commission has taken the position that the British definition of "like" work is too narrow in that it expressly requires that the woman's work be broadly similar to that of the man. The Irish statute does not require broadly similar work; it simply lists some factors which may be taken into consideration when attempting to determine whether two jobs are of equal value.

In general, Irish industry classifies jobs along traditional lines using categories such as unskilled, semi-skilled, skilled, etc. Except in relatively large or foreign companies, job evaluation techniques are rarely used.

Since sex segregation in employment is common in Ireland, most of the equal pay cases which have arisen are based, to some extent, on a comparable worth theory.[33] In none of the cases litigated so far has there been a job evaluation plan. As a result, these cases have required the Irish equality officers or the Irish labor court to make subjective determinations of the value of the work performed on the basis of submissions made by both parties, a task made feasible by the fact that the Republic of Ireland has a highly homogeneous population of just over three million.

---

[31] Such an application is provided for under Article 135 of the Treaty of Accession which permits extensions if compliance would lead to serious economic deterioration within a member state.

[32] The equal pay statute, which did take effect as scheduled, did not apply initially to the public sector, because the government allowed itself a brief phase-in period. As such, there arose the anomalous situation of the government advertising for persons to monitor the implementation of the equal pay statute, yet paying those persons according to marital and sex-based wage scales.

[33] For a review of some of the leading cases, see *European Industrial Relations Review*, No. 37 (1977), pp 8–11, and No. 55 (1978), pp. 11–12.

It is difficult to determine exactly how the officers and the labor court have reached their conclusions, because their opinions often state only the arguments of both sides and then simply announce the award. Attempting to analyze the cases on the basis of their outcome is also less than fruitful. In some instances, women have been awarded equal pay when their duties differed significantly from the men's duties, yet there also are cases where women have been denied equal pay when their duties were quite similar to the men's tasks.[34]

Several highly publicized cases have touched upon issues similar to those raised in American equal pay litigation. For instance, a case[35] involving female dayshift telephone operators in Dublin raised issues similar to those in the American *Corning Class* case.[36] Also, in a case involving Waterford Glass,[37] the union initiated a claim on behalf of 457 women who performed a variety of tasks. It was argued that the women's basic rate should at least be equal to the lowest male rate. The equality officer accepted this contention, finding that the women's work was of equal value with that of male general workers. In his award, the equality officer noted that where a woman's job required "skill, dexterity and concentration," it could be "as demanding as" the more physically-demanding male job. Since this case was not appealed by the employer, it is not clear whether the principles stated in it meet with general acceptance or whether they are simply the views of one equality officer.

Considering the degree of sex segregation in employment in Ireland and the absence of job evaluation plans, section 3(b) of the 1974 Act effectively requires that a highly subjective judgment be made. At present, when awards often are simply bringing women up to the unskilled male rate, the provision has escaped criticism to a large extent. Once women begin alleging that the weightings attached to certain characteristics are discriminatory, it is likely that section 3(b) will become a hotly debated topic.

---

[34] For instance, the first time the Dublin telephone operators' case came up, it was found that the women were not entitled to equal pay even though the only difference between their work and men's work was the time at which it was performed and the men were receiving a shift premium. Yet in a case involving police men and police women, the men performed extra duties at night but the women were still found to be entitled to equal pay. It should be noted that the second time the Dublin case came up, after the operators engaged in industrial action, it was found that they were engaged in like work with the male operators.

[35] See note 34 *supra*. This case involved 3000 female day telephone operators employed by the Irish Dept. of Posts and Telegraphs. The case is discussed in *European Industrial Relations Review*, No. 69 (1979), p. 3.

[36] *Corning Glass Works v. Brennan*, 417 U.S. 188 (1974). In *Corning Glass*, the United States Supreme Court held that the employer violated the Equal Pay Act by paying male night inspection workers at a higher base wage than it paid to female inspectors performing the same tasks on the day shift. The higher wage was paid in addition to separate night shift differential paid to all employees for night work.

[37] *Waterford Glass v. Amalgamated Transport and General Workers Union*, case reported in *European Industrial Relations Review*, No. 55 (1978), p. 12.

D. *Denmark*

Prior to 1973, explicit sex-based wage differentials were commonly found in Danish collective agreements. In April 1973, the Confederation of Employees (LO) and the Confederation of Employers (DA) concluded a national agreement which pledged the parties to abolish any wage discrimination still existing in national collective agreements. The Danish government believed that this agreement was sufficient implementation of the principle of equal pay, but at the urging of the European Commission, the government did introduce a bill to comply with the requirements of the equal pay directive. In February 1976, Law No. 32 on equal pay for men and women was enacted.

In March 1979, the European Commission initiated infringement proceedings against Denmark on the grounds that the 1976 equal pay statute did not comply with the equal pay directive because the statutory equal pay guarantee extended only to women performing the "same" work and not to women engaged in work of equal value.

Once Denmark amends the 1976 statute to meet the European Commission's objection, it will still be difficult for women to utilize the statute. At present, most Danish collective agreements classify jobs into such traditional categories as unskilled, semi-skilled, skilled, etc. The distinction between skilled and unskilled, which is of critical importance, is based upon the completion of an apprenticeship. As might be expected, very few women in Denmark have served an apprenticeship. Also, except for very large or foreign companies, job evaluation plans are not commonly found in Denmark.

E. *France*

Since the end of World War II, there has been little or no official discrimination between men and women in France with regard to pay matters. The French constitution of November, 1946, guarantees equality between the sexes and a decree promulgated that same year eliminated explicit sex-based differentials in basic wage rates as fixed by collective agreements. The Law of February 11, 1950, mandated that collectively bargained wage rates comply with the principle of equal pay for equal work. Then, in 1972, France enacted equal pay legislation, the Law of December 22, 1972, which was implemented by the Decree of March 27, 1973. The statute requires that women receive equal pay when performing work of equal value.

Formal job evaluation exercises are not commonly undertaken in French industry except in large enterprises. Most collective agreements establish a hierarchical ranking of jobs which assigns jobs to predetermined grades by matching the definition of the job's requirements with the description of the job grade. This system originated after the end of the Second World War in order to comply with the then existing government wage policy. Within the past few years, there has been a tendency to modify existing job grades to remove the strict distinction between blue-collar and white-collar jobs. How a job grading hierarchy should correspond to a wage scale is a matter for collective bargaining and wide variations between companies are not unknown.

Although the language of the French equal pay statute arguably incorporates the comparable worth theory, there have been few cases on point, and it is difficult to tell if, let alone how, the theory of comparable worth is being applied. The French government's submission to the European Commission denied the existence of wage discrimination in France today, an opinion somewhat suspect in light of the government's explanation that one reason most women fill a limited number of job classifications is their natural aptitude for those jobs. Given the governmental attitude, it is unlikely that France will be one of the first countries to consider seriously the underlying implications of the theory of comparable worth.

F. Belgium

A national collective agreement between employers and trade unions concerning equal pay for men and women was concluded on October 15, 1975. Known as Collective Labor Agreement No. 25, it was made legally binding by the Royal Decree of December 9, 1975. The agreement complies with the equal pay directive in that it provides for equal pay for work of equal value and, in Article 3, it states that job evaluation methods must not discriminate on the basis of sex in the choice of criteria, their weighting or the manner in which evaluation factors are translated into pay scales.

Very few equal pay cases have arisen under Agreement No. 25. The Belgian government attributes this to the fact that complaints are normally processed by the trade unions and settled at the workplace, thereby escaping official notice. Also, it believes that women either are not aware of any discrimination or hesitate to complain about it.

A Commission on the Employment of Women (CTF)[38] was established at the end of 1974 as an administrative unit of the Ministry of Labor and Employment. It is a tripartite advisory body which can act at the request of the Minister or at its own discretion. To determine whether women are receiving equal pay for work of equal value, the CTF conducted an analysis of collective agreements negotiated at the industry level. In its report,[39] the CTF discussed whether women were being indirectly discriminated against through the use of such techniques as according a disproportionate weighting to factors such as physical strength or dirty working conditions, which are found in traditionally male jobs. The report also mentioned several industries, singling out the food industry as the worst offender in undervaluing women's work. At the recommendation of the CTF, the Minister of Labor and Employment appointed an ad hoc committee to review thoroughly the

---

[38] See C. Pichault, "The Belgian Commission on the Employment of Women," *International Labour Review*, Vol. 115 (1977), pp. 157–74.

[39] A summary of this CTF report appeared in *European Industrial Relations Review*, No. 52 (1978), pp. 4–5.

question of job evaluation and its effect on the implementation of the principle of equal pay for men and women. The findings of this committee, which have not yet been reported, undoubtedly will have an impact on the European Commission, which has displayed a great interest in determining whether sex bias is built into traditional job evaluation schemes.

Since the CTF was instrumental in the preparation of the Belgian government's submission to the European Commission, it is not surprising that the Commission reported that the Belgian government believed that the implementation of the principle of equal pay for work of equal value would encounter the greatest difficulty in the area of job classifications. The forthcoming report of the ad hoc committee should reveal, at least, the dimensions of the problem.

G. *Luxembourg*

The Law of June 12, 1965, requires that all collective agreements lay down procedures for implementing the principle of equal pay. To comply fully with the equal pay directive, a Grand Ducal regulation was promulgated on July 10, 1974.

The most common method of job classification in Luxembourg is the traditional method of slotting jobs into categories on the basis of skill level. The analytical factor comparison method of job evaluation is used only in the rubber industry, while the points rating method can be found in the synthetic fibers and mechanical engineering industries.

There has been virtually no equal pay litigation in Luxembourg, and the works inspectorate reported to the European Commission that it had received no complaints and had uncovered no violations of the equal pay statute.[40] Such a record may result from the fact that Luxembourg has an extremely small population and its economy is dominated by heavy industry. In other countries it has been argued that assembly line jobs in light manufacturing industry have been undervalued, but few jobs of this kind exist in Luxembourg.

H. *Netherlands*

The Netherlands is the one country in Europe which had, at one time, a system of national job evaluation which was used as an instrument of government pay policy.[41] Although this is no longer the case, most firms still utilize some form of job evaluation.

Following the end of World War II, the Dutch government introduced a wage freeze. During this period, wages could be increased only if an anomaly

---

[40] The works inspectorate is a unit within Luxembourg's Ministry of Labor.

[41] See Christine Craig, "Towards National Job Evaluation: Trends and Attitudes in Britain and in the Netherlands," *Industrial Relations Journal*, Vol. 8 (1977), pp. 23–36. See also, John P. Windmuller, *Labor Relations in the Netherlands* (Ithaca, Cornell University Press, 1969), chapters 8 and 9.

in a job-evaluated wage structure could be shown. Employers and unions agreed to administer jointly a points rating system referred to as the Standardized Method, or "GM." By 1959, when job evaluation ceased to be an instrument of pay policy, nearly 60 percent of blue-collar workers were subject to the GM job evaluation plan or some variant on it. In the 1960s, job evaluation for white-collar jobs became increasingly popular. Job evaluation techniques became highly refined, in part because of the trend in Dutch political opinion which supported the elimination of traditional blue-collar/white-collar distinctions in employment as a means of achieving a more egalitarian society. Since 1965, two integrated job evaluation systems, those which can evaluate both blue-collar and white-collar jobs, have been developed but they have met with limited success.

At present, about 80 percent of blue-collar workers and 40 percent of white-collar workers are covered by job evaluation plans. There are about ten major evaluation systems, all but one of which use the points rating method. An increasing number of companies are turning to such systems as the Hay-MSL scale to provide job evaluation for their management and professional positions, but in most companies these jobs remain outside of any major job evaluation plan.

Responding to the equal pay directive, the Netherlands enacted the Law of March 20, 1975, mandating equal pay for work of equal value. The European Commission has praised the Dutch statute, because it does not require a woman complainant to compare herself to a man who is in the same firm working on substantially similar work. Instead, a female complainant may compare her wage to that commonly paid by the employer to a male employee performing work of equal value or broadly similar work. If no such comparable man is employed, the female claimant may attempt to find a comparable man in a similar company, although the wage scales of that company would be compared to those prevailing in her company. The Dutch statute also expressly addresses the problem of the value of work and states that value is to be determined by reference to the work's value under a job evaluation system. If the particular job in question has not been evaluated under a system, the statute provides that the job's value will be determined "on an equitable basis" by the Equal Pay Commission of the Netherlands.

With the coverage of job evaluation very widespread and with the techniques of job evaluation fairly well-known as a result of the plans being jointly administered,[42] it might have been predicted that the Netherlands would have the least difficulty in implementing the principle of equal pay for work of equal value. This does not seem to be the case, although there has

---

[42] At various times in the last twenty-five years, unions and employers have agreed to change the relative weightings accorded certain factors in a given plan to achieve a desired modification of job rankings. For instance, in 1958, the points for "power of expression" doubled and the points available for dexterity increased. In 1963–64, the points for factors relating to unpleasant working conditions increased reflecting the growing distaste for certain jobs.

been some discussion of the relative weight given the factor of physical strength as opposed to mental tension in the main GM plans.[43]

The Dutch government believes that the job evaluation plans as embodied in collective agreements are applied equally to men and women and at present, there seems to be little controversy over the points rating allotted to certain factors more likely to be found in traditionally female jobs. This lack of controversy may result from the publication of a Dutch wages office survey of 899 firms employing nearly 300,000 workers, about 80 percent of whom are female, which concluded that women tended to be in lower-paying jobs due to a lack of training and less seniority and not because of sex-based wage discrimination. The Equal Pay Commission has had a small caseload, a fact which even the government finds curious and which may change once the female workforce becomes more familiar with the notion of comparability.

I. *Germany*

The German federal constitution of 1949 guarantees equality of treatment to all persons regardless of sex. In 1955, the German federal labor court interpreted Article 3 of the federal constitution to require equal pay for work of equal value. Believing that the provisions in its constitution were sufficient implementation of the principle of equal pay, Germany did not take legislative action to comply with the requirements of the equal pay directive until the European Commission initiated infringement proceedings against it. In June 1979, the government introduced a bill designed to meet the requirements of the European Community's three equality directives.

Job evaluation is fairly common in Germany, with the best known plans being the six regional plans in the metalworking industry. In general, job evaluation plans are jointly administered by employers and unions and are embodied in collective agreements. Two methods of job evaluation are commonly used, factor comparison and points rating. Both types aim to quantify such factors as training, experience, skill, responsibility, mental effort, physical effort and working conditions. The German educational system provides training and certification of qualifications for many more occupations than do other countries and, as might be expected, men tend to stay on in school until they have attained a trade certificate in much larger numbers than do women. In describing the skills required by a job, it is commonly stated that the person must be certified, e.g., a certified cook, and the possession of a certificate would normally be a factor garnering points in job rankings. The correlation between job rankings and wage scales is a matter for collective bargaining.

The issue of the possible undervaluing of certain factors most often found in jobs traditionally held by females is a subject of sharp controversy in Germany. In particular, the greater number of points assigned to physically

---

[43] This was mentioned by the government in its submission to the European Commission.

demanding jobs as opposed to what the Germans call "light work" has been attacked as sex discrimination in disguise.

The historical roots of "light work" grades in Germany make them especially suspect. Following the 1955 equal pay decision of the federal labor court which held that the traditional "women's deduction," whereby women's wage rates were calculated as a percentage of the male rates, was unconstitutional, many employers introduced new "light work" grades based on the physical demands of the job rather than the sex of the worker. In practice, however, these "light work" grades quickly became exclusively female. Hence, the pay rates for the grades, typically wage grades I and II in collective agreements, were viewed by some as female rates for all practical purposes.

Shortly after the introduction of these "light work" grades, the German Federation of Trade Unions (DGB) protested that women's work was being systematically downgraded. The Federation of German Employers (BDA) took the position that the categories were open to both sexes and that the differentiation between physically light and heavy work was based on objective criteria without regard to sex. The federal government entered the dispute to the limited extent of having the Ministry of Labor and Social Affairs appoint a committee to study the measures required to guarantee the application of the principle of equal pay for work of equal value, and to recommend appropriate criteria for the evaluation of traditionally female work. The first committee, formed in the late 1950's, was composed of representatives from both employer groups and unions. It never produced any recommendations, because it simply ceased to meet after it became clear that the differences between the two sides were irreconcilable.

In the late 1960's, the question whether these "light work" grades were, in fact, discriminatory female grades came up once again in the Bundestag, and the federal government responded by reconvening the committee in 1969. When it became obvious that the matter was still too highly controversial for a committee to formulate recommendations, the Minister of Labor and Social Affairs commissioned Professors Rohmert and Rutenfranz to undertake a study of job evaluation and its effect on the guarantee of equal pay for work of equal value.

In conducting their study, the professors focused on the factor of stress, or mental tension, as it was rated in heavy and light work. In so doing, they did not rely solely on the traditional methods of job evaluation, i.e., analyzing the work based on an assessment of the objective demands or requirements of the job, but also attempted to assess the effects of the job on the worker. Specifically, an effort was made to quantify and characterize the stress imposed upon the worker by the job. In their 1975 report to the Bundestag, the professors recommended that a new kind of job evaluation system be developed which would reflect both an objective assessment of a job's demands and a subjective assessment of its effects. This latter assessment would take into account such factors as the job's practicability, tolerability, and its satisfaction level. The professors recognized that translating such subjective assessments into quantifiable ratings would be such a highly subjective matter that it would require the agreement of both employers and unions. They noted that any consensus reached would be subject to modification as subjective assessments would vary according to the social climate at any given time. Also, the professors recommended that there be changes in the method of job evaluation rating, but they did not propose a specific new method. In the following year, Professor Rohmert undertook a study to draft a workable job analysis questionnaire which would take into account the impact of the work and the working environment on the employee.

The response of the federal government has been to reiterate its position that any change in the form of job evaluation is a matter for employers and unions as signatories to collective agreements regulating job evaluation plans. Along these lines, the Ministry of Labor and Social Affairs has sent copies of the Rohmert and Rutenfranz studies to employers and trade union federations in the hope that the parties will move jointly to resolve any problems in this area, but there has been no official attempt to compel changes in the way job evaluation is applied.

The hopes of the Labor Ministry are not unfounded. There have been moves in several industries to re-grade "light work" jobs or to raise the wages of the persons in those jobs.[44] It is clear, though, that the issue of the undervaluing of factors found in traditionally female jobs is more hotly debated in Germany than in any other European country at the present time, and another report to the Bundestag on this subject is expected in 1980. In light of the studies that have been done and the activism of German women's groups, it is very likely that the issue of what constitutes work of equal value will be litigated once Germany's equal pay statute takes effect.

III. OTHER COUNTRIES

In surveying other countries on the issue of equality for women, one often looks to Sweden due to its reputation as the leader in removing all barriers which cause different treatment of the sexes. The attention of Americans is understandably also drawn to other English-speaking countries, such as Canada, Australia and New Zealand, which are viewed as having a common heritage and similar problems. After briefly describing the very different industrial relations system in each of these four countries, their attitudes toward the problem of implementing the guarantee of equal pay for women will be examined.

---

[44] For example, see J. T. Addison, "Gleichblerechtigung—The German Experience," in *Equal Pay for Women*, ed., Barrie O. Pettman (Washington and London: Hemisphere Publishing Corp., 1977), pp. 112–13.

A. *Sweden*

The Swedish system of industrial relations is characterized by remarkably centralized organization of employers and of unions at the national level. Exercising considerable control over their members, the Swedish Confederation of Trade Unions (LO), the Central Organization of Salaried Employees (TCO), and the Swedish Employers' Federation (SAF) each manage to maintain a united front at the bargaining table. As a result, many developments in Swedish industrial relations are accomplished through an industrywide collective bargaining agreement rather than by legislation. Equal pay for women is one example of this.

The SAF and the LO, which represents 90 percent of blue-collar workers, agreed in 1960 to implement the principle of equal pay by removing from collective agreements by 1965 any clauses which discriminated against women. A specific recommendation to this effect in 1962 by the SAF and the LO caused such significant progress to be made that, by 1965, most collective agreements had made provision for the elimination of separate female wage categories with the result that many collective agreements contained a smaller number of wage grades than had previously been the case.

In the early 1960's, the TCO, which represents about 50 percent of white-collar employees, entered into discussions with the SAF concerning the implementation of equal pay for women. In 1963, a joint SAF/TCO committee was formed to engage in a type of job evaluation exercise, called the position classification system, as a means of introducing equal pay. This system classified jobs in terms of their characteristics and is similar to a national job evaluation plan for white-collar employees. It is widely used whenever the TCO represents white-collar employees. The impact of this joint exercise can be appreciated when it is noted that the number of firms using job evaluation doubled between 1965 and 1970.[45]

From a practical standpoint, the principle of equal pay was implemented with relative ease for two reasons. First, prior to 1960 blue-collar jobs were commonly covered by job evaluation plans, and, second, the attitudes of the Swedish labor movement towards wage differentials in general were conducive to the concept of equal pay for women.

Job evaluation exercises covering blue-collar jobs began to be undertaken in Sweden in the late 1940's. In the 1950's, a number of industrywide job evaluation schemes were introduced. There are effectively six major job evaluation plans covering blue-collar workers in the private sector, all of the points rating type,[46] with the plan covering metalworkers being the most complex and highly developed. The relationship between a job's points rating and its wage rate is a matter for collective bargaining. The fact that job

---

[45] ILO, *Equal Remuneration*, p. 49.

[46] For a review of Swedish practice, see Great Britain, National Board for Prices and Incomes, Report No. 83, *Job Evaluation* (1968), pp. 29–31.

evaluation plans were implemented at industry level is attributable to the fact that by the 1940's, industrywide bargaining had, for the most part, supplanted local bargaining for blue-collar workers in Sweden.

Since there is no equal pay statute or government regulation on equal pay in Sweden, there is no official, standard version of the equal pay formulation. Each industrywide agreement establishes its own standard. In industries where job evaluation is used, it is usually interpreted to mean equal pay for work rated as equivalent under the evaluation plan,[47] with equal pay applying to the basic wage rate. Since the equal pay principle has been negotiated rather than legislated, it is enforceable like other terms in a collective agreement, through the Swedish labor court.

Resistance to the introduction of equal pay for women was not substantial. It has been pointed out that in 1951, when the LO adopted its policy of wage solidarity, the principle of equal pay for work of equal value for men was seen as the first stage in achieving equal pay for all.[48] As part of the LO's policy of compressing wage differentials, the elimination of sex-based differentials was a natural component. It should be emphasized that the Swedes, when they speak of wage solidarity and equal pay, do not have in mind exactly the same concept that Americans mean by the term equal pay. Swedish trade unions have consciously set out to reduce the number of wage grades so that ultimately, the wage range will be so compressed as to be levelled. In such a system, everyone would receive "equal" pay, namely the same pay. In the United States, however, advocates of equal pay usually mean that persons performing similar work should be paid similarly but they do not question the basic wage range in the country or wage variations between industries.

Sweden was one of the first countries to implement effectively the principle of equal pay for working women, yet only recently has it tackled the question of equal opportunity. In so doing, attention has focused on the fact that women tend to be found predominantly in certain occupational classifications and it has been alleged that true equal access to all jobs does not exist. There does not seem, however, to have been any discontent with the way in which traditionally female jobs are evaluated.

In July 1979, the Swedish parliament enacted the Equal Treatment in Working Life Act, a rather weak statute expressing general principles of nondiscrimination with regard to working conditions, and equal access to employment, training and education. The statute reflects the belief of both political parties that measures to abolish sex-based discrimination in employment are more effective if embodied in collective agreements rather than legislated. In light of their successful experience with equal pay, this is very likely a correct assumption.

---

[47] Great Britain, Office of Manpower Economics, First Report on the Implementation of the Equal Pay Act 1970, *Equal Pay* (1972), pp. 101–02.

[48] Karl O. Faxen, "Wage Policy and Attitudes of Industrial Relations Parties in Sweden," *Labour and Society*, Vol. 2 (1977), pp. 63 and 68.

B. *Canada*

Under the Canadian constitution, legislation relating to labor relations and civil rights matters comes under provincial rather than federal jurisdiction. Covering less than ten percent of the country's workforce, federal statutes apply to employees in jobs of an interprovincial or international nature, such as in communications, transportation and shipping. As a result, provincial developments can have more impact than federal statutes.

In 1951, Ontario became the first province to enact an equal pay statute, the Female Employees Fair Remuneration Act. By 1956, four other provinces had passed equal pay legislation, and in that year, the Parliament of Canada enacted the Female Employees Equal Pay Act. By 1972, when Canada ratified Equal Remuneration Convention No. 100 of the ILO, every province except Quebec had adopted equal pay legislation.

The phrase "equal pay for equal work" does not appear in the 1956 federal statute nor in any provincial statute.[49] The formulation most commonly employed was equal pay for the "same, similar, or substantially similar" work performed within the same establishment. Several statutes also required that such work be performed under the same or similar working conditions. For all practical purposes, these Canadian formulations approximated what Americans mean by equal pay for equal work. It should be noted that many provincial statutes did not cover part-time workers, the vast majority of whom are female.

Job evaluation is fairly prevalent in Canada with nearly all large employers using some form of job evaluation. Most job evaluation plans are administered solely by the employer, in much the same way as found in the United States. Prior to 1976, little attention was focused on the factors analyzed and the weights accorded them in job evaluation plans. To the extent that the 1968 Ontario statute mandates equal pay for work of equal skill, effort and responsibility, one may have anticipated some scrutinization of job evaluation techniques. This did not occur, however, perhaps because the Ontario legislation also required that the work be performed under the same or similar working conditions.

Canada, like many other industrialized countries, witnessed a sharp growth in its female labor force participation rate in the 1960's. This led, in the 1970's, to a heightened interest in the status of working women and an increasing dissatisfaction with the status quo. In 1970, the Royal Commission on the Status of Women reported that no equal pay law in Canada had been effective.[50] A year later, the Canadian Women's Bureau criticized the

---

[49] For a detailed examination of the Canadian statutes, see Richard J. Osborne, "Equal Pay for Equal Work: A Study of the Legislation in the United States, Canada, the United Kingdom, and New Zealand" (J.S.D. dissertation, Cornell University, 1976), pp. 265–89 and Appendix 3.

[50] *Report of the Royal Commission on the Status of Women in Canada*, Information Canada (Ottawa, 1970), pp. 74–75.

enforcement mechanisms provided for in most provincial statutes which required female employees to activate the process by filing a formal complaint, usually with the employment standards branch of the provincial department of labor.[51] In 1972, an article was published which criticized Canadian trade unions for not being committed to the principle of equal pay. The article noted that collective bargaining agreements expressly mentioning equal pay were extremely rare.[52] Although this criticism may be well taken, the efficacy of such agreements might be questioned since less than 25 percent of Canadian working women are union members.[53]

Prior to 1976, no Canadian equal pay statute incorporated the comparable worth theory or used the formulation of equal pay for work of equal value even though Canada had ratified ILO Convention No. 100, which is based on the principle of equal pay for work of equal value. Since 1976, the province of Quebec has enacted its first equal pay statute. Although the Quebec legislation does not expressly provide for equal pay for work of equal value, the province's initial enforcement activities in this area indicate that the provincial authorities are interpreting the formulation as being broader than equal pay for substantially similar work. Whether this reflects an official tendency to accept the comparable worth theory or whether it merely reflects the government's condoning the use of the statute to raise women's wages is not yet clear.

In late 1978, the Parliament of Canada enacted the Human Rights Act which tracks the language of ILO Convention No. 100 and expressly provides for equal pay for work of equal value. This federal statute has been in force for too short a time to make any assessment of its impact throughout Canada, let alone on the ten percent of the workforce to which it applies. Federal statutes in Canada often provide a model for provincial legislation, and it is likely that this reformulation of the equal pay standard may crop up in future amendments to provincial equal pay legislation.

Equal pay legislation has been on the books in Canada for over twenty years, but unlike in the United States, the existence of such legislation has not resulted in a significant amount of litigation. There have been too few cases for a consistent pattern of interpretation to emerge, although in the cases that have arisen, it can be said that the courts have tended to give the statutes a broad interpretation.[54] With a dearth of cases on the issue of what constitutes

[51] *Women's Bureau '71*, Information Canada (Ottawa, 1971), p. 24.

[52] *Women's Bureau '72*, Information Canada (Ottawa, 1972), p. 10.

[53] Estimate of Mary Eady, Director, Women's Bureau, Dept. of Labour, Province of Manitoba, made in comments at the International Conference of Trends in Industrial and Labour Relations, Montreal, Quebec, Canada, May 24–28, 1976. Report of Proceedings, pp. 261–65. This estimate takes into account the fact that while about 35 percent of the labor force is unionized, women tend to be found in the unorganized sectors of the economy in disproportionately high numbers.

[54] M. Gunderson, "Equal Pay in Canada: History, Progress and Problems," in Pettman, *Equal Pay for Women*, pp. 129–46.

work of a broadly similar nature, it is not surprising that there has been virtually no judicial examination of the meaning of broadly similar work in the context of wage rates determined by reference to a job evaluation plan. With the 1978 federal statute expressly based on a more flexible formulation of the equal pay guarantee, judicial attention may well be directed to this issue in the future.

C. *Australia*

Under the Australian federal system of government, most matters relating to industrial and labor relations come within the jurisdiction of the states. The federal constitution, however, gives the Australian Parliament the authority to enact legislation providing for the conciliation and arbitration of potential or actual industrial disputes extending beyond the limits of any one state.

Following a wave of severe strikes in the 1890's, Parliament enacted the Conciliation and Arbitration Act of 1904 which set up an independent court system to handle all interstate industrial relations.[55] In 1956, the court system was restructured so that, today, the Commonwealth Conciliation and Arbitration Commission carries out arbitral functions and the Commonwealth Industrial Court handles judicial matters. Each state has also enacted legislation which sets up tribunals to handle potential or actual intrastate industrial grievances and disputes. State tribunals generally follow the awards and standards handed down by the federal tribunal, with the federal award taking precedence if there is any conflict. Of particular importance is the nationally publicized federal award for the metalworking trades, setting wages for over 300 job classifications. Because of the Australian interpretation of "interstate," about one-half of Australian workers are covered by federal awards.

Traditionally, industrial tribunals in Australia have applied concepts of justice and fairness in making wage awards in the belief that this would encourage a more equitable wage structure consonant with an egalitarian society. This approach is based on a theory of "comparative wage justice" which

> . . . implies that a particular occupation in one industry should receive the same wage rate paid to that same occupation in other industries, irrespective of productivity variations among industries. That is, wages are set solely according to the task the individual performs, instead of also taking into account the industry in which he works.[56]

---

[55] About one-half of Australian workers are directly covered by Commonwealth Commission awards.

[56] John Niland, *Collective Bargaining and Compulsory Arbitration in Australia* (Kensington, Australia, New South Wales University Press Ltd., 1978), p. 61.

In applying the comparative wage justice principle in wage awards, the Australian tribunals consciously ignore the fact that the inherent bargaining power of an occupational group differs within different industries.[57]

Prior to 1967, when a "total wages" concept was put forward, arbitration awards were calculated by determining a "basic wage" and the "margin" for the particular occupational group which was added to the "basic wage." The "basic wage" was, in effect, a minimum wage. Originally, it was calculated at the minimum level necessary to maintain an average employee and his family in a reasonable state of comfort. This concept of the "basic wage" later evolved so that it was calculated at the maximum level the economy could sustain with the critical factor being the capacity of the community to carry the resulting wage levels.[58] The "margin" which was added to the "basic wage" was designed to compensate the differing levels of skill, responsibility, training, etc., demanded in different occupations. The "margin" component of the wage rate was calculated without regard to the sex of the workers involved. The "basic wage" component was calculated on the basis of sex; a man was assumed to be maintaining a family whereas a woman was assumed to be maintained by her family.[59] As a result, although Australia has long proceeded on the premise that work of equal worth should be compensated equally, women did not, until recently, receive equal pay for work of equal value.

Under the 1949–50 Basic Wage Enquiry, the "basic wage" for females under Commonwealth awards was increased to 75 percent of the male "basic wage" rate, and it remained at that level until 1969. In handing down an award in two applications in June 1969, the Commonwealth Conciliation and Arbitration Commission accepted the principle of equal pay for work of "the same or a like nature and of equal value."[60] The Commission proposed to implement this principle in stages so that by January 1972, the female rate would reach 100 percent of the male rate.

In late 1972, another equal pay case came before the Commonwealth Commission.[61] In reconsidering its 1969 pronouncement, the Commonwealth Commission rejected its earlier formulation as being too narrow and stated that the principle of equal pay for work of equal value would, in the future, be applied to all awards of the Commission. As such, sixteen of the eighteen most important awards covering working women were affected by this award. In announcing its award, the Commission noted that it had

---

[57] Ibid., pp. 70–73.

[58] Commonwealth Arbitration Reports, Vol. 77, p. 494, as quoted in *Official Yearbook of the Commonwealth of Australia 1966*, p. 364.

[59] This distinction was made in the first case in which female rates were at issue. For a discussion of the Fruit Packers case, see J. Nieuwenhuysen and J. Hicks, "Equal Pay for Women in Australia and New Zealand," in Pettman, *Equal Pay for Women*, pp. 76–77.

[60] Equal Pay Cases Judgement, June 19, 1969.

[61] National Wage and Equal Pay Cases Judgement, December 15, 1972.

been influenced by equal pay legislation enacted by four of the states and by the submissions of the newly-elected Labour government supporting equal pay. It would seem that the latter must have been more persuasive because the states' statutes used the equal pay for equal work formulation.

The sole remaining discriminatory aspect of wage policy related to the decision in 1967 to abolish the two-tier method of wage fixation. In declaring that it would henceforth award only a "total wages" rate, the Commission announced that it would also set a minimum wage. In 1972, however, the Commonwealth Commission stated that only men would be guaranteed a wage at a level above this minimum wage. In the 1974 National Wage judgment, at a time when most female workers were above the minimum wage, the Commission reversed itself and held that the minimum wage would be applied to both males and females.

The cost of granting equal pay has been considerable. In its 1972 award, the Commonwealth Commission directly confronted this issue and observed, "the community is prepared to accept the concept of equal pay for females and should therefore be prepared to accept the economic consequences of this decision."[62]

The implementation of equal pay has been rapid. From a 25 percent differential in wage rates in 1969, the differential between male and female rates for a given job classification declined to 7 percent in 1977. Since the Commonwealth Commission's 1972 judgment anticipated full implementation of equal pay by 1975, it might be asked why the differential still persists. The answer, in large measure, is the result of what Australians term "over-awards."[63] With the state or federal tribunal award establishing the legally-binding minimum terms of employment, the parties are then free to negotiate over-award wages through a modified collective bargaining procedure. The over-award wage is sensitive to market factors and the inherent bargaining power of certain groups of workers. Consequently, unions in male-dominated industries are often able to secure large over-award payments which workers in female-dominated industries do not receive.

It is extremely difficult to gauge what impact the implementation of equal pay has had on the Australian economy, since the 1970's were marked by high inflation and unemployment attributable to a variety of factors. Women's wages have risen much faster than men's, but it is unclear whether there has been any attempt to restore traditional pay relativities. In addition, it should be noted that the application of the principle of equal pay for work of equal value in Australia has not been controversial in those positions in which men and women perform similar jobs, because a national unisex job evaluation was performed when the male "basic wage" rate and

---

[62] Pettman, *Equal Pay for Women*, p. 80.

[63] For a discussion of over-awards, see Russell D. Lansbury, "The Return of Arbitration: Recent Trends in Dispute Settlement and Wages Policy in Australia," *International Labour Review*, Vol. 117 (1978), pp. 611-24.

the "margin" was originally fixed. In areas such as the clerical grades of the civil service, where women fill jobs once held only by men, the impact has been great but uncontroversial.

It should be emphasized that there have already been questions raised concerning the validity of the evaluation of the worth of traditionally female jobs, namely, those which were filled by women when the basic wage rates were originally fixed, such as nursing.[64] It is felt by some that these historically female jobs were under-valued in the original wage-fixing process and that their relative valuation has not changed over the years. At this time, it remains unclear whether Australia's equal pay formulation, equal pay for work of equal value, incorporates the comparable worth theory, because there has not been any concrete application of the principle of equal pay for work of equal value in instances where a job is performed overwhelmingly by women. Once this issue is raised and fully debated,[65] the true meaning of Australia's equal pay formulation will become apparent.

D. *New Zealand*

New Zealand's experience with working women's pay rates is similar to that of Australia's. The custom of fixing women's wage rates as a percentage of the male wage rate can be traced to the Arbitration Court's 1903 Christchurch Tailoring Trades Awards, which prescribed a female rate at about 50 percent of the male rate. This custom received statutory sanction in the 1936 Industrial Conciliation and Arbitration Amendment Act which specified that the Arbitration Court should fix the male basic wage rate at a sufficient level to enable a man to support a family of five in a reasonable standard of comfort. Although the 1954 version of this statute omitted the family support section, the tradition of fixing sex-based rates continued.

Along the lines of the Australian development, the Arbitration Court raised the women's rate to 70 percent of the male rate shortly after World War II. Unlike its Australian counterpart, however, the New Zealand court resisted abolishing the sex-based wage differential on the grounds that such an important social and economic issue was a matter for Parliament, a matter which was not taken up until 1972.

In 1960, New Zealand's Parliament passed the Government Services Equal Pay Act which provided for equal pay where women performed equal work under equal conditions. By 1965, the principle of equal pay had been

---

[64] See, e.g., the submission of the Women's Electoral Lobby to the Australian Conciliation and Arbitration Commission, *Inquiry into Principles of Wage Fixation* (1978), pp. 166–80. In 1969, the Department of Labour specifically considered the problem of comparing the worth of different jobs and applying an equal pay guarantee. Such an approach was rejected on the grounds that it would cause "considerable problems." Australian Dept. of Labour and National Service, Review of Australian Law and Practice Relating to Conventions Adopted by the International Labour Conference (1969), p. 90.

[65] This matter could arise in a future wage determination application.

implemented in the public services but, despite hopes to the contrary, there seemed to be little carryover effect in the private sector.

Responding to the lobbying efforts of women's groups, the government appointed a Commission of Inquiry into Equal Pay in 1970.[66] The Commission carefully reviewed American, British and Australian experience in preparing its recommendation on the standard for equal pay. The Commission specifically rejected the standard embodied in ILO Convention No. 100, equal pay for work of equal value, because it felt that job evaluation was not sufficiently developed in New Zealand to make such an approach practicable.

Following the submission of the Commission's report to Parliament, a bill was introduced and in 1972, the Equal Pay Act was passed. The following year, an amendment was passed modifying the timetable for implementation of equal pay with a projected implementation date of April 1, 1978. In 1973, Parliament also enacted the Industrial Relations Act, which both limited the role of the Arbitration Court to ratifying conciliated settlements and which emphasized free collective bargaining in wage determination. The statute marks a significant departure from New Zealand's pattern of paralleling Australian wage determination policy, and accounts, no doubt, for New Zealand's preference for legislation as the means of implementing equal pay.

Section 3(1)(a) of the Equal Pay Act of 1972 provides that where work is not exclusively or predominantly performed by females, women are entitled to equal pay where they perform work which calls for "the same, or substantially similar, degrees of skill, effort, and responsibility" under the same or substantially similar conditions.

The New Zealand statute expressly covers situations where work is exclusively or predominantly performed by females. In effect, section 3(1)(b) requires that consideration be given to what a notional or hypothetical man would be paid if he were performing the job. Although the statute does not mention job evaluation, section 3(1)(b) does seem to require that a highly speculative job evaluation exercise of sorts take place, an exercise which may be possible in a country with a little over 3 million persons and where agriculture is still an important industry.

Under the Equal Pay Act, aggrieved female workers can bring the matter before the Industrial Court if satisfactory wage rates cannot be agreed to voluntarily. It is still too early to determine what impact the Equal Pay Act will have, but there are some indications that, as the Commission of inquiry into Equal Pay feared, the concept of a notional man's rate is not easily susceptible to practical implementation.[67]

---

[66] For a discussion of the submissions made to the Commission, see J. Nieuwenhuysen and J. Hicks, "Equal Pay for Women in Australia and New Zealand," in Pettman, *Equal Pay for Women*, pp. 93–95.

[67] Osborne, "Equal Pay for Equal Work," pp. 349–56.

IV. CONCLUSION

Any country which sets out to implement an equal pay guarantee incorporating the comparable worth theory must devise a means of determining that two dissimilar jobs are of equal value if the guarantee is to have any practical effect. This implies that some sort of evaluation of the two jobs must take place. Such an evaluation may be the result of a thorough, empirical exercise covering many jobs, such as occurs in a job evaluation plan, or it may be the result of a subjective review of only the two jobs alleged to be equal undertaken by some type of government tribunal. In both instances, the evaluator must have some way of calculating a job's worth. This calculation may be arrived at by using a formal, quantitative approach or by comparing the two jobs in an informal, qualitative way. Regardless of the methodology of evaluation, the evaluator's notions of worth invariably will relate to his or her perceptions of the value the market places on various factors, such as skill, responsibility and effort, required in performing the job.[68]

As the preceding discussion has noted, most countries whose equal pay statutes or regulations contain the formulation "equal pay for work of equal value" have not yet had sufficient experience with the implications and application of this guarantee to determine with any accuracy whether it represents a significantly more far-reaching guarantee than the American "equal pay for equal work." If a country's equal pay formulation does incorporate the comparable worth theory, it must be interpreted as guaranteeing equal pay to a woman who is performing a job which is of equal value but is dissimilar to that of the man with whom she compares herself. None of the thirteen countries studied can be confidently placed in the category of applying the comparable worth doctrine in equal pay matters, although several of the countries clearly subscribe to it in theory.

The equal pay activity in a few of the countries studied should not be mistaken as indicating an acceptance of the comparable worth theory. In Ireland and Italy, particularly, whole groups of female workers are being awarded equal pay with the lowest-paid men at their workplace. Such awards represent an attempt to eliminate the most blatant form of sex discrimination in wage setting, namely, placing the female rate below that of the unskilled male rate regardless of the jobs the women perform. In correcting this inequity, the government tribunals or employer-union working parties do not rigorously scrutinize the female jobs in comparison with the male jobs; rather, it is recognized that the female wage ladder should cease to exist and

---

[68] See the paper by Donald P. Schwab in this volume, beginning on p. 49, for a discussion of how job evaluation in practice, correlates evaluations with market variables.

that female jobs should be integrated into the male wage ladder in order to create a unisex pay scale.[69]

Of the countries studied, four come closest to subscribing to the comparable worth theory: the Netherlands, Sweden, Australia and New Zealand. In the Netherlands and New Zealand, statutes explicitly contemplate that women who are not employed on similar work with men may still want to claim equal pay. Thus, these two countries can be said to accept the guarantee of equal pay for work of equal value, although too few equal pay cases have arisen in either country to confirm this statutory acceptance. It is possible that the Australian and Swedish systems could also accommodate the comparable worth theory. Both countries have remarkably centralized methods of wage setting—Australia through government arbitration awards and Sweden through private collective bargaining. The Netherlands, Sweden, Australia and New Zealand all have a history of widespread job evaluation, usually at the industry level. Compared to the American workforce, the workers in these four countries have, to a much greater extent, understood the techniques of job evaluation and wage setting. In addition, the trade unions in these four countries have sanctioned the relative equalization of wage rates in the belief that the existing wage range was too great and should be compressed. It can be seriously questioned whether any American union would support such a stance.

Although Article 119 of the European Community's Treaty of Rome mandates equal pay for work of equal value, most European Community countries which have incorporated this standard into their equal pay legislation have yet to probe seriously what work of "equal value" means. In Germany, Belgium and the United Kingdom, equal pay advocates are beginning to debate this issue publicly. The debate in these countries has been generated by the requirement that member states of the European Community meet the requirements imposed by the European Commission's 1975 equal pay directive which was issued to implement the equal pay guarantee of Article 119 of the Treaty of Rome.

The 1975 equal pay directive states that women shall receive equal pay "for the same work or for work to which equal value is attributed." The directive does not state who shall attribute value nor how such an evaluation should be done. Such issues are left to the discretion of the member states. The directive does state, however, ". . . where a job classification system is used for determining pay, it must be based on the same criteria for both men and women and so drawn up as to exclude any discrimination on grounds of

---

[69] The Irish *Waterford Glass* case is an example, discussed in note 37 *supra* and the accompanying text. There, 457 women, performing a variety of different jobs, were being paid the "female rate," which was lower than the male general worker's rate. In their equal pay claim, they sought to have their rate increased to the higher male rate. In upholding their claim, the Irish equality officer made no attempt to compare each and every female job with a male job which might be of equal value. In effect, the award simply eliminated the discriminatory female rate, which reflected the sex of the worker rather than the job performed.

sex." This statement, which strikes at the heart of the controversy by requiring a sexually-neutral job valuation, has received public attention in only three countries—Germany, Belgium and the United Kingdom.

The United Kingdom was the only member of the European Community to consider directly how the worth of a job would be determined when it was in the process of drafting a statute which would guarantee equal pay for work of equal value. The United Kingdom's equal pay statute is novel in that it adopts a two-track approach. If the woman's job and the man's job have been evaluated in the course of a job evaluation exercise at their workplace, the woman is entitled to equal pay if her job has been rated as equivalent to his job. If the two jobs have not been subject to such an evaluation, then a government tribunal must determine that they are substantially similar for the woman to receive equal pay. The European Commission has expressed dissatisfaction with this approach, noting that where no job evaluation exercise has occurred, a woman may be performing work of equal value with that of a man but nonetheless would not be guaranteed equal pay because her job is not substantially similar to his. The British statute clearly does not meet the full requirements of the European Commission's equal pay directive in this regard. Yet, one of Britain's leading equal rights advocates, Baroness Seear, has argued that a blanket "equal pay for work of equal value" guarantee should not be written into law, because it could not be implemented in any meaningful sense without first making job evaluation mandatory on all employers.

Only in Germany, Belgium and the United Kingdom can there be said to be some degree of official recognition that standard job evaluation techniques may discriminate against women by awarding greater points to factors more common to traditionally male jobs than to female positions. At the present time, all three countries have working groups studying the impact that job evaluation, as it is currently practiced, has on the guarantee of equal pay for working women. The question has already been raised whether any of the currently-practiced forms of job evaluation would award unskilled, light repetitive work a sufficient number of points so that it might be rated equivalent with the typical heavy work found in manufacturing industries. In Germany, a negative answer has been given to this question, leading some equal pay proponents to support the development of a new type of job evaluation that would take into consideration such factors as the amount of mental stress a given job inflicts on a worker, a consideration which is not part of existing job evaluation methods.

As a survey of the trends in various industrialized countries over the past ten years indicates, it seems likely that many proponents of equal opportunity for working women have seized upon equal pay legislation as a panacea for the numerous problems which are actually caused by sex segregation in employment. Unfortunately, it also has become evident over the last decade that it is extremely difficult to eradicate deeply-ingrained, sex-segregated patterns of employment within a set time period. Thus, it might be more profitable to confront sex segregation directly rather than trying to equalize pay rates for jobs which, under any normal understanding of the word, are not equal.

1977 Male and Female Participation Rates by Country[a]

Country	Population	Male Labor Force Participation Rate	Female Labor Force Participation Rate[b]
U.S.A.	216,332,000	56.5%	36.1%
Italy	55,573,000	54.1%	24.4%
Ireland[1]	3,102,500	53.1%	20.6%
Denmark	5,093,586	59.2%	42.3%
France[2]	52,841,746	54.6%	29.6%
Belgium	9,837,413	54.3%	28.7%
Luxembourg[1]	355,400	57.5%	20.3%
Netherlands	13,549,400	53.9%	21.4%
Germany	61,420,000	57.2%	31.4%
United Kingdom[2]	55,959,000	59.4%	34.3%
Sweden	8,208,544	54.7%	39.2%
Canada[2]	22,992,605	55.6%	33.8%
Australia[1]	13,809,000	57.8%	27.3%
New Zealand	3,140,300	56.0%	26.2%

Source: International Labour Organisation, *1978 Year Book of Labour Statistics*, 38th ed. (Geneva, 1978).

[1]Statistics given are for 1975.

[2]Statistics given are for 1976.

[a]In calculating the labor force participation rate, the ILO includes the entire population, unlike the United States which excludes persons under 16. As a result, the rate for these countries will be lower than expected. These rates are given for the purpose of comparison only.

[b]The ILO cautions that female rates are frequently not comparable internationally since the treatment of women working on farms or in family-owned businesses varies by country.

STATISTICAL BIASES IN THE MEASUREMENT OF EMPLOYMENT DISCRIMINATION

by
Harry V. Roberts

Professor Roberts contends that, while statistical studies of individual organizations and of the labor force in general seem to support the presumption that there is widespread employment discrimination against females, there is reason to believe that the impression of discrimination is largely a function of three biases in the statistical methodologies common to these studies. The most important of these is that most methodologies fail to make allowances for the fact that the average woman has less education, experience and other job qualifications than her male counterpart. The second stems from a tendency to assume that salary differences between occupational job groups with different male-female representation must reflect discrimination and not the effect of earnings differentials properly ascribable to job groups as such. The third bias arises from the difficulty of statistical modeling of salary-seniority relationships when there are large variations in seniority. Professor Roberts concludes that once data are adjusted for these biases, they are more consistent with an assumption of nondiscrimination than with an assumption of discrimination.

Harry V. Roberts is a Professor of Statistics at the University of Chicago's Graduate School of Business. A former Associate Editor of the *American Statistician* and the *Journal of Marketing*, he currently holds a similar position with the *Journal of the American Statistical Association*. Dr. Roberts has served as a member of the American Statistical Association's Advisory Committee to the U.S. Census Bureau and is a member of the planning committee for the conference on the 1980 Census undercount. He is the author of numerous texts and articles on statistics and their use in business management and EEO regulation and affirmative action planning. These include *Conventional Statistics* (The Scientific Press, 1974); "Committee Selection by Statistical Sampling" in *American Statistician* (1971); with Franklin B. Evans, "Fords, Chevrolets and the Problem of Discrimination" in the *Journal of Business* (1963); and with William H. Kruskal, "Affirmative Action and Chance" in the *University of Chicago Record* (1978). Dr. Roberts received all of his degrees from the University of Chicago, earning his Ph.D. there in 1955.

STATISTICAL BIASES IN THE MEASUREMENT OF EMPLOYMENT DISCRIMINATION

The current interest in measurement of comparable worth is based on the assumption that there is pervasive, systematic, and substantial salary and job discrimination against females.[1] Where discrimination exists, measurement of comparable worth would be one conceivable route to its elimination or prevention. Where discrimination does not exist, the concept of comparable worth has no contribution to make in the domain of public policy, since its advocacy is based on the premise of discrimination against females.

There is often a presumption that overwhelming evidence, both impressionistic and statistical, demonstrates that discrimination against females is indeed systematic, substantial, and pervasive. Recent legal cases have focused attention on the evidence that can be assembled in concrete instances of organizations accused of violation of equal employment opportunity obligations. That some of these cases have been vigorously contested suggests that there is reason to examine more carefully what the evidence may be and how it should be evaluated.

My personal involvement in two of the cases as an expert statistical witness on the side of the defendants[2] has led me to such an examination. I do not intend to make empirical assertions about the existence or extent of discrimination in the economy at large. I do, however, want to present what I have learned about the hazards of common statistical approaches to the measurement of discrimination, hazards that are unknown to many, and that may have contributed to the impression that the weight of statistical evidence points toward discrimination. Further, I want to outline positive suggestions for statistical investigation. The suggestions do not guarantee freedom from all possible dangers of faulty statistical inference, but I believe that they point the way around the hazards that I discuss. My presentation is a simple

---

[1] Other papers in this volume raise questions as to whether comparable worth has been, or even can be, defined in operational terms. Although this question is not my prime focus, it does have a connection with my development, and this is treated in the section on nondiscrimination and comparable worth, p. 181.

[2] See "Statistical Study of Equality of Employment Opportunity at United Airlines: Methods and Findings," Harry V. Roberts with Henry F. Field, Mary Townsend Kimpton, and David W. McGee, CMSBE Report No. 7824, The University of Chicago, May, 1978; a condensation of which may be found in the *Journal of Contemporary Business*, Vol. 8, No. 3, 1979. See also "Harris Trust and Savings Bank: An Analysis of Employee Compensation," CMSBE Report No. 7946, The University of Chicago, October, 1979; an expanded version of which was submitted as offer of proof in the Harris Bank Case, September, 1979.

statement of the key statistical issues, and it is hoped that any reader, regardless of technical background, can judge the soundness of my conclusions.

To begin, a simple observation should be made, one that can be found in virtually every elementary statistics text and course: statistical correlations do not necessarily imply causation. This trite but profound truth always needs to be kept in mind, lest serious misinterpretations arise. For readers who have not been exposed to statistics texts or courses, an example may be helpful. A study of elementary school children once showed a positive correlation between quality of handwriting and size of feet. That is, although there may have been many individual exceptions, it was true that, on average, children with larger feet had better handwriting. A naive imputation of causation would suggest that bigger feet are an aid to good handwriting. A more sophisticated interpretation is that, on the average, children with bigger feet are older and have more training and practice in handwriting.

Suppose that, in a particular organization, females have lower mean (arithmetic average) salaries than do males. Again, we have a statistical correlation. Whether or not the correlation signifies discrimination—causation of a particular kind—is not obvious. My central purpose is to illustrate how the use of statistics may help to clarify the issues entailed in deciding about causation. My major conclusion is that there are three statistical biases that can lead to correlations suggesting discrimination when, in fact, none exists. The existence of these biases is not simply conjectural; there is good reason to believe that they are as pervasive as the statistical findings of female salary shortfalls.

The first step in my development is consideration of a question that has received curiously little attention: how should wage and employment discrimination be defined for purposes of statistical investigation? One's definition— whether or not it is made explicit—has inescapable implications for statistical studies of discrimination. Most of these studies utilize a technique called linear regression, of which simple tabular comparisons can be regarded as a special case. My preferred definition is presented in the section beginning on page 179, and other definitions briefly treated in the section beginning on page 188. Presented in the affirmative, the most practical definition is that nondiscrimination with respect to salary means that all employees are paid according to expected productivity. Similarly, nondiscrimination with respect to employment indicates that all initial placement decisions are made in light of expected productivity. With this definition of discrimination in mind, we then turn to the next step, which is the identification of three important statistical biases.

The first bias is the bias of underadjustment or undermatching. This bias is intimately bound up in the standard statistical approach to the study of possible discrimination, which is aimed at finding whether nondiscriminatory variables, such as seniority, appear to "explain" some or all of a salary shortfall.[3] Variables omitted from a statistical analysis could alter the picture if they were subsequently included. Similarly, improved measurements of variables actually used in the analysis also could alter the picture. The adjusted salary differential after subsequent inclusion of omitted variables or improved measurements of the variables used could, in principle, become either larger or smaller than originally. There is good reason to expect, however, that the omission of variables or errors of measurement may have a biasing effect, tending to give the appearance of discrimination when, in fact, none exists. Moreover, the danger of underadjustment is more than an unlikely or rare possibility; it can be expected to affect almost all statistical studies of possible discrimination.[4]

The second bias stems from failure to make adequate allowance for elements of noncompetition between entering job groups in organizations. This bias relates closely to what has been called occupational segregation in the literature on comparable worth.[5]

The third bias is a consequence of failure to make paper allowances for differences in seniority in studies of comparative salaries in organizations.[6]

Purely for purposes of illustration, I also discuss the effects of these three biases in studies done in the current case of United States Department of the Treasury v. Harris Trust and Savings Bank. In this example, an attempt to deal with the three biases led, in my judgment, to a statistical picture that is more probable given the assumption of nondiscrimination than given various assumptions of discrimination. The paper concludes with a brief comment on the possible role of the three biases in studies of discrimination in the labor force at large, that is, in studies based on labor force data rather than data of individual companies or other organizations.

I. CORRELATION AND CAUSATION

Suppose that in a particular organization or in the economy at large, it is found that the mean (arithmetic average) salary of females is only 58 percent of male mean salary, or, equivalently, that females have a salary shortfall of 42 percent relative to males. Sometimes such statistical comparisons are cited as evidence of discrimination. At one extreme these citations take the form of an assertion that the entire shortfall of 42 percent can be attributed to nothing other than discrimination. More cautious claims are also made. For example,

---

[3] In this paper, I use "seniority" to mean simply "years of service with an organization" rather than any of the technical and specialized uses of the term. Thus, seniority is regarded as a job qualification in the same sense as "years of experience in previous jobs."

[4] The underadjustment bias is discussed in the section beginning on page 183, which also includes a description of a technique called reverse regression that can cope with this bias.

[5] The bias is discussed in the section on page 192.

[6] The bias is discussed in the section on page 193.

it may be contended that a 42 percent shortfall is too large to be explained by factors other than discrimination and that some part of it, perhaps unspecified, does reflect discrimination.

Any such assertion runs in the face of the truth that, aside from special situations involving what is known as randomized experimentation, statistical correlations, such as that between salary and sex, do not imply causal inferences, such as the inference of discrimination. The example of a 42 percent female salary shortfall is consistent with the hypothesis of discrimination, but the example is also consistent with many scenarios in which there is no discrimination. For example, suppose that there is a salary shortfall for females in an organization in which salaries are the same for everyone of the same seniority. Suppose further that salaries increase linearly (that is, by a particular mathematical formula) with increasing seniority. If females have on average less seniority than do males, there will also be a female shortfall in salary, but it can reflect nothing other than the female shortfall in seniority.

The task of statistical analysis of possible discrimination is to make some kind of reasoned allowance for alternative explanations of salary differentials. Its purpose is to say something about the possibility of the statistical evidence given discrimination and also about the probability of the evidence given nondiscrimination. The statistician as a statistician cannot go beyond this because, in the domain of public policy, the determination of whether or not actual discrimination exists is a decision that must take into account nonstatistical as well as statistical evidence. For example, when disagreements about possible discrimination are litigated, the decisionmaker is usually a judge, who may take into account organizational documents, testimony of individual employees, company history, etc., in addition to statistical analyses.

The statistician's approach to the goal can be thought of as one form of regression analysis, a tool that permits investigation of variables other than sex that may contribute to understanding of salary differentials between males and females. One elementary form of regression analysis consists of display of simple tables in which mean salaries are tabulated against other characteristics such as sex and years of education.

Regression methodology as ordinarily applied tends to produce correlations between salaries and sex or race. The particular organization studied doesn't seem to affect this result. It could be United Airlines or the Harris Bank, or it could be the former Department of Health, Education, and Welfare, Congressional Staffs, the Federal Judiciary, the World Council of Churches, the University of Chicago, the Rockefeller Foundation, or the March of Dimes. It could also be the labor force as a whole. The interesting question is whether this common pattern of statistical findings could have, at least in part, a plausible explanation arising from limitations of the statistical methods themselves as they have been used. My major thesis is an affirmative answer to this question.

A. *Correlation and the "Prima Facie" Case of Discrimination*

In equal economic opportunity litigation, there is a requirement for a plaintiff to establish a *prima facie* case of discrimination, which then shifts the burden of proof to the defendant. Using the most naive interpretation, a *prima facie* case can be established by demonstrating any adverse-appearing correlation between salaries and sex. There is some requirement, however, for further analysis to make a minimal allowance for explanations other than discrimination—such as seniority—that may illuminate the causal interpretation of the correlation.

In science, it is natural to pursue vigorously the search for alternative explanations of correlations, and to regard any explanation as tentative, subject to revision or rejection in the light of new evidence. Thus, even after decades of study, there are scientists who can make a surprisingly cogent case that the correlation between smoking and disease does not mean that smoking causes disease. The legal concept of a *prima facie* case is philosophically far removed from the scientific paradigm. In science, descriptive correlations, such as those between smoking and disease or salaries and sex, are not to be regarded as justifying causal interpretations unless painstaking additional work is pursued. Even then, inferences about causation are made with circumspection.

II. STATISTICAL DEFINITION OF DISCRIMINATION

In this paper, the central concern is organizations, sometimes called meritocracies, in which attempts are made to compensate employees according to their contributions to the goals of the organization. In the absence of monopolistic restraints, organizations in the market sector can be expected to fit within this classification, as can some organizations in the nonmarket sector. There are of course other kinds of organizations, which are discussed briefly, in the section beginning on page 188.

As in scientific work generally, statistical studies should be tied to definitions of the concepts under study. Often the appropriate definitions are self-evident, and explicit discussion is unnecessary. Definition of employment discrimination is not, however, self-evident. In presenting a definition, it is necessary to start from economic theory and the concept of productivity or, more technically, the concept of marginal productivity. The standard definition will not be sufficient for statistical needs, because it is a deterministic definition. That is, it is assumed in the classical theory that productivity is known precisely. In the definition of discrimination used in this paper, no such assumption is made. If precise measurements were possible, the ascertainment of whether discrimination occurs would be trivial and compliance with the requirement of nondiscrimination could be achieved automatically.

The key to this definition is the concept of expected productivity, that is, the best judgmental assessment that an employer can make of an employee's productivity. Of course, an employer may be aided by statistical studies in making this judgment. In making the assessment, it is assumed that the employer is not only "blind" to race or sex but also to any variable unrelated to productivity that might be correlated with race or sex.

Consequently, *nondiscrimination with respect to salary* means that all employees are paid according to expected productivity. Similarly, *nondiscrimination with respect to employment* indicates that all initial placement decisions are made in the light of expected productivity.

Among other things, this definition signifies that in hiring, the employer should always offer a given job to the applicant with the highest expected productivity, the one who appears best qualified, and that in making any promotion, the employer should offer the promotion to the employee who appears best qualified in the light of expected productivity. Salary advances, whether or not connected with promotions, also should be made in the light of expected productivity.[7]

If we are studying the possibility of discrimination against a protected class of individuals, such as white females, the definition suggests the making of two kinds of comparisons:

(1) *Comparison of average qualifications of males and females hired into the same types of jobs.* Higher average qualifications for the females would be consistent with the hypothesis of discrimination in starting jobs, although it would not prove discrimination because some relevant qualifications may not have been taken into account.

(2) *Comparison of average qualifications of males and females who are making about the same salaries.* Again, higher average qualifications for the females would be consistent with the hypothesis of discrimination in salary.

A. *Productivity Proxies and Job Qualifications*

In statistical implementation of the definition, one ordinarily must be content with proxies or surrogate measures of productivity, which are often called job qualifications. Examples of qualifications are years of schooling, prior experience, seniority, and particular job skills. Qualifications also can refer to direct measures of performance on the job, such as letters per day typed by a secretary, lines of code per month by a computer programmer, pages of research publications in refereed journals by a professor in a year, or last season's earned run average for a baseball pitcher.

---

[7] The definition does not, however, indicate what should be meant by "affirmative action" in the sense of searching for job applicants. An attempt to do so could be based on the cost of search and the expected return from search, but it might not be easy to translate such a definition into statistical studies.

Ordinarily, information on several qualifications will be available. There are important legal questions as to whether a given qualification such as a score on a typing test, test of programming aptitude, or test of academic achievement can be properly used in a statistical study. The problem is that the qualification may be indirectly discriminatory, that is, unrelated to productivity, but related to sex or other protected classes, and used at least as one factor in decisions about hiring and promoting. Initially, attention is given to a single qualification and it is assumed that this qualification is not indirectly discriminatory. Although the reader should keep in mind that a qualification could be something as concrete as years of education, it is best to think of it abstractly as simply a proxy for productivity.

B. *The Logic of Statistical Comparisons*

The reader will recall that the above definition of nondiscrimination calls for comparisons of measured qualifications of males and females who are making about the same salaries, rather than comparison of mean salaries of males and females with the same measured qualifications. At first, it appears that these two comparisons are similar. If salaries can be perfectly predicted from the available information on measured qualifications, the two comparisons are equivalent. In most applications, however, there is no deterministic relationship between salaries and measured qualifications. Individual salaries tend to deviate at least a little from any statistical relationship fitted to the data on measured qualifications, that is, the statistical correlation is imperfect. In the presence of imperfect correlation, it is entirely possible that for given *measured* qualifications, females can have lower mean salaries, while for given salaries, males can have the same (or even higher) mean of measured qualifications. This is not a remote possibility. For example, in the studies done for Harris Bank[8] white males tended to have higher mean salaries for given measured qualifications than did white females, but for given salaries, males tended to have at least as high mean measured qualifications.

The problem posed by the limited availability of measured qualifications or productivity proxies leads directly to the underadjustment problem, which will be taken up in the section on page 183. First, however, the relationship between the definition of nondiscrimination proposed here and the idea of comparable worth will be discussed briefly.

C. *Nondiscrimination and Comparable Worth*

Our definition of a nondiscriminating employer can be reconciled with one definition of comparative worth. Consider the phrase, "equal pay for work of equal worth." If "equal worth" is interpreted to mean "equal

---

[8] Harry V. Roberts, "Harris Trust and Savings Bank: An Analysis of Employee Compensation," Center for Mathematical Studies in Business and Economics, University of Chicago (1979).

expected productivity," we have precisely the definition above. In this interpretation, the idea of "worth" is tied to the value to an organization of an employee's output; the employer assesses (at the margin) the value of the output to the firm. The assessment is necessarily imperfect, even crude, because it depends on many things that cannot ordinarily be known precisely.

Moreover, in the absence of collusion by employers, the collective assessments of expected productivity by employers are one input, the demand component, to a market process that sets and changes salaries across individuals and jobs. In making hiring and advancement decisions, employers will often have rough ideas of market salaries in mind, but they also will be looking at the assessment of what individuals are worth to the organization in terms of expected productivity.

The definition of a nondiscriminating employer states explicitly that such an employer does not use sex or race in the assessment of expected productivity. Nor will the employer use information unrelated to expected productivity but correlated with sex or race in arriving at an assessment of expected productivity; this additional prohibition is necessary to rule out the possibility of indirect discrimination. It should be noted, however, that it is conceivable that sex or race is directly related to productivity; if this possibility occurs, our definition departs from a purely economic one.

In most situations, economic theory suggests that an employer following the dictates of self-interest alone would want to be nondiscriminatory since discrimination ordinarily does not pay. Two examples in which discrimination can pay are those in which there is prejudice by fellow employees or customers of the firm. Then sex or race can be directly related to productivity. These possibilities, which are dealt with in our definition of nondiscrimination, provide a rationale for legislation of equal pay or equal economic opportunity even in a world of competitive job markets in which employment decisions are made in the light of expected productivity. That is why our definition of a nondiscriminatory employer says something more than that the employer always pursues purely economic goals.

In our definition, then, expected productivity can be connected with "worth," a concept of "worth" that is related to the market in the sense that market salaries (in the absence of discrimination by customers or fellow employees) reflect a consensus by many employers on monetary valuations of productivity. Many who are interested in comparable worth would, however, reject any concept of worth that is tied, however indirectly, to markets or to judgmental evaluations of expected productivity. Instead, there is an idea of intrinsic worth that is to be measured by some kind of job evaluation procedure that focuses on specified job inputs, such as strength or dexterity, rather than outputs, such as productivity. Worth as measured by the market can change, however, even when the employee inputs are essentially unchanged; for example, earnings of lawyers, accountants, and statisticians may rise with increased demand for litigation concerned with equal employment opportunity, even though job evaluations of the lawyers, accountants, and statisticians would be unchanged.

III. THE UNDERADJUSTMENT BIAS

In the usual statistical approach to the study of discrimination, broadly termed regression, the aim is to compare male and female salaries for given measured qualifications, where the measured qualifications may be measured imperfectly and typically do not include all qualifications pertinent to productivity.[9] If the males have, on the average, higher qualifications, the usual approach can lead to a statistical bias that would suggest discrimination when none exists. It is consistent with statistical terminology to give the name *underadjustment bias* to this source of bias.

The underadjustment bias is perhaps the most important of the statistical biases that must be dealt with in the statistical study of employment discrimination. The underlying concept is elementary but not easy. It relates to what is usually called the regression fallacy, a subject that has ensnared many a scientific investigator and that I have always found hard to explain to students. There is, however, a simple numerical example that brings out the point in terms that require only simple arithmetic for explanation.

Consider a hypothetical illustration in which there are 24 males and 24 females and a nondiscriminatory employer. For each employee we are given salary and true productivity. Salary is in dollars; productivity is scaled from 10 to 15. In reality, true productivity is unknown, but we assume in our hypothetical illustration that we know true productivity even though the employer does not.

In Figure 1, on the next page, there is a representation of the picture on true productivity for the 24 male employees and for 24 females.

Clearly, the employer is nondiscriminatory. For any given productivity, males and females are paid the same, and for any given salary, males and females have the same productivity. On the average, however, the females have both lower productivity and lower salaries than do the males, as shown by the distribution of frequencies in the total row (beneath the tables) and in the total column (at the right hand of the tables). The assumption that females have lower productivity is here made to bring out a point of methodology. The point could equally well have been made, perhaps better made from the standpoint of psychology, if the words "male" and "female" were everywhere switched throughout the example. The present construction, however, is more easily related to empirical studies.

Now, suppose that a statistician comes on the scene. The statistician, like the employer, is unable to observe true productivity. What the statistician can observe is a proxy for productivity; recall that a proxy is ordinarily

---

[9] Note the difference here from the approach of comparison of mean measured qualifications for given salaries, which would be appropriate under the definition found on page 180.

Figure 1

SALARY VERSUS TRUE PRODUCTIVITY FOR MALES

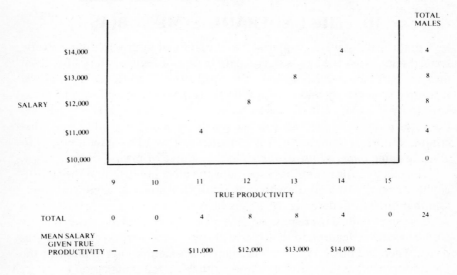

SALARY VERSUS TRUE PRODUCTIVITY FOR FEMALES

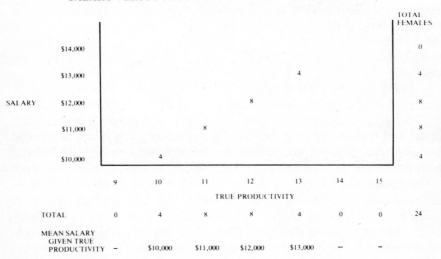

not a perfect substitute for productivity itself. With probability of ½ the proxy actually equals true productivity. With probability of ¼, the proxy is one unit higher than true productivity, and with probability of ¼, the proxy is one unit lower than true productivity. The statistician's observations for the 24 males and 24 females are shown in Figure 2.

Regression analysis, as applied to this example, is essentially a computation to estimate the difference in mean male and female salaries for any given

Figure 2

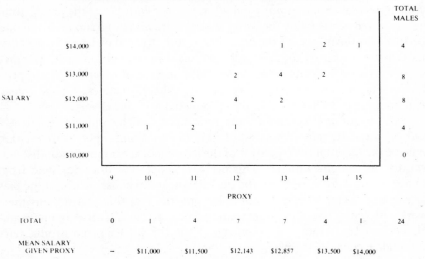

SALARY VERSUS PRODUCTIVITY PROXY FOR MALES

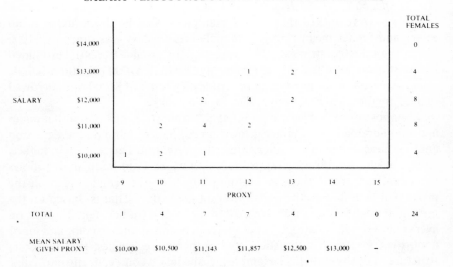

SALARY VERSUS PRODUCTIVITY PROXY FOR FEMALES

value of the productivity proxy. The computation assumes that there is a "true" but unobservable difference that is constant over all values of the proxy. The hypothetical example has been devised so that elementary arithmetic will bring out the essence: the means in the bottom rows of the two tables can be compared. For example, for the value 12 for the proxy, the male mean is $12,143, while the female is $11,857. For every value of the proxy for which there is at least one male and one female, the male mean is higher.

The reader is urged to check the arithmetic of the example. The value 12 of the proxy can be used as an illustration to reveal the essence of this otherwise mysterious result. Among the seven females with 12 for the proxy, four are measured correctly by the proxy, but two are measured too high and one too low. For the males, on the other hand, four are also measured correctly, but two are measured too low and only one is measured too high. The difference between males and females arises because the distribution of true productivity for males is displaced to the right of that of females—that is, males tend on balance to have higher true productivity in this example.

The traditional computational procedure used by the statistician will pick up a female salary shortfall of $353 (with a standard error of $184) in spite of the fact that the employer of the hypothetical example is nondiscriminatory, as explained above. This perverse conclusion does not stem from some technical error made by the statistician. It is a consequence of the bias of the traditional regression approach and the fact that statisticians must work with (crude) proxies rather than true productivity. It arises in this example because males have, on the average, both a higher mean productivity and higher mean of the proxy.

A. *Applicability of the Hypothetical Example*

We have remarked that, in the example, males had both higher mean salary and higher mean proxy. The male mean salary was precisely $1000 higher than the female mean. The regression-adjusted differential estimated by the statistician was $353, considerably less than $1000 but still a female salary shortfall. We may say that the crude difference of $1000 was narrowed to $353 by the statistical adjustment for the proxy.

Suppose now that we are told that an actual study has found that males had a higher unadjusted salary mean than did females, and that a regression analysis has resulted in a smaller adjusted differential. This pattern is, in fact, typical of almost all salary regressions with which I am familiar. It follows mathematically from these two assumptions that the female mean on the proxy will be less than the male mean on the proxy. That is, based on the measured qualifications that are used in regression studies, females have on average lower qualifications. A parallel conclusion applies to comparisons of minorities. Hence, the statistical studies themselves suggest that the basic structure of the hypothetical example is realistic. Of course, in any particular study, one may check actual proxies to compare male and female mean years of education, mean job related experience, mean seniority, etc.

B. *Reverse Regression*

The example just given has displayed the bias of underadjustment. Is there any way to get around this bias? The answer has been anticipated by the definition of nondiscrimination given above. The statistician need merely compare mean values of the proxy between males and females at each given salary level. Since this approach reverses the direction of the traditional (or direct) approach, it is natural to call it reverse regression.

The example has been set up so that the reverse regression can be performed by simple inspection. The reader can verify that for each salary level, males and females have exactly the mean value for the proxy. Hence the difference between average values for the proxy is precisely zero at every level of salary.

My purpose is not to argue that the reverse regression approach is the only proper statistical approach. In general, both approaches are needed, but it is unwise to try to base conclusions about shortfalls and possible discrimination on the traditional or direct regression alone.

There is a simple numerical approximation relating the estimated shortfalls or longfalls of salary from direct regression to estimated longfalls or shortfalls of qualifications (expressed in salary units) that would be found from the corresponding reverse regression. The relationship can be expressed in words as follows:

ESTIMATED QUALIFICATIONS DIFFERENTIAL EQUALS CRUDE SALARY DIFFERENTIAL TIMES AN ADJUSTMENT PLUS REFINED SALARY DIFFERENTIAL

The formula will be illustrated in terms of the example above, in which the original salary shortfall was $1000 and the adjusted shortfall was $353. The mean of female salaries minus that of males is − $1000. The estimated salary differential, females minus males, after direct regression adjustment, is − $353. The approximation of the qualifications differential (expressed in dollars units) can then be expressed:

$$-\$1000(1 - \text{RSQUARE}) - (-\$353),$$

where RSQUARE is the squared correlation R between salary and the proxy for males separately or females separately.[10]

In many regression studies of possible salary discrimination, R tends to be about 0.8 and RSQUARE, about 0.64. If this value is substituted in the formula, the estimated qualification differential expressed in salary units would be − $7, given the slight qualification edge to males. The exact value in this hypothetical example is of course zero, because the original construction specified a nondiscriminatory employer and the symmetrical distribution of errors of measurement about true productivity were built in.

---

[10] For readers familiar with statistical terminology, RSQUARE measures the fraction of total salary variation that is "explained" by the regression for males separately and females separately. It is not the overall RSQUARE that is usually reported.

To illustrate another application of the approximation formula, suppose that the mean female salary, without regression adjustment for a proxy, is 58 percent of that of males. If we equate the male mean with a parity of 100 percent, the crude estimated differential will be $58 - 100 = -42$. Suppose that after regression adjustment, the estimated differential narrows to -15. Application of the approximation formula will show that the qualification differential estimated by reverse regression is virtually zero.[11]

In the Harris study,[12] the formula proved to be a good approximation for direct regressions performed both by plaintiff and defendant, and the reverse regression estimates of differential qualifications for given salary were consistently close to zero.

The formula shows also that a narrowing through time in female salary shortfalls estimated by direct regression does not necessarily mean that there is discrimination that is narrowing through time. If the unadjusted differential in mean salaries is narrowing through time, one can have essential parity on reverse regression combined with narrowing adjusted shortfalls on direct regression. The unadjusted differential in mean salaries can be narrowing because true productivity differences are narrowing. Whether or not this explanation is correct can be checked by examination of the unadjusted differential in the mean of productivity proxies, that is, in mean qualifications. In the Harris example, this phenomenon was in fact occurring. It could be checked directly, for example, that the differential in mean years of education between males and females was narrowing. It could be checked indirectly because the difference between the unadjusted and adjusted female shortfall is equal to the difference in mean proxies (expressed in salary units). This difference, too, was decreasing through time.

C. *The Role of Measurement Errors*

This section deals with interesting subtleties suggested by the definition of productivity introduced in Section II, but it is not essential to the main development of the paper. Some readers may wish to skim or skip it.

In our numerical illustration of underadjustment at the start of this section, the result was due to the fact that the variable PROXY can be thought of as an imperfect measurement of true productivity. In this sense underadjustment appears as a consequence of what can be called measurement error. Here, we do not have in mind that possibility that there are measurement errors in the proxy itself, although these can contribute to the overall result. Thus, if the proxy is years of education, years of education can be perfectly measured, but even perfectly-measured years of education is an imperfect measure of true productivity.

---

[11] In practice, we would, of course, want to use the actual R for males separately or females separately in the formula; here the value of 0.8 has been assumed for illustration.

[12] Roberts, *supra*, note 8.

The illustration can be altered in a way suggested by Arthur P. Dempster to bring out an additional idea of importance.[13] Suppose that for the second pair of tables presented in Figure 2, we reinterpret the proxy to be true productivity. These new tables in Figure 3 reflect this one change of labeling of the horizontal axis.

Figure 3

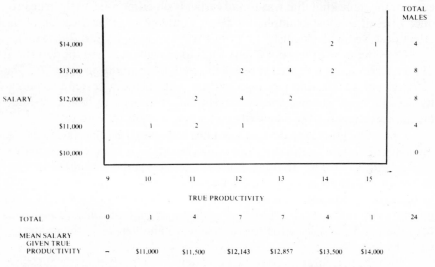

SALARY VERSUS TRUE PRODUCTIVITY FOR MALES

SALARY		9	10	11	12	13	14	15	TOTAL MALES
	$14,000					1	2	1	4
	$13,000				2	4	2		8
	$12,000			2	4	2			8
	$11,000		1	2	1				4
	$10,000								0

TRUE PRODUCTIVITY

TOTAL	0	1	4	7	7	4	1	24
MEAN SALARY GIVEN TRUE PRODUCTIVITY	—	$11,000	$11,500	$12,143	$12,857	$13,500	$14,000	

SALARY VERSUS TRUE PRODUCTIVITY FOR FEMALES

SALARY		9	10	11	12	13	14	15	TOTAL FEMALES
	$14,000								0
	$13,000				1	2	1		4
	$12,000			2	4	2			8
	$11,000		2	4	2				8
	$10,000	1	2	1					4

TRUE PRODUCTIVITY

TOTAL	1	4	7	7	4	1	0	24
MEAN SALARY GIVEN TRUE PRODUCTIVITY	$10,000	$10,500	$11,143	$11,857	$12,500	$13,000	—	

---

[13] A. P. Dempster, "Statistical Concepts of Discrimination," Statistics Department, Harvard University (1979).

There is now a shortfall of female mean salaries even for the same true productivity, but at the same time, mean productivity will be the same for a given salary. This is caused by the fact that (1) at a given salary, the distribution of true productivity is identical for males and females, just as was true earlier for the distribution of proxy; and (2) females have, on the average, lower salaries, which also was true in the earlier example. Hence, we see that the imperfect correlation between salaries and true productivity can lead to surprising results even in the absence of measurement error. If measurement error of the same kind that was found earlier is superimposed on the true productivities of this last example, the result would be an intensification of the effect observed with the distributions of true productivity just illustrated.

Consideration of this possibility leads to an elaboration of the definition of nondiscrimination treated above in the section beginning on page 179. The definition of nondiscrimination given there is called the Assessed Productivity definition, in which employers try to equate salaries to their best judgmental assessments of productivity, taking no account of race or sex.

Up to this point, the development has been based on the Assessed Productivity definition of nondiscrimination, because it is the most reasonable, useful, and defensible. There is, however, an alternative definition of nondiscrimination that can be called the True Productivity definition. According to this latter definition, nondiscrimination means the same mean salary for given true productivity. It is possible to have discrimination according to one definition and nondiscrimination according to another, as in the numerical example just given.

With the presentation of this second definition, several subtle questions are raised that cannot be carried further within current limitations of space. One persuasive argument for the Assessed Productivity definition is that it depends on something knowable--assessed productivity--as opposed to the True Productivity definition, which depends on the unknowable true productivity.

There is room for further study of statistical definitions of nondiscrimination and of their implications for practical work. For example, it is useful to distinguish systematic errors of measurement from the random errors of measurement illustrated in the example above. Dempster has referred to the problem raised by systematic errors of measurement as a problem of incomplete adjustment as opposed to a problem of underadjustment.[14] For example, if a given number of years of education bears a different relationship to true productivity for whites and minorities, due to differing qualities of schools, there is another statistical bias, distinct from the one treated above or from the other two on the list of three biases presented earlier. In the example of education just given, which is the one usually mentioned, the effect of this new bias works against the employer's side of a dispute in affirmative

---

[14] *Ibid.*

action. But this bias, unlike the underadjustment bias, is likely in some circumstances to work in the opposite direction. For example, suppose that only the most able female college graduates tend to apply to an organization while all male graduates tend to apply. There is therefore less of a presumption that this source of bias will work against employers than is true for the three major biases treated in this paper.

D. *Payment for Employee Qualifications*

In oral testimony during the Harris case, Dr. Stephan Michelson offered a rationale that can be extended into an alternative definition for nondiscrimination, one that differs from either the Assessed Productivity or the True Productivity definitions. Michelson thinks of employers as paying for specific employee qualifications, such as the possession of a bachelor's degree. One can even think of a salary formula that looks like the fitted equation in a regression, in which salary is a function of several employee qualifications. Such a model may, in some organizations, be a good approximation to reality. If the salaries are supposed to be determined strictly by formula, standard regression methodology would be the correct means for an investigation of whether a formula was being followed for everyone, male and female, even if the specific formula were unknown to the statistician.

More realistically, one might think of such a formula as indicating a target salary for the given employee qualifications, with some flexibility for going higher or lower in individual cases. Suppose that the policy on deviations requires that, at each target salary, deviations be determined so as to add up to zero. Then again, traditional regression methodology would be appropriate.

Such a policy on deviations from target would be very difficult to implement. My position would be that, at least for meritocracies, deviations would be made on the basis of assessed productivity, and that would lead us directly to the Assessed Productivity definition of nondiscrimination. The salary formula would be no more than an initial calibration.

E. *Multiple Proxies*

For simplicity of exposition, I have confined attention to the case of a single qualification or proxy for productivity. In practice, there will usually be several available proxies (although they are usually meager by comparison with what one would hope for!). The essential ideas are the same. In studying discrimination, the statistician using direct regression now asks about mean salary differentials at any combination of values of the proxies, because it is assumed that the true differential is constant. One way to implement reverse regression is to do the corresponding direct regression and use the proxy weights thereby developed in order to get an index of qualifications or productivity proxies. In reverse regression, this index, in turn, is compared for males and females at each salary level. Details are given in the Harris study.[15]

IV. NONCOMPETING GROUPS AND "JOB SEGREGATION"

In this section, we discuss the second of the three major biases. Our main conclusions for statistical studies of discrimination are these: (1) for salary comparisons between males and females, employees should be subdivided into homogeneous entering job groups for relatively narrow periods of time, and salary comparisons should be made within these groups; (2) there should be a separate statistical study of the possibility of shunting highly qualified females (or minorities) into lower entering job groups, which would entail comparisons of mean qualifications of males and females coming into the same entering job groups (at about the same time); and (3) there should be study by statistical or other means of any possible barriers to entry to job groups, whether legitimate or illegitimate. Job preference studies are also relevant in understanding what is happening.

Let us turn then to a detailed examination of issues. Suppose that in the early 1970's, a statistician is studying possible discrimination among flight personnel of Skyways Airlines. Direct regression is used. After statistical adjustment for a proxy—say years of schooling—the statistician finds that the males have mean annual incomes that are $70,000 higher than those of females.

After finishing the study, the statistician learns that all the males are pilots and that all the females are flight attendants.

This additional information shows that the question of drawing inferences about possible sex discrimination in salaries goes beyond the information available in the data base. From the perspective of a discrimination study, there is one overriding question: why are all the females flight attendants and all the males pilots? If there is some artificial restraint on female entry into pilot jobs, whether imposed by the company or union or by governmental regulation, this additional evidence (typically nonstatistical in nature) would point in the direction of discrimination. If the occupational specialization reflected qualifications and preferences of the individuals concerned, the additional evidence would point in the opposite direction. In either event, the fact that pilots earn more than flight attendants is not of itself the key question in the investigation of possible discrimination. Possible restraints on entry into occupations or jobs, not the valuation of the jobs themselves, would appear to pose the real threat of discrimination, and equally, the real challenge to the statistician.

---

[15] Roberts, *supra*, note 8.

Thus, the possibility of noncompeting job groups raises serious hazards for statistical analyses, lest estimates of sex differentials (whether by direct or reverse regression) be confounded with salary differences ascribable to sources of noncompetition that have nothing to do with discrimination. A natural way to deal with the question is to make special studies of entering job groups to complement studies of salary differentials. The reverse regression approach applies equally to each type of study. Thus, one can compare mean education of males and females entering relatively homogeneous job groups within an organization. If the qualifications of males and females are similar, then, in effect, salary regressions can be performed within each entering job group. If they are dissimilar, then further investigation—only partly statistical—is needed to explore reasons for the dissimilarities.

Comparisons of males and females within entering job groups are important in their own right for investigation of possible job discrimination. The definition of nondiscrimination given on page 180 requires, for example, that within any entering job group, expected productivity—measured by mean qualifications—should be the same for males and females. If, for example, females entering clerical jobs have higher mean qualifications than do males, this evidence can be construed as being consistent with a kind of discrimination called shunting. Shunting studies are, thus, an essential part of statistical study of possible discrimination, because shunting can exist even if salary discrimination does not. They are also important as one step in the investigation of possible salary discrimination, as is vividly brought out by the example of pilots and flight attendants at Skyways Airlines.

In the Harris study, the shunting studies showed essential parity of qualifications (actually a slight edge to males) within entering job groups, a finding consistent with the assumption of nondiscrimination.[16] The subsequent use of entering job groups in salary regressions almost always reduced the estimated female shortfalls by comparison with the corresponding regression models that did not include entering job groups. Although the use of reverse regression analysis showed essential parity of males and females even without taking the entering job group into consideration, the failure to take account of the entering job group is a source of potential statistical bias.

V. SENIORITY AND OTHER STATISTICAL DETAILS

The third of the three biases enumerated at the outset of this paper concerns the failure to make proper allowances for differences in seniority. This paper has said almost nothing about the technicalities of regression. In all regression studies, including affirmative action studies, the adequacy of the statistical model is an important technicality. Adequacy refers to the extent to

---

[16] In these studies, the definition of entering job groups was jointly determined by the company and the enforcement agency.

which the data conform to the mathematical specifications on which the fitting process is based. A detailed discussion of adequacy in the context of affirmative action studies is provided in Roberts.[17] One example is the specification that expected salary should be related in a linear way to each individual independent variable, regardless of values taken by the others. For common proxies such as years of education, years of experience, age, and seniority, this specification is seldom satisfied without transformations of such variables. The seniority variable is particularly hard to handle because it is often implicated in two types of nonlinearities. First, any given level of other variables, the relationship between expected salary and seniority tends to be nonlinear and, second, there tend to be what are known as interactions between seniority and other variables. This means that the relationship of expected salary to the other variables may itself change as seniority changes.

The best method of handling this problem is to disaggregate a large regression study into smaller groups of employees, sometimes called cohorts, which are defined by relatively narrow periods of time at which initial employment occurred. Such a disaggregation also serves as a means of studying possible discrimination by specific time periods of hire. Failure to disaggregate confounds the more distant past with the recent past. If there were discrimination in the distant past or if disparities in employee qualifications between males and females were then more substantial, the statistician gets a single picture that is influenced strongly by events that may no longer be relevant for policy purposes.

Of course, any technical inadequacy of regression can distort conclusions. In my experience, however, the main technical inadequacy that is likely to lead to a biasing effect is the flawed treatment of seniority.

VI. REMARKS ON LABOR FORCE DISCRIMINATION STUDIES

The methodological biases treated in this paper have been exposited within the illustrative framework of discrimination studies of a single organization. These same statistical biases must affect broader studies of the labor force, since these tend to mirror in essential respects the circumstances found in studies within organizations, such as lower mean qualifications for females and minorities and reduction of crude salary differentials after regression adjustment on available proxies. The differences in circumstances between the different organizations represented by the employees in labor force studies simply make it much harder to know what is happening or to investigate in detail the subtle questions that must be studied to obtain insight into discrimination.

---

[17] Roberts, *supra*, note 8.

VII. IMPLICATIONS FOR COMPARABLE WORTH

As explained in the introduction, the main connection between my theme and comparable worth is that the implications of the latter for public policy become less and less important to the extent that the statistical biases outlined here inaccurately create the impression of discrimination when none exists or exaggerate the extent of actual discrimination.

However, investigations of the concept of comparable worth often lead to regression-type studies (including simple tabular comparisons of means) in which, for example, measures of worth obtained from job evaluation plans are related to actual salaries in an organization. From this perspective, worth—or individual dimensions thereof—plays a curious role. Insofar as it attaches to the individuals holding the jobs, worth is like a productivity proxy. Insofar as it attaches to the job, it is one device by which homogeneous entering job groups can be defined. These groups can in turn serve as the vehicle for investigations of shunting of females into less desirable jobs.

But insofar as some groups appear to be largely or wholly "segregated," there is little room for *statistical* investigation of problems of salary discrimination. These problems can best be investigated statistically, according to the position of this paper, by comparing male and female qualifications at *given* salaries or in *given* job groups at which both males and females are to be found. If an occupation is "segregated," the important question is "why," and an investigation of mobility and possible constraints on mobility is crucial.

THE LEGAL FRAMEWORK

by
Robert E. Williams and Douglas S. McDowell

The authors' thesis is that there is no statutory authority for a finding of liability based on a comparison of the wages paid for jobs which are dissimilar in content. They contend that the Equal Pay Act of 1963 and Title VII of the Civil Rights Act of 1964 must be construed harmoniously and, thus, unless the former's standard of equal pay for equal work is violated, a claim of compensation discrimination based on the comparable worth theory cannot be maintained under Title VII. To support their thesis, they review the legislative history of the Equal Pay Act and Title VII, as well as the experience of the War Labor Board during World War II. The paper then analyzes federal district and appellate court decisions which discuss the standard of proof in cases involving compensation differentials between men and women. The authors conclude with an examination of the practical and administrative difficulties which will arise if the courts are required to determine the relative worth of jobs.

Robert E. Williams is a partner in the Washington, D.C., law firm of McGuiness & Williams, which specializes in EEO and labor law. A graduate of Beloit College, he received his law degree from the University of Illinois in 1967. For the next five years, he served on the National Labor Relations Board staff, concluding his work there as a supervisory attorney in the Appellate Court Branch. Mr. Williams is a member of the Illinois and District of Columbia Bars and was a co-author of *NLRB Regulation of Election Conduct*, which was published in 1974.

Douglas S. McDowell is the Administrative Counsel for the Equal Employment Advisory Council and is associated with the law firm of McGuiness & Williams. A former attorney at the National Labor Relations Board, he is the co-author of *NLRB Remedies for Unfair Labor Practices*, which was published in 1976. Mr. McDowell received his undergraduate and law degrees from the University of Michigan in 1964 and 1971 respectively. He is a member of the Michigan and District of Columbia Bars and the Committee on Equal Employment Opportunity Law of the Labor Relations Law Section of the American Bar Association.

THE LEGAL FRAMEWORK

The problems confronting a comparable worth approach to job evaluation or some related method for equalizing male and female pay differentials
are not exclusively technical in nature, limited only to considerations of feasibility, practicality and desirability. Any substitution of a standard which
involves a comparison of the relative worth or value of jobs for the Congres-
sionally legislated doctrine of "equal pay for equal work" raises an additional issue. Can authority for the alternative standard be found within the
existing legal framework?

The principal federal laws prohibiting sex-based discrimination in employment compensation are the Equal Pay Act of 1963 and Title VII of the
Civil Rights Act of 1964. Of the two, the Equal Pay Act is by far the more explicit in its application to issues involving pay differentials between men and
women. Its basic standard is embodied in the "equal pay for equal work"
maxim. It requires employers to pay men and women the same wages if they
work in the same establishment under similar working conditions, performing "equal work" on jobs that require equal skill, effort and responsibility. It
permits pay differentials, however, based on length of service, merit, quantity or quality of production, or any other factor aside from sex.

Title VII, on the other hand, while less specific in its reference to sex-
based pay discrepancies, sets forth a general ban on employment practices
that discriminate on the basis of race, color, religion, sex or national origin.
There can be no question that Title VII's general prohibitory language is
broad enough to reach sex discrimination in compensation and, thus, to
overlap with the Equal Pay Act. Controversy has developed, however, about
whether Title VII goes beyond the Equal Pay Act to require parity in compensation between men and women performing jobs that are not "equal" under
the standards of the latter Act, but are viewed as being of "comparable
worth" to the employer or perhaps, in a broader sense, to society at large.

Advocates of the view that Title VII requires equal pay for jobs of "comparable worth" contend that employers have historically discriminated by
setting lower rates of compensation for jobs held predominantly by women
than for traditionally male-dominated jobs, even though the work performed
by the women is of as much value to the employer as that of the men. Moreover, the view has been expressed that the market wage for such jobs may
reflect sex discrimination and that reliance upon the market, therefore, is not

justifiable. This practice, they maintain, is a form of sex-based discrimination in employment which Title VII prohibits.

Opponents of this "comparable worth" theory respond that the generally lower wage rates paid to women in certain jobs result not from discrimination by their employers, but rather from various social, cultural and economic factors whose combined effect has been to hold down the levels of compensation that women competing for such jobs can command in the market. The resultant pay differentials, they say, stem from social forces beyond the control of particular employers, and, as such, are beyond the intended reach of Title VII. They also argue that "comparable worth" is unworkable as a legal standard, because there is no existing methodology by which the worth or value of dissimilar jobs can be compared with legal certainty.

Since the passage of these two federal statutes in the early 1960's, the vast majority of equal pay claims taken to the federal courts have been prosecuted under the "equal work" standards of the Equal Pay Act. Recently, however, increasing numbers of claimants have sought redress under Title VII for pay discrepancies which, because of the dissimilarity of the jobs in question, could not be found to violate the Equal Pay Act. Their reliance on the "comparable worth" theory has produced a substantial and growing body of opinion in the lower federal courts as to the validity of this application of the sex discrimination ban of Title VII. The issue has yet to be addressed by the United States Supreme Court.

With notable exceptions, the courts that have considered such claims have decided that the Equal Pay Act and Title VII must be construed in harmony with one another, and that unless the Equal Pay Act standards are violated, a claim of compensation discrimination based on sex cannot be maintained under Title VII. To date, the Ninth Circuit has ruled directly to the contrary,[1] but even that court stated that when Title VII plaintiffs attempt to establish wage discrimination based solely on comparisons of jobs, their claims must be evaluated under an "equal" work standard, not a "comparable" work standard.[2]

Nevertheless, despite its repeated rejection by the courts, the theory that Title VII requires comparison of dissimilar jobs on the basis of their relative "worth" has increasingly been advocated, or at least seriously discussed, by

---

[1] *Gunther v. County of Washington,* 602 F.2d 882, 20 FEP Cases 792 (9th Cir. 1979), *pet. for reh'g denied,* 22 FEP Cases 1650 (1980), *petition for cert. filed.*

[2] *Gunther* is discussed more fully below (pp. 237–40 and footnotes 133 and 137). As of the printing date of this book, several important cases await resolution by either the courts of appeals or the United States Supreme Court. *See, e.g., Gunther; Lemons v. Denver,* 620 F.2d 228 (10th Cir. 1980) *petition for cert. filed* (No. 80–82); and *IUE v. Westinghouse Electric Corp.,* 19 FEP Cases 1028 (D.N.J. 1979), *appeal docketed.* The discussion below presents many of the legal issues and arguments which have been and will be urged in such cases. The status of *Westinghouse* is updated in the Editor's Note at the end of this paper.

government agencies, women's rights groups and commentators. Of particular importance is the attention this theory has received from the Equal Employment Opportunity Commission (EEOC), the federal agency which now administers both Title VII and the Equal Pay Act.[3] EEOC has participated as amicus curiae in several court cases brought under Title VII by private female plaintiffs charging that they had been denied equal pay for work that was comparable to that performed by men.[4] In these amicus briefs, EEOC has supported plaintiffs' arguments that the sex discrimination provisions of Title VII are broad enough to support a finding of compensation discrimination even when it is clear that the "equal work" standard of the Equal Pay Act could not be met.[5]

Additionally, in one instance in 1977, the EEOC entered into a contract with Lester B. Knight Associates, a private consulting firm, to conduct an investigation of General Telephone & Electronics Corporation, which allegedly was paying less for traditional female jobs than for dissimilar traditional male jobs. See Contract No. EEO-W-77088. The contract required the consulting firm to provide sufficient documentary evidence to reach a conclusion that the employer had violated Title VII. This evidence was to be based upon a methodology, to be developed by the contractor, for determining the comparable worth of the jobs. No discrimination charge was ever filed against the employer, however, because the target employer refused to respond to the private contractors' request for information and no court proceedings were ever initiated by EEOC.

In recognition of its lack of expertise in this area, the EEOC, later in 1977, entered into its current agreement with the National Academy of Sciences (NAS) to review the feasibility and desirability of using the comparable worth theory to identify sex discrimination in compensation. The study is specifically addressed to the question of comparing jobs that would not be equivalent for purposes of the Equal Pay Act. It will look into the techniques and criteria for setting compensation levels for jobs, along with related issues concerning the implications of such a system for collective bargaining agreements and for the economy as a whole. The NAS is also to consider whether

---

[3] On July 1, 1979, responsibility for enforcement of the Equal Pay Act was transferred to EEOC from the Wage and Hour Administrator of the United States Department of Labor. See Reorganization Plan No. 1 of 1978, 43 FR 19807.

[4] See EEOC amicus curiae briefs filed in *Christensen v. State of Iowa*, 563 F.2d 353 (8th Cir. 1977); and *IUE v. Westinghouse Electric Corporation*, Nos. 79-1893 and 79-1894 (3d. Cir.) (EEOC also participated in the oral argument).

[5] Under Title VII, EEOC can either file its own discrimination charges or process those filed by private individuals. EEOC is required to attempt to conciliate and settle those cases. If that is not possible, the agency has the authority to either file its own lawsuit against the employer in a federal district court or give the private party a "right-to-sue" letter which permits him/her to file his/her own suit. Significantly, it does not appear that, since the enactment of Title VII, the Commission has ever filed a Title VII suit alleging that an employer had committed a violation by paying women less than men even though the women were performing jobs with admittedly dissimilar or unequal job content.

the evidence produced under such a system would meet the evidentiary standards required under the law, and whether additional legislation would be required to enforce the comparable worth theory. The publication date for the final NAS report has been postponed to an undetermined date. Pending the outcome of the NAS study, EEOC has announced that it "does not adopt as its interpretation of the Equal Pay Act the interpretations of the Wage and Hour Administrator."[6] EEOC also stated it will issue its interpretation of the relationship between Title VII and the Equal Pay Act "so as to harmonize the two statutes."[7]

The Commission also held hearings on "Job Segregation and Wage Discrimination Under Title VII and the Equal Pay Act" on April 28–30, 1980. The stated purpose of the hearings was to "determine whether the wage rates of jobs in which minorities and women have been historically segregated are likely to be depressed because those jobs are largely occupied by members of these groups. . . ."[8] In announcing its hearings, the Commission added the caveat that it "is not specifically exploring any theory that would compare the worth of different jobs by some abstract standard determined and administered by the government, as is sometimes implied in the concept of 'comparable worth.' "[9] This caveat, coupled with the delay in the issuance of the final NAS report, suggests that the Commission has not yet decided what course of action to take, nor what standard to apply, when dealing with allegations of wage discrimination based upon sex.

It should be noted, however, that whether a job segregation/wage discrimination or "comparable worth" approach is taken, illegal discrimination cannot be established unless it can be shown that there is an improper wage differential between various groups for which their employer bears legal responsibility. Consequently, when sex discrimination in wages is alleged, a comparison between predominantly male and predominantly female jobs would be necessary. Thus, both the job segregation and "comparable worth" theories would have to confront the fact that many courts have not accepted such comparisons when dissimilar jobs are involved. Moreover, because such comparisons would be required, it would appear that the job segregation theory actually is a variant of the "comparable worth" approach.[10]

---

[6] 44 Fed. Reg. 3867 (1979). Before its authority to administer the Equal Pay Act was transferred to EEOC, the Wage and Hour Administrator of the U.S. Department of Labor issued bulletins interpreting the Equal Pay Act.

[7] Id.

[8] 44 Fed. Reg. 63485, November 2, 1979; 45 Fed. Reg. 11659, February 21, 1980; 45 Fed. Reg. 13816, March 3, 1980.

[9] 45 Fed. Reg. 11659, February 21, 1980.

[10] The most complete exposition of the job segregation/wage discrimination theory is contained in R. Blumrosen, *Wage Discrimination, Job Segregation, and Title VII of the Civil Rights Act of 1964*, 12 U. Mich. J.L. Ref. 399 (1979). A detailed, critical discussion of that article can be found in B. Nelson, *Wage Discrimination and the "Comparable Worth" Theory in Perspective,*

Aside from EEOC's amicus efforts (see p. 201, note 4, *supra*.), the only formal proceeding in which a federal government agency has advocated a comparable worth standard for determining sex discrimination in pay rates was an administrative action brought against Kerr Glass Manufacturing Corporation by the Labor Department's Office of Federal Contract Compliance Programs (OFCCP). The complaint in that case[11] alleges that Kerr used a job evaluation system which, by reason of its discriminatory origin and application, resulted in an unfairly low rate of pay for traditionally female jobs and an unfairly high rate of pay for certain traditionally male jobs. The results of the suit are inconclusive at this time. The hearing before an administrative law judge consumed about 123 days and no judge's decision has yet been issued. Thus, the Labor Department's legal theory has never been tested by court review. Furthermore, no administrative law judge nor court has yet ruled on the relationship between equal pay requirements of the federal antidiscrimination statutes and the Federal Contract Compliance Program under Executive Order 11246. It remains undecided, therefore, whether sex-based compensation claims which do not violate either the Equal Pay Act or Title VII, could nevertheless be held by the Labor Department to constitute a violation of the Order.[12] In short, neither the EEOC nor the Department of Labor has had much experience with either the practical or the legal problems posed by the "comparable worth" approach.

This paper will explore the legal aspects of this controversy, primarily from the historical perspective. First, there will be a brief discussion of the

---

13 U. Mich. J. L. Ref. 231 (1980), and therefore the Blumrosen article will not be discussed in detail here. It should be pointed out, however, that close attention should be given to any wage discrimination theory that is based upon statistical evidence. First, courts are giving ever-increasing scrutiny to such evidence, and it is clear that a statistical showing of a predominance of a certain race or sex in a particular job category has been found by the court to be insufficient to establish a *prima facie* case of discrimination in job placement or assignment. See, *e.g., Rich v. Martin Marietta*, 467 F.Supp. 587, 611–12 (D. Col. 1979).

Moreover, theories of wage discrimination often rely upon evidence which allegedly demonstrates decades of discrimination against females. Such assertions are questionable (see Nelson above, at 233–64), but in any event, evidence of alleged discrimination which occurred *before* the enactment of either Title VII or the Equal Pay Act is not properly considered in determining whether a case of discrimination can be established under those statutes. See, *e.g., EEOC v. United Virginia Bank*, 21 FEP Cases 1405, 1407 (4th Cir. 1980). Moroever, under Title VII, charges of discriminatory hiring or placement practices must be filed within 180 days of the alleged discriminatory act. If such timely charges are not made, the past alleged discriminatory act has no present legal consequences and cannot be relied upon for a finding of discrimination. See *United Air Lines v. Evans*, 431 U.S. 553 (1977).

[11] Case Number OFCCP-CR-1977-4. OFCCP administers Executive Order 11246, which requires federal contractors and subcontractors to include an equal opportunity clause in their contracts under which they agree not to discriminate on the basis of sex, race, color, religion or national origin.

[12] Other aspects of the Executive Order program have been found subordinate to judicial interpretations of Title VII. See, *United States v. East Texas Motor Freight System, Inc.*, 564 F.2d 179 (5th Cir. 1977); and *United States v. Trucking Management, Inc.*, 20 FEP Cases 342 (D. D.C. 1979), *appeal pending* No. 79-2103 (D.C. Cir.). Both cases held that seniority systems that are valid under Title VII may not be found to violate Executive Order 11246.

government's only prior attempt to deal with sex-based compensation discrimination claims—*i.e.,* the experience of the National War Labor Board during World War II. An examination of the Board's history demonstrates that it had virtually no first-hand experience in evaluating the relative worth of "comparable" jobs.

Second, the history of the proceedings in Congress leading up to the enactment of the Equal Pay Act in 1963 will be reviewed. The legislative history makes it quite clear that Congress, after analyzing and debating the issue at length, decisively rejected the "comparable work" approach and adopted instead the "equal work" standard as the measure of employers' equal pay obligations. Attention will then focus on the proceedings in Congress the following year, when, despite the lack of opportunity for debate on the effects of the hasty addition of sex discrimination to the purview of Title VII, legislative steps were taken to assure that the limitations carefully imposed in the Equal Pay Act would not be swept aside. More particularly, the Bennett Amendment to Title VII will be examined. It was added specifically to assure that "discrimination in compensation on account of sex does not violate Title VII unless it also violates the Equal Pay Act."[13]

The paper will conclude with an examination of the courts' treatment of the "comparable worth" theory, as reflected in published opinions in cases arising under the Equal Pay Act and Title VII. This discussion will analyze whether existing case law affords a basis to challenge an employer's compensation system on grounds of sex discrimination unless it can be shown that women are being paid less than men for performing jobs that are "substantially equal" in job content, skill, effort, responsibility and working conditions. Moreover, many employers have successfully defended against wage discrimination claims by demonstrating that they relied upon the prevailing market wage for predominantly female jobs.

To summarize the legal precedents, it can be argued that Title VII and the Equal Pay Act, read together, provide a statutory scheme whereby qualified female employees are guaranteed access to all jobs. At the same time, Congress intended that federal agencies and the courts should not become involved in evaluating the relative worth of dissimilar jobs. If an employer discriminates against female employees in hiring, promotions, transfers or other employment practices prohibited by Title VII, then a violation may be established and a remedy obtained. Moreover, males and females doing the same work are now guaranteed equal pay. Courts are experienced in making such determinations, but have no experience in evaluating the economic factors that make up compensation systems, such as collective bargaining forces, the comparative strength of intra-union pressure groups, the market price and market demands for persons with various skills and the myriad other factors that establish the relationships between the thousands of jobs in

---

[13] 111 Cong. Rec. 13359 (1965) (remarks of Sen. Bennett).

the economy. Congress recognized in 1963 and 1964 that to interject courts and agencies into this difficult and complex process would be administratively infeasible and severely disruptive to both the judiciary and the economy. The reasons for Congress' rejection of the "comparable worth" theory are as valid today as they were then.

I. THE NATIONAL WAR LABOR
BOARD EXPERIENCE

To gain historical perspective on the legal framework surrounding the concepts of "equal work" and "comparable worth," it is useful to consider briefly the experience of the World War II National War Labor Board ("Board").[14] Some of the Board's decisions have been cited as precedent for examining the value of "women's jobs" in determining whether discrimination has occurred.[15] It has been said that the Board engaged in a process of evaluating dissimilar male and female jobs to determine whether the tasks were "comparable," thereby requiring equal pay. In fact, however, the concept of "comparable worth" is quite unlike the principles applied in actual Board practice. Moreover, the extraordinary purposes for which the Board was created, and the circumstances under which it operated, demonstrate that its history provides little guidance for those attempting to construct a practical methodology for implementing the comparable worth theory.

The Board was established as an emergency wartime measure by Presidential Executive Order 9017 in January 1942, with the primary purpose of restraining wage increases in order to prevent inflation. Increases in wage rates could be approved only to correct gross inequities or to aid in the effective prosecution of the war.[16] The Board was created at the request of both union and management as a means of carrying out their wartime no strike-no lockout commitment and to provide a means of resolving issues which could not be solved by bargaining. Employers found the Board beneficial because it contributed to the stability of industrial relations; the unions went along with Board determinations, in part, because they provided a method to obtain wage increases which otherwise were frozen by the Emergency Price Control Act.

---

[14] Three of the authors of other papers in this study—Professors George H. Hildebrand, E. Robert Livernash and Herbert R. Northrup—served as officers of the War Labor Board. Their experience at the Board, along with the other authorities cited, have been relied upon in this discussion.

[15] See *e.g.* Gitt, *Beyond the Equal Pay Act: Expanding Wage Differential Protections Under Title VII*, Vol. 8 Loyola L. J. 723, 732 (1977), citing *General Electric Co.* and *Westinghouse Electric Corp.*, 28 War Lab. Rep. 666 (1945).

[16] National War Labor Board, Termination Report (1945), Vol. 1, 8–9.

The Board was in no sense a judicial or juridical body, nor could it be compared to a modern-type administrative agency such as the National Labor Relations Board, which makes quasi-judicial administrative determinations concerning allegations that employers or unions have violated federal labor relations laws. The Board's functions could more readily be analogized loosely to those of the Federal Mediation and Conciliation Service or the Council on Wage and Price Stability.

The National War Labor Board was a tripartite body composed of an equal number (four each) of public, industry and labor representatives. In addition to the National Board, there were twelve Regional Boards. The Regional Boards handled the bulk of the day-to-day work, with the National Board acting much like a supreme court in overseeing the Regions' work. The Board had the authority to resolve issues in dispute by mediation or arbitration, but its recommendations did not have the force and effect of law, nor were they enforced by court order.[17] Congress left the problem of compliance to executive action, such as the withholding or withdrawing of government contracts, benefits or privileges from the noncomplying employer where necessary.[18] The actual enforcement powers of the Board were never established or tested to any degree.

The Board's procedures, unlike those of a court, were highly informal.[19] Employer and union representatives discussed their cases freely with Board and staff members. The contesting parties had "an open invitation . . . to come in and talk things over."[20] Unlike the rigorous judicial, procedural and evidentiary requirements imposed by the Equal Pay Act and Title VII, the Board relied primarily on its mediation and persuasion functions, and its "findings" or recommendations were not equivalent to formal findings of fact made by judicial tribunals. As Former Chairman Garrison stated:

> The reason for this [lack of written pleadings and formal advocacy] is that in labor disputes there is no rule of law upon which to base the decision and no judicial sanctions by which to enforce it. The decision simply will not stick unless it falls within a fairly narrow zone of acceptability or tolerability whose ascertainment can only be arrived at through an intimate understanding of the inmost positions of both sides and of all the forces which are playing upon their representatives both within their own group (corporate or labor) and from the outside.[21]

---

[17] *Id.*, at 7, XXVI.

[18] *Id.*, at 10.

[19] *Id.* at XXV–XXVI (Statement of Chairman Lloyd K. Garrison).

[20] *Id.* at XXVI.

[21] *Id.* at XXVI.

Ultimately, the Board's program rested on its status as an "emergency agency" whose

> only purpose was to settle disputes in the interests of the war effort. In these circumstances, people's patriotic instincts predisposed them to accept the Board's decisions and the Board was able to appeal to those instincts very effectively.[22]

In short, whatever acceptance the Board achieved appears to have resulted more from a recognition of the war emergency than from any inherent efficacy of government control of compensation structures. It remains open to question, therefore, whether such wide-scale government participation in wage regulation in a peacetime economy would be tolerated. Moreover, the informal and non-legal nature of the Board's operations render questionable any argument that a similar administrative structure could be transposed readily into a present-day administrative or judicial system designed to enforce nondiscrimination laws dealing with compensation. The Board's experiences provide little practical guidance for courts or federal agencies which are required to operate under due process and procedural constraints, often in an adversarial atmosphere. Accusations of wage discrimination which are stated as broadly as under the comparable worth theory rarely are made in a manner that would encourage easy resolution by the parties, or in the alternative, through informal and nonbinding mediation or arbitration.

With respect to the Board's policies concerning equal pay for women, the Board issued General Order No. 16, in November 1942, which provided that employers could make adjustments which "equalize the wage or salary rates paid to females with the rates paid to males for *comparable quality and quantity of work on the same or similar operations* . . ." without approval of the National Board.[23] This order has led to the conclusion by some (including one member of Congress during the Equal Pay Act debates, discussed below at p. 215) that the Board was engaged in applying a "comparable work" standard. To the contrary, however, "[c]omparatively few dispute cases involving the 'equal pay' principle came to the level of the National Board for Determination."[24] Moreover, almost all of the comparisons undertaken by the Board at either the national or regional level involved determinations of whether women were being paid less for performing the *same* duties as men.[25] In short, the standard applied in practice by the Board was that of "equal work" (such as was adopted in the Equal Pay Act), not that of "comparable work" mentioned in General Order No. 16.

---

[22] *Id.* at XXVII.

[23] *Id.* at 290 (emphasis added).

[24] *Id.*

[25] See generally, *Id.* at 291–97 and cases there cited.

Employers were allowed to make appropriate adjustments within their own wage structures as long as they were in conformity with the requirements of General Order No. 16 and other orders and regulations. Most often, determinations were required when women were hired during the war to replace men on jobs which were not changed, or when downward adjustments in women's wages were necessary because the functions of jobs in which they replaced men were lightened or rearranged.[26]

Only when unions objected to existing wages or employer adjustments would complaints be made to the War Labor Board, generally to one of the twelve regional Boards. Allegations of wage inequities were made by unions as a means of obtaining wage increases because peacetime collective bargaining and market forces were foreclosed as an alternative source.

Several basic precedents were established by the National Board in the sex compensation area. These were summarized by the Board as follows:[27]

1. Where women are working on the same jobs as men or on jobs formerly performed by men or on jobs performed interchangeably by men and women, or on jobs which differ only inconsequently, and not in measurable job content, from jobs performed by men, the women should receive the same rates of pay as the men, unless (a) their output is less in quantity or quality than the output of men, or (b) there are ascertainable and specific added costs to the company resulting from the use of women, such as provision for extra helpers or for rest periods not provided in the case of men. In the case of (a) or (b), appropriate adjustment in rates may be made.

2. Intangible alleged cost factors incident to the employment of women (such as absenteeism, lack of qualification for other work to which they are not assigned, relative impermanence in industry, legal restrictions, lack of prior training in industry, necessity of providing sanitary facilities, etc.) cannot legitimately be used to reduce the rates to which the woman would otherwise be entitled on the basis of job content.

3. *The rates for jobs which have historically been performed by women only and which differ measurably from the jobs performed by men are presumed to be correct in relation to the men's rates in the plant, especially where they are of long standing and have been accepted in collective bargaining.*

4. *This presumption can be overcome by affirmative evidence of the existence of an intra-plant inequity derived from a compari-*

---

[26] *Id.* at 291.

[27] *Id.* at 296–97; and *General Electric Co. and Westinghouse Electric Corp.*, 28 War Lab. Rep. 666, 677 (1945) (industry members dissenting).

*son of the content of the jobs in question with the content of the
jobs performed by men.* Some consideration, however, may be
given in such cases, in modifying long established rate relationships
to the collective bargaining history.

5. In particular cases, under a proper evaluation, there may be
women's jobs which warrant a lower rate than the rate assigned to
the lowest men's jobs, depending entirely on the circumstances.

6. *The determination of proper rates for men's and women's
jobs cannot be made by rule of thumb;* it calls for judgment; and,
*wherever possible, it should be made through collective bargaining
conducted in good faith.*
(Emphasis added).

Principles 3 and 4 were based on the Board's view that the existing rates
paid for "womens' jobs" would be presumed to be correct, particularly when
they were longstanding and developed through collective bargaining. Principle 4 allows this presumption to be overcome if intraplant inequity can be
shown by a comparison of the content of predominantly male and female
jobs. Principle 6 states that broad blanket rules were not to be used; rather
collective bargaining should be relied upon. As noted above, however, the
Board, in practice, limited its inquiry to the "equal work" standard.

When discrepancies between "women's jobs" and "men's jobs" were
questioned, the Board took one of three positions:

1. it presumed that rates for jobs traditionally performed by
   women were correctly rated in relation to the general wage
   schedule of the plant, especially if such rates were established
   through collective bargaining;
2. it remanded the issue to the parties for further negotiations as to
   the jobs which were performed historically by women, and the
   appropriate rates for such classification; [or]
3. it suggested or ordered the institution of a job evaluation to establish the worth of a job on the basis of content irrespective of
   the sex of any incumbent.[28]

Thus, proper wages for dissimilar male and female jobs were not set by
Board fiat but were left to the parties. Moreover, in establishing the "equal
pay for equal work" standard, "the Board did not contemplate that the doctrine would be applied to those occupations which were limited to women
employees only."[29]

One of the Board's final decisions often is cited inappropriately for the
proposition that the Board was deeply engaged in making comparisons

[28] Termination Report at 294.
[29] *Id.*

between, and requiring equal pay for, male and female jobs that were "comparable." In *General Electric and Westinghouse Electric,*[30] the issue arose whether the Board should require rates for women's jobs to be set in accordance with point values assigned to the jobs by the employers. The union protested to the Board that sex discrimination was responsible for jobs customarily performed by women being paid less, on a comparative job content basis, than jobs usually performed by men. The union alleged that there was a substantial difference between the wage rates for male and female jobs on the basis of comparative job content. The job evaluations involved were performed by the employers, not the Board. The Board's decision stated that "the exact extent of the differentials ascribable to sex cannot now be precisely determined nor can we say that they are the same in all plants or with respect to all jobs."[31] Moreover, of the several wage differentials alleged, the Board was unable to determine whether there was any particular figure which needed to be corrected.[32]

Although many women's jobs were alleged to receive less than the lowest male common labor rate, the Board also recognized that, because of the wartime pressures that resulted in a shortage of male workers, "the male common labor rates may be unstable and out of balance with the semi-skilled and skilled jobs."[33] Furthermore, even when the male common labor rate was in balance with the higher rates, the Board was unable to tell from the record that the lowest rated women's job would necessarily be moved up in every plant to the lowest rated male job.[34] Thus, for all these reasons, the Board concluded that:

> when it comes to attaching rates to the [women's] jobs it is not possible to find that there is any one figure representing this undervaluation in the case of any given plant, much less in the case of all plants of a company combined together.[35]

Because of these difficulties the Board concluded that it should limit its recommendations to a partial reduction in these differentials without attempting to indicate which of them should be corrected by collective bargaining. Rather, it approved the principle of a single evaluation line for all jobs in a plant regardless of whether the jobs are performed by men or women, but recommended that the *parties* negotiate a formula for narrowing any reason-

---

[30] 28 War Lab. Rep. 666 (1945).

[31] *Id.* at 685, 689.

[32] *Id.* at 689.

[33] *Id.*

[34] *Id.*

[35] *Id.*

able wage rate differentials existing between men's and women's jobs.[36] The parties were unable to come to an agreement, however, and the Board's final recommendation was that a fund should be established to increase the rates of certain women's jobs by four cents per hour.

A close examination of the *General Electric and Westinghouse* decision shows, therefore, that in one instance in which it clearly had an opportunity to do otherwise, the War Labor Board chose not to engage itself in job evaluation or job comparisons to determine whether specific job wage rates were the result of sex discrimination. Instead, it recognized the difficulties in making such determinations and relied upon the evaluations performed by the particular employers.[37] Because the Board's term ended on December 31, 1945, just two days after *General Electric and Westinghouse* was made public, there is no later experience to indicate whether there was any practical way in which the Board might have made the comparisons sought by the unions.

For the most part, then, the sex-related wage claims considered by the War Labor Board involved an "equal pay for equal work" doctrine,[38] that is, equal payment for the same tasks on jobs presently or formerly performed by males. When comparisons of dissimilar jobs were requested, the Board generally presumed that the existing wage rates were correct and referred the cases to the disputing parties for negotiation, with the suggestion or order that a job evaluation system be instituted to consider the worth of the job on the basis of content, irrespective of the sex of any incumbent.[39] Generally, however, the Board did not attempt to establish the relative worth of dissimilar jobs and, as the *General Electric and Westinghouse* decision indicates, it found the comparison task beyond its capabilities.

Moreover, as the following section demonstrates, when Congress, nearly twenty years later, considered the problem of sex-based wage discrimination, it was unwilling to adopt even the standard of General Order No. 16, which stated that females should be paid the same rates as males for "comparable quality and quantity of work on the same or similar operations."[40] Rather, in the debates on the Equal Pay Act, Congress specifically deleted from the original bills language that would have prohibited an employer from paying different wages for work of "comparable" character on jobs

---

[36] *Id.* at 691.

[37] This is not to say that job evaluation concepts and their application were not given a boost by War Labor Board policies. Job evaluation was undertaken increasingly by employers to establish or justify wage rates for jobs within certain wage brackets that were worked out with Board officials.

[38] Termination Report at 294.

[39] *Id.*

[40] See pp. 213–16, below.

which required "comparable" skills.[41] In these debates, Congress clearly indicated its rejection of the "comparable work" standard.[42]

II. LEGISLATIVE HISTORY OF THE EQUAL PAY ACT

A. *Congressional Consideration of Sex-Based Compensation Discrimination*

The only time Congress has considered in any detail the question of sex-based compensation discrimination was during the extensive 1962 and 1963 House and Senate Committee Hearings and floor deliberations related to the Equal Pay Act.[43] The legislative history of that act demonstrates Congress' intention to assure that neither courts nor government agencies be given so much discretion that they would become bogged down in attempting to re-structure existing wage compensation systems. The extent to which Congress examined sex-based wage discrimination prior to enactment of the Equal Pay Act contrasts sharply with the hasty and cursory treatment it gave the subject in 1964 in its consideration of Title VII.[44] The 1964 legislative history of Title VII's sex discrimination provision is "notable primarily for its brevity."[45] By comparison, the 1962 and 1963 Equal Pay Act history is unusual in the degree to which Congress sought to eliminate the ambiguities and lack of standards inherent in broad, undefined concepts such as "comparable work" and to substitute and define carefully the standard of "equal work" which it finally adopted.

From a close look at the legislative history of the Equal Pay Act, it is apparent that Congress intended to set strict limits on the standards to be applied in judging claims of sex discrimination in wage compensation. In fact, as discussed below, Congress examined and rejected a theory of discrimination which would have allowed findings of discrimination to be based upon pay differentials for "comparable" male and female jobs. No similar specificity can be found in the history of the sex discrimination provision of Title VII. This contrast is important, because it is a basic principle of statutory construction that a statute dealing with a narrow, precise and specific

---

[41] See the discussion below on pp. 213–16.

[42] *Lemons v. City and County of Denver*, 620 F.2d 228, 22 FEP Cases 959 (10th Cir. 1980) *petition for cert. filed* (No. 80–82); *Schultz v. Wheaton Glass Co.*, 421 F.2d 259, 265 (3rd Cir. 1970), *cert. denied*, 398 U.S. 905 (1970); *Angelo v. Bacharach Instrument Co.*, 555 F.2d 1164, 1174 (3rd Cir. 1977); and *IUE v. Westinghouse*, 17 FEP Cases 16, 21 (M.D. W.Va. 1977).

[43] Fair Labor Standards Act, 29 U.S.C. § 206(d).

[44] See below, pp. 223–30.

[45] *General Electrtic Co. v. Gilbert*, 429 U.S. 125, 143 (1976).

subject should prevail over another governing the subject in more general terms, regardless of the sequence of passage.[46]

In its final form, the Equal Pay Act adopted the "equal work" standard with the requirement that a violation of the Act could not be established unless females were paid less for jobs involving the same skill, effort, responsibility and working conditions as performed by males in the same establishment. As the Supreme Court pointed out in *Corning Glass Works v. Brennan*,[47] Congress intended by passing the Equal Pay Act to prevent "second-guessing the validity of a company's evaluation system."[48] Thus, Congress "did not authorize the Secretary [of Labor] or the Courts to engage in wholesale reevaluation of any employer's pay structure in order to enforce their own conception of economic worth."[49]

B. *The 1962 Congressional Deliberations*

The 1963 Equal Pay Act—the first federal legislation dealing with sex-based compensation discrimination—was the final product of eighteen months of exhaustive committee consideration, hearings, and floor debate over two sessions of Congress in 1962 and 1963.

The initial bills considered by the House in 1962 would have prohibited employers from paying different wages "for work of *comparable* character on jobs the performance of which requires *comparable* skills."[50] The Kennedy Administration strongly supported this concept, and Secretary of Labor Goldberg testified that "I am not impressed when the argument is made that it is difficult or impossible to determine work that is comparable."[51] Both Secretary of Labor Goldberg and Assistant Secretary Esther Peterson urged that the concept of comparable work to determine the

---

[46] *Radzanower v. Touche Ross & Co.*, 426 U.S. 148, 153 (1976); and *Morton v. Mancari*, 417 U.S. 535, 550–51 (1974). In *Mancari*, the Supreme Court found that Title VII's race discrimination provision did not preclude application of an earlier statute giving hiring preferences to Indians. The Court stated that:
> Where there is no clear intention otherwise, a specific statute will not be controlled or nullified by a general one, regardless of the priority of enactment.
417 U.S. at 550–51.

[47] 417 U.S. 188 (1974).

[48] 417 U.S. at 200.

[49] *Brennan v. Prince William Hospital Corp.*; 503 F.2d 282, 285 (4th Cir. 1974), *cert. denied*, 420 U.S. 972 (1975); *Christopher v. State of Iowa*, 559 F.2d 1135, 20 FEP Cases 829, 832 (8th Cir. 1977) (Comparability of jobs insufficient to establish an Equal Pay Act violation); *Horner v. Mary Institute*, 21 FEP Cases 1069, 1074 (8th Cir. 1980); *Kohne v. Imco Container*, 20 EPD ¶30,168 at 11,876 (same) (W.D.Va. 1979); and *Thompson v. Boyle*, 21 FEP Cases 57, 73 (D.D.C. 1979).

[50] See H.R. 8898, 87th Cong., 1st Sess.; and H.R. 10226, 87th Cong. 2d Sess. (emphasis added). Texts of these bills are found in *Hearings Before the Select Subcommittee of Labor on the House Committee on Education & Labor on H.R. 8898, 10266, Part 1*, 87th Cong., 2d Sess. 2–10 (1962) (hereinafter "*1962 House Hearings*").

[51] *1962 House Hearings* at 17.

economic worth of different jobs could be carried out by applying job evalu-
tion systems then in use by industry.[52]

The "comparable work" approach was given additional support by
unions and women's groups. For example, James Carey, who testified on behalf of the Industrial Union Department of the AFL-CIO, stated that the
concept of equal pay for "comparable work" would eliminate three forms of
unequal pay:

(1) Paying lower wages to women on the same job as men.
(2) Changing a man's job by modifying it slightly at a much lower
    rate of pay for women, a rate change not justified by the modi-
    fication.
(3) *Paying women lower wages irrespective of the value of the work
    performed. This occurs in situations where men and women
    work in different types of jobs in the same plant.*[53]

Carey urged that, where the skill, training, education, working conditions,
and other factors "make the value of the job the same, workers should
receive equal pay."[54]

On the other hand, the National Association of Manufacturers warned
that "comparable" was a dubious word, fraught with dispute inviting complications."[55] It cautioned that the bill did not provide any specific basis for
determining which jobs were comparable, and argued that the standard was
"so general and so vague as to give an administrator a grant of power which
could destroy the sound wage structure which many industrial companies
have worked for years to perfect."[56] In its deliberations, Congress adopted
this latter view.

When the House debated the proposed legislation later in 1962, it
amended the bill in order to reject the "comparable work" approach. Representative St. George introduced an amendment to provide for equal pay for
"equal work." As she explained, there is a great difference between the terms
"equal" and "comparable": "The word 'comparable' opens up great
vistas. It gives tremendous latitude to whoever is to be arbitrator in these
disputes."[57] She added that the purpose of the bill was to "produce and
foster equality," and that [w]hen you give this latitude [to the Secretary of
Labor] by using the word 'comparable', you are destroying the main purpose

---

[52] *Id.* at 15–16, 27, 216.

[53] *Id.* at 172–73 (emphasis added).

[54] *Id.* at 173. Similarly, Mort Furay, representing the Restaurant Employees and
Bartenders International Union, argued for the adoption of the concept of equal pay for "equal
value." *1962 House Hearings, Part 1,* at 112–13.

[55] *1962 House Hearings* at 166.

[56] *Id.* at 166.

[57] 108 Cong. Rec. 14767.

of the bill."[58] Similarly, Representative Landrum explained that the "equal work" amendment would prevent:

> the trooping around all over the country of employees of the Labor Department harassing business with their various interpretations of the term "comparable" when "equal" is capable of the same definition throughout the United States.[59]

Representative Zelenko, the Chairman of the Subcommittee that considered the bill, opposed the St. George amendment and read into the record a letter from the Secretary of Labor which argued that "comparable" was a key word in the Administration's proposal and its deletion "could spell defeat for the bill's purpose."[60] He added that he felt legal precedent for using the term "comparable" could be found in the National War Labor Board's use of the term during World War II.[61] Representative St. George responded that "of course, the National [War] Labor Board to which the gentleman refers is rather old hat. I mean it goes back quite a long way."[62] She also stated that the concept of comparability being urged by Congressman Zelenko was actually "equality" for women, which was confused "when we go into these hazy words [such as comparable]."[63]

Congressman Zelenko then mentioned several War Labor Board cases which he asserted applied the standard, set out in General Order No. 16,[64] of equal wage or salary rates for women and men for "comparable quality and quantity of work on the same or similar operations."[65] Despite his objections, the House adopted the St. George amendment and changed the proposed equal pay legislation to require equal pay for "equal work on jobs the performance of which requires equal skills."[66]

In 1962, the Senate also passed a version of the equal pay bill containing the St. George "equal work" amendment, but the Senate bill was a rider to a bill originating in the Foreign Affairs Committee of the House. As a result, there was a conflict between two House committees concerning jurisdiction over the equal pay legislation and the dispute was not resolved in time to have

---

[58] *Id*. at 14768.

[59] *Id*. at 14767. Representative Landrum also objected that the term "comparable" was not defined in the bill and that it gave too much latitude to the Secretary of Labor. June 14, 1962, Cong. Rec. 9726 (daily edition).

[60] 108 Cong. Rec. 14768.

[61] *Id*. See the discussion at pp. 205–12 *supra*.

[62] *Id*.

[63] *Id*.

[64] See pp. 207–08 *supra*.

[65] 108 Cong. Rec. 14769.

[66] 108 Cong. Rec. 14768, and Section 4 of H.R. 11677, as amended.

a conference with the Senate Committee prior to the adjournment of the 87th Congress.[67]

C. *The 1963 Congressional Deliberations*

In early 1963, the House Special Subcommittee on Labor reconvened to consider H.R. 3861 and related bills. H.R. 3861 incorporated the St. George Amendment and would have prohibited employers from paying different wages on the basis of sex "for equal work on jobs the performance of which requires equal skills . . ."[68] As the Supreme Court later noted:

> In both the House and Senate committee hearings, witnesses were highly critical of the Act's definition of equal work and of its exemptions. Many noted that most of American industry used formal, systematic job evaluation plans to establish equitable wage structures in their plants. Such systems, as explained coincidentally by a representative of Corning Glass Works who testified at both hearings, took into consideration four separate factors in determining job value—skill, effort, responsibility and working conditions—and each of these four components was further systematically divided into various subcomponents. Under a job evaluation plan, point values are assigned to each of the subcomponents of a given job, resulting in a total point figure representing a relatively objective measure of the job's value.
>
> In comparison to the rather complex evaluation plans used by industry, the definition of equal work used in the first drafts of the Equal Pay bill was criticized as unduly vague and incomplete. Industry representatives feared that as a result of the bill's definition of equal work, the Secretary of Labor would be cast in the position of second-guessing the validity of a company's job evaluation system. They repeatedly urged that the bill be amended to include an exception for job classification systems, or otherwise to incorporate the language of job evaluation into the bill. Thus Corning's own representative testified:
>
> "Job evaluation is an accepted and tested method of attaining equity in wage relationship.
>
> "A great part of industry is committed to job evaluation by past practice and by contractual agreement as the basis for wage administration.
>
> " 'Skill' alone, as a criterion, fails to recognize other aspects of the job situation that affect job worth.

---

[67] *Hearings Before the House Special Subcommittee on Labor of the Committee on Education and Labor on H.R. 3861 and related bills*, 88th Cong., 1st Sess. 1, No. 284 (1963) (hereinafter *"1963 House Hearings"*).

[68] *Id.* at 3.

"We sincerely hope that this committee in passing legislation to eliminate wage differences based on sex alone, will recognize in its language the general role of job evaluation in establishing equitable rate relationships."[69]

After the 1963 testimony of the Corning Glass Representative, Congressman O'Hara stated: "I think I can speak for all members of the subcommittee when I say that we have no desire to disturb job classification rates established in a particular industry based upon the factors that you have described [i.e., skill, effort, responsibility and working conditions]."[70] Although indicating that the same pay should be given to women who perform the same work as men, he added: "I don't think any of us want to get into a kind of situation where we are trying to equate skill and work input into entirely different kinds of jobs."[71] As an example, he noted that "none of us wants to get into" comparing "the clerk-typist or the stenographer in the business office and the drill press operator in the shop."[72] He then asked Corning's representative how Congress "could make it clear that we do not intend to go around disturbing these relationships based on the factors you described in your testimony. . . ." The response was that the definition of equal work should be changed to include the factors of skill, effort, responsibility and working conditions.[73] The importance of this testimony was later highlighted by the Supreme Court in the *Corning Glass* decision when it observed that:

Indeed, the most telling evidence of congressional intent is the fact that the Act's amended definition of equal work incorporated the specific language of the job evaluation plan described at the hearings by Corning's own representative—that is, the concepts of "skill," "effort," "responsibility," and "working conditions."[74]

Language tracking that proposed by the Corning representative was contained in H.R. 6060, which was reported out of the House Committee and considered by the House as the final Equal Pay Act.[75] This bill, initially introduced by Congressman Goodell, was drafted to amend the Fair Labor Standards Act. It provided for equal pay for "equal work on jobs the performance of which requires equal skill, effort and responsibility and

---

[69] *Corning Glass Works v. Brennan*, 417 U.S. 188, 199–200 (1974) (footnotes omitted).

[70] 1963 *House Hearings* at 239–40.

[71] *Id.* at 240.

[72] *Id.*

[73] *Id.*

[74] 417 U.S. at 201.

[75] 109 Cong. Rec. 9195.

which are performed under similar working conditions"—the standard finally enacted by Congress.[76]

The House debates on H.R. 6060 are unusual in the degree to which several Congressmen set out in detail their understanding of the intent of Congress to prevent the courts and government agencies from requiring the modification of wage rates except in the narrow "equal work" situation envisioned by the bill. These comments are remarkably consistent and indicate that the bill was a bipartisan effort which had received almost unanimous approval of the full Education and Labor Committee after extensive examination of the issues.[77] Several interrelated themes can be found in the House floor debates, most notably the congressional mandates that: (1) dissimilar jobs are not to be compared for purposes of determining whether wage discrimination has occurred; and (2) the role of the courts and federal agencies in this subject area is to be strictly limited.

The remarks of Representative Frelinghuysen are illustrative. He began by noting the differences between the present bill and those considered the previous year, which include the following:

> Sixth. The concept of equal pay for jobs demanding equal skill has been expanded to require also equal effort, responsibility, and similar working conditions. These factors are the core of all job classification systems. They form a legitimate basis for differentials in pay.[78]

Representative Frelinghuysen also stated that administration of the equal pay concept would be expected to be neither "excessive nor excessively wide ranging."[79] He indicated that Congress was seeking to insure that where women and men were performing the same task under the same working con-

---

[76] The Equal Pay Act, § 6 (d) of the Fair Labor Standards Act (29 U.S.C. § 206 (d) (1) (1970)) provides:

> No employer having employees subject to any provisions of this section shall discriminate within any establishment in which such employees are employed, between employees on the basis of sex by paying wages to employees in such establishment at a rate less than the rate at which he pays wages to employees of the opposite sex in such establishment for *equal work on jobs the performance of which requires equal skill, effort and responsibility, and which are performed under similar working conditions*, except where such payment is made pursuant to (i) a seniority system; (ii) a merit system; (iii) a system which measures earnings by quantity or quality of production; or (iv) a differential based on any other factor other than sex: Provided, That an employer who is paying a wage rate differential in violation of this subsection shall not, in order to comply with the provisions of this subsection, reduce the wage rate of any employee (emphasis added).

[77] See 109 Cong. Rec. 9197 (remarks of Reps. Thompson and Griffin) and 109 Cong. Rec. 9198 (remarks of Rep. Halleck).

[78] 109 Cong. Rec. 9195.

[79] *Id.*

ditions, they would be paid the same. But he added that "[i]t is not intended that either the Labor Department or individual employees will be equipped with hunting licenses."[80]

Representative Frelinghuysen also gave several examples of the types of wage differentials which were *not* to be disturbed. He noted that male and female packagers might perform jobs that were identical in every respect except that the male packager might be required to lift the finished heavy crates off the assembly line. The lifting would be a significant difference justifying a different level of pay.[81] Similarly, he cited the wide variety of sales positions, and stated that "mechanical and surface similarities are not to be confused with, or viewed as, basic job evaluation characteristics."[82] Representative Frelinghuysen ended these remarks by noting that:

> Finally, jobs in dispute must be the same in work content, effort, skill and responsibility requirements, and in working conditions. As indicated earlier, it is not intended to compare unrelated jobs, or jobs that have been historically and normally considered by the industry to be different. Violations usually will be apparent, and will almost always occur in the same work area and where the same tasks are performed.[83]

Representative Thompson, Chairman of the Subcommittee that considered the bill, agreed with this explanation, and added that "[t]he language recognizes that there are many factors used to measure the relationship between jobs and which establish a valid basis for a difference in pay. *We do not want to disturb these.*"[84]

Representative Goodell, the sponsor of H.R. 6060, joined the discussion and stated that:

> Last year when the House changed the word "comparable" to "equal" the clear intention was to narrow the whole concept. We went from "comparable" to "equal" meaning that the jobs involved should be virtually identical, that is they would be very much alike or closely related to each other.
>
> We do not expect the Labor Department people to go into an establishment and attempt to rate jobs that are not equal. We do not want to hear the Department say, "Well, they amount to the same thing," and evaluate them so they come up to the same skill or point. We expect this to apply only to jobs that are substantially identical or equal. I think that the language in the bill last year

---

[80] *Id.* at 9196.

[81] *Id.*

[82] *Id.*

[83] *Id. Accord*, 109 Cong. Rec. 9209 (remarks of Rep. Goodell).

[84] *Id.* (emphasis added).

which has been adopted this year, and has been further expanded by reference to equal skill, effort, and working conditions, is intended to make this point very clear.[85]

Representative Goodell then agreed with the statement of Representative Griffin that there would be no basis under the statute for comparing an inspector's job with that of an assembler, or that of an inspector who examined a complicated part with a job which involved only a cursory inspection.[86] Representative Thompson added that if two inspectors were doing the same job on the line, but one of them lifted the parts off the line and carried them away, this would be "an additional matter which clearly obliterates any question that they would be the same [work]."[87]

Moreover, Representative Goodell rejected oversimplified comparisons of male and female wages as the basis invoking the Equal Pay Act:

> We do not have in mind the Secretary of Labor's going into an establishment and saying, "Look you are paying the women here $1.75 and the men $2.10. Come on in here, Mr. Employer, and you prove that you are not discriminating on the basis of sex." That would be just the opposite of what we are doing.[88]

Congressman Goodell added that it was the intention of "both sides of the aisle" with respect to the terms skill, effort, responsibility and working conditions to provide:

> A maximum area for the interplay of intangible factors that justify a measurement which does not have to be given a point-by-point evaluation. In this concept, we want the private enterprise system, employer and employees and a union, if there is a union, and the employers and employees if there is not a union, to have a *maximum degree of discretion* in working out the evaluation of the employee's work and how much he should be paid for it.[89]

He explained further:

> It is not necessary for an employer to have an elaborate and formal or written job classification system to qualify for exemptions under this bill *or to prove that he is not discriminating on the basis of sex.* If he has a reasonable standard of differentiation, the Labor Department is not to come in, even, and judge the reasonableness or

---

[85] *Id.* at 9197.

[86] *Id.* at 9197–98.

[87] *Id.* at 9198.

[88] *Id.* at 9208.

[89] *Id.* at 9198 (emphasis added). See also *Id.* at 9209 (remarks of Rep. Goodell).

unreasonableness of this differentiation among employees, except as it shows a clear pattern of discrimination against sex.[90]

Finally, Congressman Goodell described the limited role of the Secretary of Labor and courts in this subject area:

> It is not intended that the Secretary of Labor or the courts will substitute their judgment for the judgment of the employer and his experts who have established and applied a bona fide job rating system. It is not the business of the Secretary of Labor to write job evaluations or judge the merits of job evaluation systems.[91]

As this review of the history of the Equal Pay Act demonstrates, Congress expended a great deal of effort over a two-year period in determining precisely what conduct could be considered compensation discrimination based upon sex. Congress rejected the concept that the courts or administrative agencies should become involved in the application of a standard based upon the undefinable concept of "comparable work."[92] It chose, rather, the equal work standard and determined that wage discrimination claims could not be maintained in the absence of a showing that the female claimants were performing substantially the same work as males. To accept the theory that Title VII permits the courts to make a comparison of the value contributed to the employer by "comparable" jobs would undo this painstaking work of Congress and place the courts and agencies into an area of inquiry which Congress specifically indicated should not be entered.

III. APPLYING THE EQUAL PAY ACT'S EQUAL WORK STANDARD

As already discussed, the Equal Pay Act is quite specific in detailing what the government (formerly the Department of Labor, now the EEOC) must show to prove a violation.[93] It must establish that the employer pays differing wages to employees of opposite sexes:

- Within the same establishment;
- For equal work on jobs the performance of which requires equal skill, effort and responsibility; and
- Which are performed under similar working conditions.

---

[90] *Id.* at 9208 (emphasis added).

[91] *Id.* at 9209.

[92] See the cases cited in note 42, *supra*.

[93] The text of the Equal Pay Act is set out in note 76, *supra*.

If the jobs are not "equal" under all of these standards, no violation will be found. Obviously, a factual analysis of each particular case is required.

Furthermore, if the EEOC shows that the employer is paying women less than men for equal work, there are four statutory exceptions (also called affirmative defenses) which may permit such pay differentials. These are situations in which the unequal payments are made pursuant to:

- A seniority system;
- A merit system;
- A system which measures earnings by quantity or quality of production; or
- A differential based on any other factor other than sex.

The employer has the burden of proving if any of these exceptions applies.

For the purpose of this discussion, the most important aspect of the statute is its requirement that the employer pay men and women equally for work on jobs which require equal (a) skill, (b) effort, and (c) responsibility and (d) are performed under similar working conditions. To establish the employer's liability, the EEOC must show that the relevant jobs are equal under all four of these factors.[94] If one element is not shown, the jobs are not considered equal. The four factors are not defined by the statute, however, and court interpretation has been required.

The courts generally have found that to prove a violation, it is not necessary that the jobs be absolutely equal or identical. It is sufficient that they are "substantially equal."[95] This interpretation prevents employers from creating artificial job classifications which, although not substantially different, might be used as a way to escape the requirements of the Equal Pay Act.[96] Likewise, actual duties, and not mere job titles, are determinative.[97] The courts have also noted that the issue is "not what skills are possessed by the particular individuals, but whether the duties actually performed require or utilize those additional skills."[98] Perhaps most significant is the emphasis which court decisions give to the actual "job content," holding it to be the

---

[94] See *Marshall v. Building Maintenance Corp.*, 16 EPD ¶ 8153 (D. Conn. 1977) (light and heavy duty cleaning jobs compared).

[95] *Shultz v. Wheaton Glass Co.*, 421 F.2d 259, 9 FEP Cases 502, 506 (3d Cir. 1970), *cert. denied*, 398 U.S. 905 (duties of male and female selector-packers found equal); and *Angelo v. Bacharach Instrument Co.*, 555 F.2d 1164, 14 FEP Cases 1778, 1787 (3rd Cir. 1977) (light and heavy assembly jobs are not equivalent).

[96] See *Shultz v. Wheaton Glass Co.*, 421 F.2d 259.

[97] 29 C.F.R. § 800.121.

[98] *DiSalvo v. Chamber of Commerce*, 416 F. Supp. 844, 13 FEP Cases 636, 643 (W.D. Mo. 1976), *aff'd in relevant part*, 568 F.2d 593 (8th Cir. 1978), where the court found the employer unlawfully paid disparate wages to male and female associate editors.

"controlling factor" under the Equal Pay Act.[99] Accordingly, if the job functions are dissimilar, unequal pay to females probably will not establish a violation of the Equal Pay Act.

Thus, if an Equal Pay Act violation cannot be shown by evidence that an employer pays male and female employees differently on the basis of unequal job content and functions, it then becomes particularly important to determine whether such a wage differential may nevertheless violate Title VII of the Civil Rights Act. Indeed, the answer to that question may determine whether the "comparable worth" interpretation may be applied under existing statutory schemes.

IV. THE STATUTORY RELATIONSHIP BETWEEN THE EQUAL PAY ACT AND TITLE VII

A. *The Bennett Amendment*

As noted at the outset, Title VII of the Civil Rights Act of 1964[100] is a much broader statute than the Equal Pay Act in terms of prohibiting various types of discrimination. It prevents employers from discriminating on the basis of "race, color, religion, sex, or national origin." These prohibitions apply to numerous types of employment situations such as hiring, work assignment, transfers, promotions, layoffs and discharges, as well as compensation. Through Title VII, Congress assured that all qualified persons would have equal access to job opportunities. Clearly, by enacting Title VII, Congress expressed its awareness of sex discrimination and its determination to provide qualified women an equal opportunity to employment benefits on the same basis as males.

Although Title VII has a broad reach, it is significant that Congress exempted specific types of employment practices from its prohibitions. For example, Section 703(h) of the statute [101] states that it shall not be unlawful for an employer to apply different standards of compensation, or different terms, conditions, or privileges of employment where the differences are part of:

• A bona fide seniority system;

• A merit system; or

---

[99] See *Calage v. Univ. of Tennessee*, 400 F. Supp. 32, 13 FEP Cases 1147, 1141 (E.D. Tenn. 1975), *aff'd*, 544 F.2d 297, 13 FEP Cases 1153 (6th Cir. 1976) (compared duties of male and female catering managers); *Angelo v. Bacharach Instrument Co., supra*, 555 F.2d 1164, 14 FEP Cases at 1787; *Shultz v. Wheaton Glass Co., supra*, 421 F.2d at 265, 9 FEP Cases at 506; *Orr v. MacNeil & Son, Inc.*, 511 F.2d 166, 10 FEP Cases 694 (5th Cir. 1975).

[100] 42 U.S.C. §§ 2000e, *et seq.*

[101] 42 U.S.C. § 2000e-2(h) [Section 703 (h)].

224 COMPARABLE WORTH: ISSUES AND ALTERNATIVES

- A system which measures earnings by quantity or quality of production.[102]

This section has been read expansively by the courts to define what constitutes discrimination and to permit employment practices which otherwise might have been subject to statutory prohibition.[103]

Section 703(h) also contains another more specific provision—called the "Bennett Amendment"—which exempts compensation claims from Title VII's coverage if the employer's compensation system is "authorized" by the Equal Pay Act. The Bennett Amendment states:

> It shall *not be an unlawful employment practice* under this title for any employer to differentiate upon the basis of sex in determining the amount of wages or compensation paid or to be paid to employees of such employer *if such differentiation is authorized by the provisions of section 6(d) of the Fair Labor Standards Act of 1938,* as amended (29 U.S.C. 206(d) [i.e., the Equal Pay Act]. (Emphasis added).

A major area of inquiry with respect to the comparable worth interpretation of Title VII, therefore, is whether the Bennett Amendment was intended (1) to incorporate into Title VII the substantive "equal work" standard of the Equal Pay Act, and (2) to mandate that no sex-based compensation discrimination claim could be upheld unless the "equal work" standard was violated. As shown below, the legislative history and several court decisions suggest that the Equal Pay Act standard is the exclusive standard Congress intended to be used in determining whether a sex-based wage differential violates Title VII.

---

[102] The first clause of Section 703 (h) states:

(h) Notwithstanding any other provision of this title, it shall not be an unlawful employment practice for an employer to apply different standards of compensation, or different terms, conditions, or privileges of employment pursuant to a bona fide seniority or merit system, or a system which measures earnings by quantity or quality of production or to employees who work in different locations, provided that such differences are not the result of an intention to discriminate because of race, color, religion, sex or national origin; . . .

[103] See *International Brotherhood of Teamsters v. United States*, 431 U.S. 324, 353–54 (1977) (Section 703 (h) protects neutral seniority systems even if they perpetuate the effects of past discrimination); *Hinton v. Lee Way Motor Freight, Inc.*, 412 F. Supp. 625, 628–29 (E.D. Okla. 1975), *and cases there cited* (Seniority systems that are legal under Title VII may not be attacked under 42 U.S.C. § 1981); *Pettway v. American Cast Iron Pipe Co.*, 576 F.2d 1157, 1191–92 n. 37 (5th Cir. 1978), *cert. denied*, 431 U.S. 1115 (1979) (same); *United States v. East Texas Motor Freight, Inc.*, 564 F.2d 179 (5th Cir. 1977) (Title VII-sanctioned seniority systems immune from attack under Executive Order 11246); and *United States v. Trucking Management, Inc.*, 20 FEP Cases 342 (D.D.C. 1979) (same). *Cf., Great American Federal Savings & Loan Assn. v. Novotny*, 442 U.S. 366 (1979). (Deprivation of a Title VII right does not provide a right to sue under 42 U.S.C. § 1985 (c) because permitting parallel remedies would undercut Title VII's procedural and administrative requirements and permit recovery in circumstances not contemplated by Congress).

B. *The House Amendment*

H.R. 7152, the House bill ultimately enacted as the Civil Rights Act of 1964, was intended primarily to protect the rights of Blacks and other minorities.[104] As a result, when the bill went to the House floor for consideration, it did not contain any sex discrimination provision, and sex discrimination had never been considered in committee hearings. In fact, "[i]n view of the political pressures which surrounded the bill, it is hardly surprising that no one viewed it as a vehicle to secure equal rights for women."[105]

House floor debates lasted almost two weeks, from January 31, to February 10, 1964. It was not until the penultimate day of debate that an amendment to add sex discrimination was introduced by Representative Howard Smith of Virginia, Chairman of the House Rules Committee and the bill's principal opponent.[106] Congressman Smith asserted that he was serious about the amendment, but then supported that statement with an irrelevant illustration about a lady constituent who had complained that there was an imbalance of spinsters, which shut off the right of every female to have a husband.[107]

The House debates show that there was very little consideration of what would constitute sex discrimination, and certainly no specific consideration of equal pay issues.[108] Indeed, "the discussion of the sex amendment lasted almost two hours, but the record provides little indication of congressional intent as to the interpretation of the amendment."[109] Accordingly,

[t]he passage of the amendment, and its subsequent enactment into law, came without even a minimum of congressional investigation into an area with implications that are only beginning to pierce the consciousness and conscience of America.[110]

Opposition to the sex discrimination amendment was led by Congresswoman Green who was concerned that it was intended to "clutter up"

---

[104] Editor's Note, *Discrimination Forbidden: Sex Discrimination*, EEOC, Legislative History of Titles VII and XI of the Civil Rights Act of 1964, 3213; Note, *Developments in the Law—Employment Discrimination and Title VII of the Civil Rights Act of 1964*, 84 Harv. L. Rev. 1109, 1166 (1971) (hereinafter "*Developments*"); and 110 Cong. Rec. 2581 (1964) (remarks of Representative Green).

[105] R. Miller, *Sex Discrimination and Title VII of the Civil Rights Act of 1964*, 51 Minn. L. Rev. 877, 880 (1967) (hereinafter "*Miller*").

[106] Miller at 880; Note, *Employer Dress and Appearance Codes and Title VII of the Civil Rights Act of 1964*, 46 So. Cal. L. Rev. 965, 968 (1973).

[107] 110 Cong. Rec. 2577 (1964). The woman had blamed the government for creating the imbalance by engaging in wars that had killed off large numbers of eligible males. *Id.*

[108] Miller, 51 Minn. L. Rev. at 880–82.

[109] *Id.* at 882.

[110] *Developments*, 84 Harv. L. Rev. at 1167. See also 46 So. Cal. L. Rev. at 968 ("The late introduction of the sex amendment precluded extensive consideration of the scope of its applicability or the broad impact that such an amendment might have on society.")

the bill to assure its defeat and destroy the primary purpose of the legislation to end discrimination against Blacks.[111] She also noted that

> those gentlemen of the House who are most strong in their support of women's rights this afternoon, probably gave us the most opposition when we considered the bill which would grant equal pay for equal work just a very few months ago. I say I welcome the conversion and hope it is of long duration.[112]

Congresswoman Green also opposed the amendment because it had never been considered by any committee prior to its introduction.[113]

Because of this history of the Title VII sex discrimination provision, one commentator has concluded:

> Hence, the sex provisions of Title VII can be viewed more as an accidental result of political maneuvering than as a clear expression of congressional intent to bring equal job opportunities to women.[114]

Similarly, the Fifth Circuit, sitting *in banc,* determined that "[w]ithout more extensive consideration, Congress in all probability did not intend for its proscription of sexual discrimination to have significant and sweeping implications."[115] The court reasoned that without a stronger congressional mandate, it "should not therefore extend the coverage of the Act to situations of questionable application. . . ."[116]

Thus, in contrast to the extensive consideration given by Congress to the implications of the Equal Pay Act for employer compensation systems, there was no discussion at all in the Title VII debates that would indicate that when the House initially passed that legislation, it had even considered the problem of sex-based compensation discrimination, much less decided to adopt a new and different approach to that problem.

C. *Senator Clark's Memorandum*

When the civil rights bill was considered by the Senate after it had passed the House, however, the Senate "paid especial attention to the provisions of the Equal Pay Act."[117] The House-passed bill with the new sex discrimina-

---

[111] 110 Cong. Rec. 2581, 2584, 2720–21.

[112] *Id.* Congresswoman Green had been a strong supporter of the Equal Pay Act and previously had introduced equal pay legislation.

[113] 110 Cong. Rec. 2582, 2720–21. *And see*, Miller, 51 Min. L. Rev. at 880. ("In fact the matter of sex discrimination had not even been considered during the hearings.")

[114] Miller, 51 Minn. L. Rev. at 884.

[115] *Willingham v. Macon Telegraph Publishing Co.*, 507 F.2d 1084, 1090 (5th Cir. 1975) (*in banc*).

[116] *Id.*

[117] *General Electric v. Gilbert*, 429 U.S. 125, 143 (1976).

tion provision went directly to the Senate floor. After three weeks of debate, Senator Clark, one of Title VII's floor managers, prepared a memorandum which was read into the Congressional Record to address questions and deal with objections that had been raised regarding the meaning of the bill. One of the explanations makes it evident that Congress intended that the Equal Pay Act standards would be controlling under the Civil Rights bill:

> Objection. The sex antidiscrimination provisions of the bill duplicate the coverage of the Equal Pay Act of 1963. But more than this, they extend far beyond the scope and coverage of the Equal Pay Act. They do not include the limitation in that act with respect to equal work on jobs requiring equal skills in the same establishments, and thus, cut across different jobs.
>
> Answer: The Equal Pay Act is a part of the wage hour law, with different coverage and with numerous exemptions unlike Title VII. Furthermore, under Title VII, jobs can no longer be classified as to sex, except where there is a rational basis for discrimination on the ground of bona fide occupational qualification. *The standards in the Equal Pay Act for determining discrimination as to wages of course, are applicable to the comparable situation under Title VII.*[118]

The significance of the memorandum is that even before any reference to the Equal Pay Act had been made in Title VII through the Bennett Amendment, the bill's sponsors understood that the Act's standards would assure that sex discrimination wage claims would not be broadened to "cut across different jobs" and be applied to jobs that were not "equal." The objection clearly expressed the concern that Title VII might be construed as permitting an equal pay violation to be found where different jobs were involved. Senator Clark's reply indicates that when different jobs were involved, the Equal Pay Act's legal standards would be applied to restrict the scope of Title VII.

D. *The Addition of the Bennett Amendment*

Later in the debates, Senator Bennett introduced his proposed amendment which, as noted above (p. 224), permits an employer to differentiate in compensation upon the basis of sex if the difference is "authorized" by the Equal Pay Act. Because cloture had been invoked before the amendment was introduced, there was almost no opportunity for debate or development of detailed legislative history. Nonetheless, Senator Bennett clearly stated that, "[t]he purpose of my amendment is to provide that in the event of

---

[118] 110 Cong. Rec. 7217 (emphasis added).

conflicts [with Title VII], the provisions of the Equal Pay Act shall not be nullified."[119]

E. *Congressman Celler's Statement*

After Title VII passed the Senate, it was sent back to the House for consideration of the Senate amendments, including the Bennett Amendment. Immediately before House passage, Congressman Celler, the bill's original sponsor and the floor leader in the House, expressed the view of the House that sex-based compensation claims would not satisfy Title VII unles the Equal Pay Act's standards were met. He stated that the Bennett Amendment:

> [p]rovides that compliance with the Fair Labor Standards Act as amended satisfies the requirement of the title barring discrimination because of sex—section 703(b) [sic] [703(h)].[120]

---

[119] *Id.* The entire debate when the Bennett Amendment was adopted is as follows:
Mr. BENNETT. Mr. President, I yield myself 2 minutes.
The PRESIDING OFFICER. The amendment will be stated.
The legislative clerk read as follows: On page 44, line 15, immediately after the period, it is proposed to insert the following new sentence: "It shall not be an unlawful employment practice under this title for any employer to differentiate upon the basis of sex in determining the amount of the wages or compensation paid or to be paid to employees of such employer if such differentiation is authorized by the provisions of section 6(d) of the Fair Labor Standards Act of 1938, as amended (29 U.S.C. 206 (d))."
Mr. BENNETT. Mr. President, after many years of yearning by members of the fair sex in this country, and after very careful study by the appropriate committees of Congress, last year Congress passed the so-called Equal Pay Act, which became effective only yesterday.
By this time, programs have been established for the effective administration of this act. Now, when the civil rights bill is under consideration, in which the word 'sex' has been inserted in many places, I do not believe sufficient attention may have been paid to possible conflicts between the wholesale insertion of the word 'sex' in the bill and in the Equal Pay Act. *The purpose of my amendment is to provide that in the event of conflicts, the provisions of the Equal Pay Act shall not be nullified.*
I understand that the leadership in charge of the bill have agreed to the amendment as a proper technical correction of the bill. If they will confirm that understanding, I shall ask that the amendment be voted on without asking for the yeas and nays.
Mr. HUMPHREY. The amendment of the Senator from Utah is helpful. I believe it is needed. I thank him for his thoughtfulness. The amendment is fully acceptable.
Mr. DIRKSEN. Mr. President, I yield myself 1 minute.
We were aware of the conflict that might develop because the Equal Pay Act was an amendment to the Fair Labor Standards Act. The Fair Labor Standards Act carries out certain exceptions.
All that the pending amendment does is recognize those exceptions, that are carried in the basic act.
Therefore, this amendment is necessary, in the interest of clarification.
The PRESIDING OFFICER (Mr. Ribicoff in the chair).
The question is on agreeing to the amendment of the Senator from Utah. (Putting the question.)
The amendment was agreed to.
110 Cong. Rec. 13647 (1964) (emphasis added).

[120] 110 Cong. Rec. 15896.

F. *Senator Bennett's 1965 Interpretation*

In 1965, Senator Bennett clarified what he felt was unwarranted confusion over the meaning of the Bennett Amendment.[121] His concern was directed specifically to a law review article[122] which had concluded that there were two possible interpretations of the amendment. The article noted the possibility that the amendment merely incorporated into Title VII the Equal Pay Act's affirmative defenses, but stated that:

> [the Equal Pay Act's language setting out the defenses] is merely clarifying language similar to that which was already in Section 703(h). If the Bennett Amendment was simply intended to incorporate by reference these exceptions into subsection (h), the amendment would have no substantive effect. 111 Cong. Rec. 13359.[123]

The article went on to conclude that if the amendment were to be given any effect, the "more plausible" view was that "it must be interpreted to mean that discrimination in compensation on account of sex does not violate Title VII unless it also violates the Equal Pay Act."[124] Senator Bennett's written interpretation, which he inserted in the record, resolved this conflict by stating in relevant part:

> The amendment therefore means that it is not an unlawful employment practice: . . . (b) to have different standards of compensation for nonexempt employees where such differentiation is not prohibited by the equal pay act amendment to the Fair Labor Standards Act.

---

[121] His remarks were made in the context of a discussion of his proposed amendment to the Senate's cloture rule. He explained that when he called up his amendment during the Title VII debates, he had compiled with the Senate leadership's urging not to explain the amendment. 111 Cong. Rec 13359 (1965). He stated that during the closing two days of the Title VII debate, there were 56 rollcall votes on amendments which were properly before the Senate, and noted that:
> [t]hose 56 votes proceeded in an atmosphere of complete chaos because most of the Senators offering amendments had already used up so much of their allotted hour of debate that there was barely time available to call up many of the amendments and no time to discuss them. This resulted in action by the Senate without the creation of any legislative history. 111 Cong. Rec. 13359.

[122] Berg, *Equal Employment Opportunity Under the Civil Rights Act of 1964*, 31 Brooklyn L. Rev. 62.

[123] As noted above (p. 223), three of the four affirmative defenses contained in the Equal Pay Act already were contained in Section 703 (h) when the Bennett Amendment was adopted. Each statute permits different compensation standards pursuant to a seniority system, a merit system, and a system which measures earnings by quantity or quality of production. The fourth Equal Pay Act defense—differentiation in wages based on a "factor other than sex"—would not need to be incorporated into Title VII by the Bennett Amendment since Title VII would not be arguably applicable unless a factor of sex was alleged as a reason for the compensation differential. For these reasons, the Bennett Amendment would be rendered superfluous and meaningless if it were interpreted only to incorporate the Equal Pay Act's affirmative defenses and not also its substantive "equal work" requirement as the sole basis for sex-based compensation claims.

[124] *Id.*

Simply stated, *the [Bennett] amendment means that discrimination in compensation on account of sex does not violate Title VII unless it also violates the Equal Pay Act.*[125]

Senator Dirksen joined the discussion and agreed that Senator Bennett's just-stated interpretation was the one which he, Senator Humphrey and their staffs had in mind when the Bennett Amendment was adopted by the Senate.[126] He added that: "I trust that this will suffice to clear up in the minds of anyone, whether in the Department of Justice or elsewhere, what the Senate intended when that amendment was accepted."[127]

These significant Congressional statements of Senators Bennett, Clark and Dirksen and Representative Celler obviously were intended to assure that the Equal Pay Act's standards would continue to be the only standard for sex discrimination wage claims under Title VII.[128]

G. *EEOC's Guidelines on Title VII and the Equal Pay Act*

In 1965, shortly after Title VII was enacted, the Equal Employment Opportunity Commission (EEOC) issued an official interpretation of the Bennett Amendment which closely followed the positions of Senators Bennett and Clark and Representative Celler. This interpretation stated:

(a) Title VII requires that its provisions be harmonized with the Equal Pay Act (section 6(d) of the Fair Labor Standards Act of 1938, 29 U.S.C. 205(d)) in order to avoid conflicting interpretations or requirements with respect to situations to which both statutes are applicable. *Accordingly, the Commission interprets section 703(h) to mean that the standards of 'equal pay for equal work' set forth in the Equal Pay Act for determining what is unlawful discrimination in compensation are applicable to Title VII.* However, it is the judgment of the Commission that the employee coverage of the prohibition against discrimination in compensation because of sex is coextensive with that of the other prohibitions in section 703, and is

---

[125] 111 Cong. Rec. 13359 (emphasis added).

[126] 111 Cong. Rec. 13360.

[127] *Id.*

[128] In *Gunther v. County of Washington,* 602 F.2d 882, 20 FEP Cases 792 (9th Cir. 1979), *pet. reh'g denied,* 22 FEP Cases 1650 (1980), *petition for cert. filed,* the court took a contrary view of the legislative history. The *Gunther* analysis of this history is discussed below at pp. 237–40.

For another approach to the relationship between the Equal Pay Act and Title VII which contrasts with and reaches opposite conclusions from those in this paper, see R. Blumrosen, *Wage Discrimination, Job Segregation, and Title VII of the Civil Rights Act of 1964,* 12 U. Mich. J. L. Ref. 399 (1979).

not limited by section 703(h) to those employees covered by the Fair Labor Standards Act (emphasis added).[129]

In 1972, however, EEOC rewrote the guideline to provide as follows:

Sec. 1604.8 Relationship of Title VII to the Equal Pay Act.

(a) The employee coverage of the prohibitions against discrimination based on sex contained in Title VII is co-extensive with that of the other prohibitions contained in Title VII and is not limited by Section 703(h) to those employees covered by the Fair Labor Standards Act.

(b) *By virtue of Section 703(h), a defense based on the Equal Pay Act may be raised in a proceeding under Title VII.*

(c) Where such a defense is raised the Commission will give appropriate consideration to the interpretations of the Administrator, Wage and Hour Division, Department of Labor, but will not be bound thereby (emphasis added).[130]

Paragraph (b) of this more recent guideline states that an Equal Pay Act defense may be raised in a Title VII proceeding. On its face, therefore, the 1972 guideline would appear to limit Title VII sex compensation suits to the Equal Pay standards. Private plaintiffs, however, have attempted to construe the 1972 guideline as supporting their view that the Bennett Amendment only was intended to incorporate the statutory exemptions of the Equal Pay Act into Title VII. But the guideline is not that specific and would appear to provide an employer *any* Equal Pay Act defense, which would include a defense that the substantive equal work requirement had not been established by the plaintiff.

Moreover, insofar as the 1972 EEOC guideline has been advanced as supporting the more limited view of the Bennett Amendment, the courts have not accepted the argument. Those courts which have considered both EEOC interpretations have held that the Bennett Amendment incorporated the "equal work" standard into Title VII. The earlier EEOC interpretation, which was contemporaneous with the enactment of Title VII, was found to be consistent with that view.[131] The courts have followed the principle established in *General Electric v. Gilbert*[132] that deference should not be given to a

---

[129] 30 Fed. Reg. 14927 (Dec. 2, 1965), formerly 29 C.F.R. § 1604.7 (1965).

[130] 29 C.F.R. § 1604.8.

[131] See *IUE v. Westinghouse Electric Corp.*, 17 FEP Cases 16, 22 (N.D. W.Va. 1977); and *IUE v. Westinghouse Electric Corp.*, 19 FEP Cases 450, 455 (D.N.J. 1979), *interlocutory appeal certified*, 19 FEP Cases 1028 (D.N.J. 1979), *appeal docketed*, Nos. 79-1893 and 79-1894 (3d Cir.), argued March 20, 1980.

[132] 429 U.S. 125, 142 (1976).

later EEOC guideline which contradicts an earlier position of the agency which was adopted at a time closer to the enactment of the statute.[133]

V. COURT DECISIONS DISCUSSING THE COMPARABLE WORTH THEORY

As previously discussed, the courts construing the Equal Pay Act have held consistently that Congress rejected the "comparable work" concept and mandated that the Act should not be applied by judges and federal administrators to enforce their own conceptions of economic worth or to require widespread reevaluation of an employer's compensation structure.[134] Many court decisions to date have held that this Congressional directive is carried out by consistent application of the "equal work" standard under both statutes.

In construing both the Equal Pay Act and Title VII's provisions, the courts have found that unequal pay for women in jobs with the same work content and the same skill, effort and responsibility requirements as jobs done by men violated both acts. For example, in *Laffey v. Northwestern Airlines,*[135] the court held that both Title VII and the Equal Pay Act could be violated by payment of lower salaries and pensions to female stewardesses whose work was "equal" to that of male pursers. Thus, it was found that employer conduct that violates the Equal Pay Act also can violate Title VII.

---

[133] In *Gunther v. County of Washington*, 602 F.2d 882, 20 FEP Cases 792, 798 & n. 10 (9th Cir. 1979), *pet. for reh'g denied*, 22 FEP Cases 1650 (1980), *petition for cert. filed*, the court stated without elaboration that the earlier EEOC guideline was not inconsistent with the court's view that the Bennett Amendment should be construed narrowly. The court, however, failed to discuss the most relevant language of the 1965 guideline which provided that the standards of the Equal Pay Act for determining discrimination would apply to Title VII. Moreover, the court did not appear to be aware that a later, and possibly inconsistent, version of the EEOC's guideline has been published. Also, the court did not comment on the fact that the 1965 guideline's language did not state that it adopted the narrowed interpretation of the Bennett Amendment—a significant omission in view of the detailed legislative history discussed above.

[134] See pp. 213 *supra*.

[135] 567 F.2d 429, 446 (D.C. Cir. 1976), *cert. denied*, 434 U.S. 1086 (1976). In *Laffey*, the court emphasized that Title VII was not intended to supplant the Equal Pay Act in cases involving sex-based wage discrimination claims, stating:

> Although Title VII reaches farther than the Equal Pay Act to protect groups other than those sex-based classes and to proscribe discrimination in many facets of employment additional to compensation, nowhere have we encountered an indication that Title VII was intended either to supplant or be supplanted by the Equal Pay Act in the relatively small area in which the two are congruent. On the contrary, we are satisfied that the provisions of both acts should be read *in pari materia*, and neither should be interpreted in a manner that would undermine the other. In *Orr v. Frank R. MacNeill & Son, Inc.*, the Fifth Circuit declared that "[t]he sex discrimination provision of Title VII of the Civil Rights Act of 1964 must be construed in harmony with the Equal Pay Act of 1963." We agree, and we now so hold (footnote omitted) 567 F.2d at 445–46.

Moreover, a widely accepted rule has developed that the wage discrimination requirements of the Equal Pay Act and Title VII must be read *"in pari materia"* (that is, in harmony) and that a person charging wage discrimination based upon sex has the same burden of proof under either statute.[136]

Under these cases, an equal pay violation under Title-VII can be shown only if the males' and females' jobs are "substantially equal"—the same standard as the Equal Pay Act. With occasional exception,[137] the decided

---

The court further held that the lower payments to female stewardesses whose work was "equal" to male pursers would be "immune from attack under Title VII only if it comes within one of the four enumerated exceptions to the Equal Pay Act." 567 F.2d at 446. This holding is consistent with the view that the same standards apply to both statutes. The issue of whether women must receive equal pay even if their jobs are *different* was not discussed by the *Laffey* decision.

[136] See, *e.g., Lemons v. City and County of Denver*, 620 F.2d 228, 22 FEP Cases 959 (10th Cir. 1980) *petition for cert. filed* (No. 80-82); *Schultz v. Wheaton Glass Co.,* 421 F.2d 259 (3d Cir. 1970), *cert. denied*, 398 U.S. 905 (1970); *Orr v. Frank R. MacNeill & Son, Inc.*, 511 F.2d 166 (5th Cir. 1975), *cert. denied*, 423 U.S. 856 (1975); *Ammons v. Zia Co.*, 448 F.2d 117 (10th Cir. 1971); *Calage v. University of Tennessee*, 544 F.2d 297 (6th Cir. 1977); *Laffey v. Northwest Airlines, Inc.*, 567 F.2d 429 (D.C. Cir. 1976); *Keyes v. Lenoir Rhyne College*, 15 FEP Cases 914 (W.D. N.C. 1976), *aff'd*, 552 F.2d 579 (4th Cir.), *cert. denied*, 434 U.S. 904 (1977); *DiSalvo v. Chamber of Commerce of Greater Kansas City*, 568 F.2d 593 (8th Cir. 1978); *Burdine v. Texas Dept. of Community Affairs*, 608 F.2d 563, 21 FEP Cases 975 (5th Cir. 1979) *cert. granted*, (No. 79-1764); *Wetzel v. Liberty Mutual Insurance Co.*, 449 F.Supp. 398, 407 (W.D. Pa. 1978); *Chrapliwy v. Uniroyal, Inc.*, 15 FEP Cases 795 (N.D. Ind. 1977); *Cullari v. East-West Gateway Council*, 21 FEP Cases 698, 707 (E.D. Mo. 1978); *Patterson v. Western Development Labs*, 13 FEP Cases 772, 775-76 (N.D. Cal. 1976); *Kohne v. Imco Container Co.*, 20 EPD ¶30,168 (W.D. Va. 1979); *Johnson v. University of Bridgeport*, 20 FEP Cases 1766, 1769-70 (D. Conn. 1979); *Molthan v. Temple University*, 442 F.Supp. 448 (E.D. Pa. 1977); and *Pedreyra v. Cornell Prescription Pharmacies, Inc.*, 465 F.Supp. 936, 944 (D. Col. 1979).

[137] A primary opposing case is *Gunther v. County of Washington*, 20 FEP Cases 792 (9th Cir. 1979) *pet. for reh'g denied*, 22 FEP Cases 1650 (1980), *petition for cert. filed*. The *Gunther* decision is discussed in detail in footnotes 128 and 133 and pp. 237-40. In *Gunther*, the Ninth Circuit based its decision in part on its application of *Manhart v. City of Los Angeles Department of Power & Water*, 553 F.2d 581 (9th Cir. 1977), *vacated and remanded*, 435 U.S. 702 (1978). That decision does not support the theory that dissimilar jobs may be compared to prove sex-based compensation claims, for the Ninth Circuit stated that the female and male employees were "identically situated." 553 F.2d at 583. The dispute, rather, concerned whether Title VII was violated by the employer's requirement that females make larger pension contributions than males and whether the employer's policy was based upon a "factor other than sex" under the Equal Pay Act's affirmative defenses. The Court's statement that "all the Bennett Amendment did was to incorporate the exemptions of the Equal Pay Act into Title VII" (553 F.2d at 590), was made in the context of the Court's conclusion that Senator Humphrey had erroneously construed the Bennett Amendment when he stated that certain types of pension plans would be exempted from Title VII's prohibitions. The Court was concerned only with defining the scope of the Equal Pay Act's exemptions and not with whether wage rate claims could be asserted in other than equal work situations. In *Greenspan v. Automobile Club of Michigan*, 22 FEP Cases 184, 203-08 & n. 23 (E.D. Mich. 1980), the court cited the *Gunther* decision for the proposition that "Title VII appears to encompass claims of comparable work not being comparably rewarded which do not achieve the specificity or detail of an Equal Pay Act claim." It should be noted, however, that the *Greenspan* decision did not analyze the issue but merely cited to the Ninth Circuit's decision. Moreover, the court's analysis of the compensation discrimination issues was limited to determining the "same jobs" as males. Accordingly, the court in *Greenspan* did not apply the comparable work approach in its actual decision. The citation to *Gunther*, therefore, should be regarded as dictum.

cases suggest that unsuccessful female plaintiffs who fail to prove equal work cannot proceed with a sex-based compensation claim under Title VII on any other basis.

For example, in *Orr v. Frank R. MacNeill & Son, Inc.*, the court dismissed a Title VII salary discrimination claim where the plaintiff was asserting that her job as a department head was *just as important* as that of the male department heads, even though the work content on the job was different.[138] She introduced evidence of intentional discrimination, and the district court specifically found that the president of the insurance agency had stated that the vice-president would not pay the plaintiff as much as he would have paid a man. The court held, therefore, that the employer had violated Title VII. The Fifth Circuit reversed holding, on the basis of the Bennett Amendment, that the Equal Pay Act test of "equal work" was the test to be applied in Title VII wage discrimination cases and that this standard had not been met by plaintiff. The Fifth Circuit explained that the Equal Pay Act and Title VII must be construed harmoniously: "To establish a case under Title VII it must be proved that a wage differential was based upon sex and that there was the performance of equal work for unequal compensation." 511 F.2d at 171.

Similarly, in *Ammons v. Zia Co.*,[139] the female plaintiff was performing a job with different content but which she claimed merited the same pay as jobs performed by men. She alleged she was denied higher compensation because of her sex in violation of Title VII. The Tenth Circuit rejected these claims, stating that "[t]o establish a case of discrimination under Title VII, one must prove a differential in pay based on sex for performing 'equal' work. . . ." 448 F.2d at 119–20. The court added that since "equal work" within the meaning of the Equal Pay Act had not been established, it did not have to reach the question of whether one of the Equal Pay Act's affirmative defenses was applicable.

The Tenth Circuit recently reaffirmed this interpretation of Title VII in *Lemons v. City and County of Denver,* stating:

> The equal pay for "comparable work" concept had been rejected by Congress in favor of "equal work" in 1962. The Bennett Amendment is generally considered to have the equal pay/equal work concept apply to Title VII in the same way as it applies in the Equal Pay Act.[140]

---

[138] 511 F.2d 166, 171 (5th Cir. 1975), *cert. denied*, 423 U.S. 865 (1965).

[139] 448 F.2d 117 (10th Cir. 1971).

[140] 620 F.2d 228, 22 FEP Cases 959, 960 (1980) *petition for cert. filed* (No. 80–82). *Fitzgerald v. Sirloin Stockade*, 22 FEP 262 (10th Cir. 1980), has been cited for the proposition that the Tenth Circuit now holds that Title VII compensation claims may be broader than those under the Equal Pay Act. That is not the view of the Tenth Circuit. The language in *Fitzgerald* is confused and it is difficult to tell what the court was holding. *Fitzgerald* involved an individual, not a class, claim. Moreover, the relevant legislative histories and cases were not discussed. In-

In *Keyes v. Lenoir Rhyne College, supra,* a female college professor sued the college under Title VII and the Equal Pay Act, seeking higher pay for herself and a class of female faculty members. She introduced evidence that they had received "less pay than *comparably situated* men." 23 WH Cases 319, 323, 15 FEP Cases 914, 918 (W.D.N.C. 1976) (emphasis added). The district court applied the "equal work" standard to plaintiff's claims as a whole without distinguishing between the wage differential claims under Title VII and the Equal Pay Act:

> Plaintiff has the initial burden of not only proving that a disparity in salary existed between male and female teachers but that such disparity existed in such positions requiring *equal work,* equal skill, effort and responsibility, and which are performed under similar working conditions. 23 WH Cases at 329 (emphasis added) (citation omitted).

The district court rejected the female faculty members' wage discrimination claim and observed that Ms. Keyes "made no attempt to show that the work performed by males and females was equal, or that the jobs were substantially equal or the same." 23 WH Cases at 329. The court also noted that the teaching positions being compared required a wide variety of skills and qualifications. The district court's judgment was affirmed by the Fourth Circuit on the basis that:

> While the evidence revealed that the average male faculty salary was higher than that of females, there was no showing of any salary differential for teaching positions which were substantially equal. . . . *Keyes v. Lenoir Rhyne College*, 552 F.2d 579, 580 (4th Cir. 1977).[141]

These decisions are typical of the cases in holding that, unless the existence of equal work can be established, a female plaintiff cannot recover under Title VII. Further, some courts have adopted the corollary that differences in male and female compensation that do not violate the Equal Pay

deed, the Tenth Circuit failed to cite even its earlier decision in *Ammons v. Zia*, 448 F.2d 117 (1971) which is one of the leading cases to hold that sex-based discrimination claims that do not meet the equal work standard *cannot* be maintained under Title VII. After *Fitzgerald*, the Tenth Circuit in *Lemons v. Denver* reaffirmed the *Ammons* decision, adopted our view of the Bennett Amendment, and stated that employer reliance upon the labor market was a defense to comparable worth claims.

[141] In *Molthan v. Temple University*, 442 F.Supp. 448 (E.D. Pa. 1977), a female physician employed by Temple University brought an action under Title VII and the Equal Pay Act wherein she alleged, *inter alia*, that she and other female physicians "earned a lesser salary than males working in comparable positions in other clinical laboratories." 442 F.Supp. at 450. The court rejected the wage claims under both Title VII and the Equal Pay Act, holding she had failed to show that she received less salary for performing work equal to work performed by men. The court held that sex-based wage discrimination claims are not actionable under Title VII unless the differentials in wages "run afoul" of the Equal Pay Act. 442 F.Supp. at 454.

Act are "authorized" by the Bennett Amendment for purposes of Title VII,[142] and that "differentiations permitted by the Equal Pay Act are *approved* by reference in Title VII cases."[143]

Patterson v. Western Development Labs[144] is particularly interesting because it holds that the "equal work" standard also sets the limits of *race-based* Title VII compensation claims. There, plaintiffs alleged that the average black worker earned substantially less than the average white employee and also that the average pay for black managerial and professional employees was less than that earned by whites. The court found that the cases dealing with sex-based compensation were analogous and that the plaintiff's burden under Title VII was the same as under the Equal Pay Act. The court stated:

> We cannot conceive of any rationale for applying a different legal standard in Title VII actions brought for compensation discrimination based on race.
>
> We conclude that the burden of proof herein is upon plaintiffs to show that different amounts of compensation have been or are being paid to blacks and whites for "equal work" and that plaintiffs herein have made no such showing.

In a number of cases, the courts have rejected assertions of female plaintiffs that a wage discrimination claim could be made under Title VII even though the plaintiffs conceded they were not attempting to prove they were engaged in work that was equal to that performed by males, but only intended to show that they were being paid less for doing jobs determined to be of equal value by the employer. Two decisions involving *Westinghouse Electric* are quite instructive.[145] In those cases, the plaintiffs argued that the employer was intentionally paying lower wages to allegedly female-dominated jobs than to jobs predominantly held by men. The male and female jobs in question admittedly were not of the same job content but the plaintiffs indicated they would show the jobs should have been evaluated as comparable. Both district courts construed the Bennett Amendment as showing that Congress intended to apply the equal work standard to Title VII cases involving sex discrimination in compensation. The legislative histories of Title VII and the Equal Pay Act were read together as evidence that Congress intended to limit the scope of judicial intervention into the business place and prevent businesses from being "subjected to massive job reevaluation which

---

[142] *Id.* at 454.

[143] *Howard v. Ward County*, 418 F.Supp. 494, 503 (D. N.D. 1976) (emphasis added).

[144] 13 FEP Cases 772 (N.D. Cal. 1976).

[145] *IUE v. Westinghouse Electric Corp.*, 17 FEP Cases 16 (N.D. W.Va. 1977); and *IUE v. Westinghouse Electric Corp.*, 19 FEP Cases 450 (D. N.J. 1979), *interlocutory appeal certified*, 19 FEP Cases 1028 (D. N.J. 1979), *appeal docketed*, Nos. 79-1893 and 79-1894 (3rd Cir.), argued orally on March 20, 1980.

would be costly and allow for varied interpretations as to what jobs are comparable."[146]

In the New Jersey *Westinghouse* case, the plaintiffs had argued that, unless Title VII were construed to permit the equal pay claim, female employees might be subjected to intentional wage discrimination in jobs where the employer only employed females. The district court rejected this argument as unrealistic. It stated:

> Before closing this opinion, we would like to briefly comment on plaintiffs' argument that Congress could not conceivably have intended to isolate one form of purposeful discrimination and exempt it from the broad prohibitions of Title VII. They refer to the hypothetical situation whereby, given this court's decision, an employer could isolate a job category which was traditionally all female, arbitrarily cut the wages of that job class in half for the sole reason that its holders were female, and yet not run afoul of the broad remedial provisions of Title VII. . . Even assuming that this would in fact be true, such discrimination could not be maintained. Title VII would still prohibit sex discrimination in hiring, firing, promotion, transfer, classification and terms and conditions of employment and any attempt to perpetuate the effects of such purposefully discriminatory yet allegedly lawful activities would run afoul of these prohibitions. We therefore do not believe that our decision will have the dire consequences predicted by the plaintiffs.[147]

The Ninth Circuit took a different, but not completely contrary approach to wage compensation claims in *Gunther v. County of Washington, Oregon*, 602 F.2d 882, 20 FEP Cases 792 (9th Cir. 1979), reh'g denied, 22 FEP Cases 1650, 23 EPD ¶30,900 (1980). There, jail matrons asserted that their employer violated Title VII by paying them less than male guards. They alleged that their jobs were substantially equal to the male jail guards, and also that even if their jobs were not substantially the same, some of the discrepancy in their wages was nevertheless due to sex discrimination.

In its opinion, the district court dismissed the claims because the female jobs entailed less effort and responsibility, and hence were not "substantially equal" to the jobs performed by the males. The Ninth Circuit affirmed the district court's finding that plaintiffs had not been denied equal pay for equal work, but nevertheless ruled that Title VII might have been violated if plaintiffs could show on remand that "some of the discrepancy in wages was due to sex discrimination." 602 F.2d at 888. In so ruling, the court stated that "problems of proof may present substantial barriers to establishing this kind of discriminatory compensation claim." 602 F.2d at 888.

---

[146] 17 FEP Cases at 21, and 19 FEP Cases at 453.
[147] 19 FEP Cases at 457.

The Ninth Circuit's initial ruling stated that there were two "plausible" interpretations of the Bennett Amendment, but held that the amendment only incorporated the Equal Pay Act's four affirmative defenses into Title VII and did not also impose the "equal work" standard on Title VII as the sole basis for sex-based compensation claims. The court concluded that there was no clear indication of Congressional intent on the question, but the only legislative history considered by the opinion was the short colloquy between Senators Bennett and Dirksen when the Bennett Amendment was passed. (See p. 228, *supra*.) The court did not mention the Clark Memorandum, the Celler statement and the 1965 written statement of Senator Bennett which also recognized the two possible interpretations of the Bennett Amendment, but resolved it by concluding that discrimination in compensation on account of sex does not violate Title VII unless it also violates the Equal Pay Act. The court's failure to fully examine the legislative history of Title VII may have been due, in part, to the failure of the parties to brief the Bennett Amendment issue when the case was first argued.

After the appellate court's initial decision, the County petitioned for rehearing, urging that the Bennett Amendment issue had not been fully presented to the court when it made its original decision. In its supplemental opinion on denial of rehearing, the Ninth Circuit acknowledged that "the parties inadequately presented this issue before the court" (22 FEP Cases at 1651), but then proceeded once again to resolve the questions presented without requesting full briefing from either plaintiffs or the County.

In its supplemental opinion, the Ninth Circuit set forth a substantially different interpretation of the legislative history surrounding the Bennett Amendment than is offered in this paper, but also went on to state that when a female plaintiff attempts to establish a prima face case of wage discrimination based solely on a comparison of the work performed, she would have to meet the equal work standard. The rationale of the Court's supplemental decision bears close examination both because of the court's treatment of the legislative history and its ultimate skepticism of a theory of compensation discrimination based upon comparable rather than equal work.

The Ninth Circuit stated that Senator Bennett's 1965 interpretation of his amendment (see p. 229, *supra*) was entitled to "no weight" because it was not expressed until the year following the amendment's adoption and, therefore, could "at best" only reflect Senator Bennett's own understanding, not "what was on Congress' collective mind when it acted" (22 FEP Cases at 1652). In this regard, however, the court omitted any mention of Senator Dirksen's statement confirming that he, Senator Humphrey and their staffs had all shared the same understanding of the amendment as was expressed by Senator Bennett. In light of this confirmation by the principal Senate floor leaders for both parties during the Title VII debates (Sen. Humphrey never disavowed this understanding), the court's refusal to give any weight whatsoever to the interpretation offered by the amendment's sponsor seems questionable, particularly in view of the circumstances of the amendment's enactment (see p. 229, *supra*) and the paucity of other evidence as to its meaning.

Also questionable is the court's reading of the Clark memorandum stating that the Equal Pay Act's standards for determining wage discrimination would be "applicable to the comparable situation under Title VII." (See p. 226, *supra.*) Focusing on the words "comparable situation" and construing them in the narrowest possible sense, the court concluded that Senator Clark was referring only to cases in which a Title VII plaintiff was claiming discrimination based on a denial of equal pay for equal work (*Id.*). But this analysis ignores the substance of the objection to which Senator Clark's statement was addressed. The objection was that Title VII would allow wage discrimination claims which "cut across different jobs." The court's conclusion that Senator Clark's answer meant only that claims based on an equal pay for equal work theory would be judged by the equal work standard makes his statement unresponsive to the objection, as well as substantially meaningless.

The court also made no effort to reconcile away Congressman Celler's statement that compliance with the Equal Pay Act would satisfy Title VII's requirement barring sex discrimination. (See p. 228, *supra.*) Instead, it simply said that "this solitary comment" was "insufficient to establish the County's interpretation of the Bennett Amendment [essentially, the interpretation offered in this paper] in view of the *contrary or inconclusive* legislative history previously discussed" (22 FEP Cases at 1652). The court's choice of the words "contrary or inconclusive" is remarkable, because, of course, the court's previous discussion had contained no reference to any legislative history affirmatively supporting its own interpretation. All of its prior discussion had been aimed at showing that the history relied on by the County was not definitive. Thus, while brushing aside an argument for which it had no real answer, the court conveyed the impression of support for a contrary interpretation where in fact none existed.

Moreover, despite the evident fact that the problem of sex-based compensation discrimination was not considered when the House added the sex discrimination provision to Title VII, the Ninth Circuit, in denying the petition for rehearing, stated that "[Congress] may have believed that the Equal Pay Act by itself was inadequate to remedy sex discrimination, or that broader protections were necessary" (22 FEP Cases at 1654). The Court cited no legislative history for this unsupported speculation, and rather cited to Gitt and Gelb, *Beyond the Equal Pay Act: Expanding Wage Differential Protections under Title VII*, 8 Loyola L. J. 723, 744–45(1977), which in turn cites to legislative history which, at most, indicates that certain female sponsors of the amendment were concerned about the denial of "equal pay for equal work." See 110 Cong. Rec. 2580-81 (1964).

The most significant aspect of the *Gunther* decision, however, is that despite the court's contrary interpretation of the Bennett Amendment, it ultimately concluded that "a comparable work standard cannot be substituted for an equal work standard" in wage discrimination cases brought under Title VII (22 FEP Cases at 1655). Rather, the court stated that a Title VII plaintiff claiming wage discrimination based solely on a comparison between men's and women's jobs would "have to show that her job requirements are substantially *equal, not comparable*, to that [sic] of a similarly situated male." (*Id.*, emphasis added.) Thus, although the *Gunther* court refused to rule out sex-based wage discrimination claims under Title VII based on some evidence other than job comparisons, that decision clearly does *not* amount to a judicial endorsement of the "comparable worth" theory.

VI. RELIANCE ON MARKET FACTORS AS A DEFENSE TO TITLE VII DISCRIMINATION CLAIMS

The courts have also been unpersuaded by arguments that employers may not rely on the market place value of certain jobs that are predominantly performed by females because such reliance perpetuates discrimination against women that has been practiced by society at large. In *Christensen v. State of Iowa*,[148] the plaintiffs contended that Title VII was violated because the employer paid clerical workers, who were exclusively female, less than it paid physical plant workers, who were mostly male, for jobs that were of allegedly equal value to the university. The university determined its wage scales for nonprofessional jobs by reference to wages paid for similar work in the local labor market. The university had attempted to determine objectively the relative worth of the jobs using the Hayes System of job evaluation. The local market, however, paid higher wages for physical plant jobs than the Hayes System might suggest, and the university modified the Hayes-suggested rate to meet the market rate.

---

[148] 563 F.2d 353, 356 (8th Cir. 1977), See also, *Kohne v. Imco Container Co.*, 480 F. Supp. 1015, 20 EPD ¶30,168 at p. 11,875 (W.D. VA. 1979) where the plaintiff was unsuccessful in arguing that "its weaker position in the market made it vulnerable to exploitation by the defendant." The plaintiff was unable to show she was performing work equal to that performed by men and her claim was dismissed.

Where plaintiffs have shown that they were paid less for performing the *same* work as males, however, an employer might not be able to defend this differential—which would violate the Equal Pay Act—by arguing that women could be found to work at the lower rates. See, *Corning Glass Works v. Brennan*, 417 U.S. 188, 207-08 (1974); *Hodgson v. Brookhaven General Hospital*, 436 F.2d 719 (5th Cir. 1970); *Brennan v. Victoria Bank & Trust Co.*, 493 F.2d 896 (5th Cir. 1974) and *Brennan v. City Stores, Inc.*, 479 F.2d 235, 241 n. 12,242 (5th Cir. 1973). On the other hand, when the plaintiff is unable to establish that the jobs in question are substantially equal to jobs performed by males, then *Corning Glass* would be inapplicable and "an employer may consider the market place value of the skills of a particular individual when determining his or her salary." See *Horner v. Mary Institute*, 21 FEP Cases 1069, 1074 (8th Cir. 1980).

The Eighth Circuit ruled that the plaintiffs had not established a *prima facie* case of Title VII discrimination, even apart from any legal dispute over the meaning of the Bennett Amendment. The court held that plaintiffs' argument, that reliance on the market merely perpetuates market discrimination, misconstrued the purposes of Title VII. It pointed out that Title VII was designed to give all persons an equal "opportunity" for employment without regard to sex and other types of discrimination. Because it was not alleged that females had been denied access to any job that males performed, the court construed the plaintiff's argument to be that Title VII was violated whenever males and females receive different compensation for work that does not command an equal price on the labor market, even though it might, subjectively, be of equal value to the employer. The court stated that:

> Appellant's theory ignores economic realities. The value of the job to the employer represents but one factor affecting wages. Other factors may include the supply of workers willing to do the job and the ability of the workers to band together to bargain collectively for higher wages. We find nothing in the text and history of Title VII suggesting that Congress intended to abrogate the laws of supply and demand or other economic principles that determine wage rates for various kinds of work. We do not interpret Title VII as requiring an employer to ignore the market in setting wage rates for genuinely different work classifications.[149]

The court also agreed with the university that it would have been economically unrealistic to adopt fully the Hayes System, because some community wage scales were higher and these had to be met by the university to compete with other employers.[150]

Also, in *Keyes v. Lenoir Rhyne College* (discussed at p. 235 *supra.*), the employer successfully defended against sex discrimination compensation allegations by female faculty members by relying on such "legitimate factors" as the area of specialization in question, the availability of qualified persons in the market place in that field at the time the plaintiffs were employed, and the need for such skills by the particular college program in question.[151]

The disruptive consequences of ignoring the market system were further illustrated in the oral opinion of Judge Winner in *Lemons v. City & County of Denver*.[152] There, nurses hired by the city alleged that the city's practice of

---

[149] 563 F.2d at 356.

[150] *Cf., Wheeler v. Armco Steel Corp.*, 20 EPD ¶30,164 (S.D. Tex. 1979) (Employer did not violate Title VII when it did not pay female employee strictly according to the Hay system, which the court found did not consider such legitimate business criteria as seniority, experience, and education).

[151] 15 FEP Cases 919, 920, 922.

[152] 17 FEP Cases 906 (D. Colo. 1978), *affirmed*, 620 F.2d 228, 22 FEP Cases 959 (10th Cir. 1980).

paying jobs at the prevailing wage in the Denver area violated Title VII because society had placed an improperly low market value on nursing work because the jobs were held by women. The judge noted that such a theory was "pregnant with the possibility of disrupting the entire economic system of the [U.S.]"[153] and that the "courts in this country would be deluged with that type of litigation and there isn't a judge in the United States, especially this Judge, qualified to set everybody else's pay. It would be an absolutely hopeless morass."[154] Judge Winner indicated he was aware that there was a history of sex discrimination in this society, but also concluded that Congress did not intend that the federal courts should "restructure the economy of the country."[155] He stated, for example, that the plaintiff's concept would require a comparison of the relative worth of jobs held by organized and unorganized workers without providing any solution as to how to make the comparison.[156]

Judge Winner also observed that Congress has not been able to repeal the law of supply and demand and found that the supply of nurses was large relative to the demand and that, as a result, nurses were put in a disadvantageous negotiating position.[157] Although it might be shown that male-dominated professions were paid more than female jobs, the court held that this alone could not establish a Title VII violation, because the only allegation against the city was that it paid the market rate, and not that it discriminated in hiring or assignment of females. Because the male and female jobs in questions were not substantially equal, the Title VII complaint was dismissed.[158]

On appeal, the Tenth Circuit agreed with Judge Winner's reasoning in *Lemons v. City and County of Denver.* The court observed that

> [t]he relationship of pay for nurses to pay for other positions is obviously a product of past attitudes, practices, and perhaps of supply and demand. . . [I]t became a part of the economic balance and

---

[153] 17 FEP Cases at 907.

[154] *Id.* at 909.

[155] *Id.* at 908.

[156] *Id.* at 909.

[157] He found that the statistical evidence demonstrated that if there was discrimination in the profession, it favored females, who "out-number males by a tremendous percentage." 17 FEP Cases at 909.

[158] In a similar case involving publicly-hired nurses, the court dismissed claims of discrimination based on the employer's payment of market wage rates. *County Employees Assn. v. Health Dept.*, 18 FEP Cases 1538 (Wash. Ct. App. 1978). The decision found that more was required than an allegation of past discrimination by other employers, which in turn influenced the specific employer in the case. The court noted that women could have applied and been hired into any department in the county and received the same wages as males holding those jobs. As in *Christensen v. Iowa*, the court found that other factors such as the supply of willing workers and the bargaining ability of the employees were ignored by the plaintiff.

relationships prevailing in the community among the myriad of positions prevailing in the job market.[159]

The court of appeals then went on to hold that wage disparities thus based on market factors are beyond the reach of existing law:

This type of disparity was not sought to be adjusted by the Civil Rights Act, and is not within the equal protection clause. The courts under existing authority cannot require the City within its employment to reassess the worth of services in each position in relation to all others, and to strike a new balance and relationship.[160]

The previous discussion illustrates the overwhelming trend of court decisions concerning whether sex-based compensation claims must conform to the "equal work" requirement of the Equal Pay Act. The decisions generally hold that Congress did not intend to permit the courts or federal agencies to restructure job evaluation systems on the basis of the economic worth of the jobs.

VII. POLICY CONSIDERATIONS

The judicial decisions discussed above are strongly supported by considerations relating to the complexity and difficulty of compensation-discrimination claims in general. In many instances it is true that jobs in the market are predominantly held by women,[161] and that market wages in some of those jobs are lower than jobs predominated by males. It does not follow, however, that either the overrepresentation of women in these particular jobs or the lower wages they receive resulted from illegal discrimination.

For example, a 1978 study by the United States Labor Department concluded that female job preference is a major factor in the imbalance of females in certain jobs.[162]

Despite affirmative action programs and publicity on the career success of women in stereotypical male positions, most women have not changed their career aspirations. They continue to plan careers

[159] 620 F.2d 228, 22 FEP Cases 959 (10th Cir. 1980).

[160] 620 F.2d at 229, 22 FEP Cases at 959-60.

[161] Women represent 97.8% of all Registered Nurses, 94.5% of elementary school teachers, 69% of retail sales clerks, 76.6% of all clerical workers (including bank tellers, bookkeepers, file clerks, secretaries, etc.), 96% of maids, 82.9% of food servers (waitresses) and 87.6% of all health service workers. See 1975 Handbook on Women Workers, U.S. Department of Labor Bulletin 297 (1975).

[162] See *Years of Decision*, Vol. 4 (1978), U.S. Dept. of Labor Employment Training Administration.

in traditionally female positions. As a result, they continue to occupy lower paying positions.[163]

. . . To the extent that women prefer a typically female occupation, affirmative action programs directed solely at employers will not substantially reduce occupational segregation. Hence, in addition to pursuing a vigorous affirmative action program, public policy undoubtedly should be concerned with counseling and educational programs if young women are to be informed about the full range of available occupations.[164]

This study indicates that there are a number of factors—aside from employer or market discrimination—that influence the choice of jobs taken by females. Adoption of the comparable worth approach would underestimate the complexity of the issues and disregard the existing market values of the jobs in question. Also, it would require the federal courts and agencies to set wage scales without regard to market factors, job preference, collective bargaining and numerous other factors that relate to the setting of wage scales. In the absence of a clear legislative mandate to do so, adoption of the comparable worth approach by the courts or agencies would be in direct conflict with the mandate of Congress.

VIII. SUMMARY AND CONCLUSION

Present law provides little, if any, support for the concept that courts enforcing federal wage discrimination legislation should become involved in comparing the relative worth or value of jobs. To the contrary, when Congress enacted the Equal Pay Act in 1963, it adopted the "equal work" standard and refused to accept language intended to create a "comparable work" criterion. Among the advantages Congress found in the more limited "equal work" concept were:

1. That it is less vague than the "comparable work" approach, and not as difficult to enforce;
2. That it recognizes that expertise and experience of private parties in job evaluation matters; and
3. That it would not inject federal regulators and the courts into an area where they had little expertise.

Although Congress thus limited the scope of sex-based compensation claims in 1963, it provided additional protection for women in employment the following year by adding a sex discrimination provision to Title VII. This

---

[163] *Id.* at iii.

[164] *Id.* at 114.

provision forbids employers from discriminating in hiring, job placement or classification, promotions, transfers, layoffs and discharges. This protection is limited, however, by the Bennett Amendment, which restricts sex-based compensation claims to those which would satisfy the Equal Pay Act's "equal work" standard. The policy reasons for this approach were set forth by the court in *Kohne v. Imco Container Co.*, 480 F. Supp. at 1039:

> Of course, sound policy underlies such a construction. Congress did not intend to put either the Secretary of Labor or the courts in the business of evaluating jobs and in determining what constitutes a proper differential for unequal work. See *Angelo v. Bacharach Instrument Co., supra; Brennan v. Prince William Hospital Corp., supra,* at 285. Sufficient remedies exist under Title VII to deal with discriminatory hiring and promotional practices, without the courts becoming embroiled in determinations of how an employer's work force ought to be paid.

The present statutory approach to wage discrimination has proven to be reasonable and workable. Barriers which once prevented women from having access to jobs have been broken down by enforcement of federal laws and regulations.[165] Today, qualified females not only have an equal opportunity to be hired into any job category, but under the "equal work" standard they also must be paid the same as males if they perform jobs that involve "equal work" and require the same skill, effort, and responsibility under the same working conditions.

A recent Wall Street Journal Article described the practical application of present law and the market place as follows:

> With a little more practice, the EEOC will likely achieve its underlying objective without interfering in the labor market. Consider what is happening now with secretaries. As discriminatory barriers against women are hacked down, in large part because of the EEOC's earlier efforts, the most talented and overqualified secretaries are leaving the secretarial labor force and taking on more responsible positions. At the same time, the demand for secretaries is increasing, with the result that pay rates have started to soar. The market may yet validate the proposition that secretaries are worth more than tool and die makers.

---

[165] Another particularly significant development has been enforcement of Federal Executive Order 11246 by the Office of Federal Contract Compliance Programs. Under its regulations, federal contractors are required to have a work force in which the percentage of females in each job category matches that of the workforce in the surrounding community. If women are underrepresented in any job category, the employer is required to establish goals and timetables to remedy this deficiency. Failure to do so can result in the loss of government contracts or other sanctions. See 43 C.F.R. Parts 60-1 and 60-2.

Decreeing that one job must be paid the same as another represents interference at its worst. But barriers that keep women or minorities from realizing their full potential also represent interference at its worst. Mounting a full-scale attack on those barriers can only help the market to be more efficient. That—and not metaphysical excursions into the murky world of comparable worth—is, and should continue to be, the primary mission of the EEOC.[166]

Application of the "equal work" standard involves primarily factual determinations and does not require the courts to engage in extensive comparisons of dissimilar jobs. The inquiry, rather, is whether or not the jobs in question are the same. As shown, when Congress adopted this approach instead of the "comparable work" standard, it did so in part because it was less vague and relatively easier to apply. Nevertheless, "the federal courts have had no small difficulty"[167] in attempting to apply even this simpler standard.

It is a common misconception that industrial job evaluation techniques are utilized solely to determine the "worth" to the employer of the various jobs throughout its organization. In fact, establishing a compensation system is not a precise science of general application. Each employer considers a number of factors such as: the market value for particular jobs; collective bargaining forces; the relative skill, effort, responsibilities and working conditions of various jobs; the relative attractiveness of merit, and direct or incentive pay schemes; and whether the employer wishes to satisfy, retain, motivate or attract persons in particular job categories. While the end result of the evaluation process must be acceptable to the employees (or risk discontent, morale problems and strike situations), it would be naive at best to conclude that the process of evaluating the relative compensation for different jobs is anything but an extremely complex and difficult process. Beyond the difficulties generally experienced by employers in evaluating their job categories, there are no established administrative or judicial standards or techniques for making comparisons between dissimilar jobs.

Adoption of the "comparable worth" approach, therefore, could make the courts' responsibility even more difficult and place an unrealistic burden on them. In contrast to the relatively straightforward factual inquiry required under the "equal work" standard, the comparable worth approach would necessitate complex subjective judgments about the relative worth of various unrelated jobs in the employer's overall operation. Comparisons between diverse categories, such as skilled technicians, line operators, clericals, truck drivers and food service personnel, would be required. The immensity of the task of making such comparisons is aptly demonstrated by the Census Bureau's Classified Index of Industries and Occupations which has approximately 19,000 industry and 23,000 occupation titles.

---

[166] G. S. Crystal, "Comparable Worth?" Wall St. J., Nov. 5, 1979, at 30, col. 3.

[167] *Angelo v. Bacharach Instrument Co.*, 555 F.2d 1164, 1170 (3d Cir. 1977).

Because there are no established judicial standards for making such comparisons, it is impossible to predict how many potential plaintiffs might attempt to pursue claims that their jobs were comparable to those of members of the opposite sex. Indeed, the logic of the comparable worth argument would permit practically any female worker to argue that her contribution was comparable to that of some male employee, and should, therefore, receive equal compensation

In the few cases in which the comparable worth approach has been litigated, judges have been apprehensive about the theory because of its disregard of long-established factors such as collective bargaining strength and labor markets.[168] There is no assurance, however, that all courts will have similar qualms about restructuring the economy of the nation.

Moreover, even if the comparable worth concept is not accepted by the courts, Congress may be asked to incorporate the theory in new legislation. In either event, the burden that would be imposed on the courts should be clearly recognized, for there can be no question that judicial resolution of compensation claims would be made much more difficult under such a standard.

In evaluating particular wage systems under a comparable worth standard, courts could be required to make value comparisons between numerous factors, including the skill, effort, responsibility and working conditions of the employer's job categories. There could be several hundred different jobs at a large employer's facility, but a comparison of a few suffices to show the detailed inquiry involved. For example, suppose females in certain clerical functions felt their jobs were worth as much as those of male employees who do routine maintenance work. The following job categories might be compared:[169]

Billing, Posting, and Calculating Machine Operations	Routine Machinery Maintenance
Bookkeeping-machine operator I	Technical testing engineer
Bookkeeping-machine operator II	Nozzle-and-sleeve worker
Food checker	Pot liner
Food-and-beverage checker	Leaf coverer
Food tabulator, cafeteria	Stem-dryer maintainer

---

[168] See *Lemons v. City and County of Denver*, 620 F.2d 228, 22 FEP Cases 959, (10th Cir. 1980) *petition for cert. filed* (No. 80-82), wherein the court of appeals observed that legal remedies which "would cross job description lines into areas of entirely different skills . . . would be a whole new world for the courts, and until some better signal from Congress is received, we cannot venture into it." 620 F.2d at 229, 22 FEP Cases at 960.

[169] 1977 Standard Occupational Classification Manual, U.S. Dept. of Commerce 145-46, 208.

Fee clerk

Interline clerk

Accounts-adjustable clerk

Billing-machine operator

Payroll clerk, data processing

Food-and-beverage controller

Check-processing clerk II

Accounting clerk, data processing

Policy-value calculator

Check-processing clerk I

Adding-machine operator

Audit-machine operator

Calculating-machine operator

Gas-volume computer

Proof-machine operator

Frame bander

Overhead cleaner maintainer

Flyer repairer

Curing-press maintainer

Knife changer

Printing-roller handler

Pattern assembler

Stroboscope operator

Oiler

Salvager

Polishing-wheel setter

Flatcar whacker

Cell installer

Pipe changer

Rubber and plastics worker

Rigger

A court attempting such comparisons would have to inquire into the employer's methods of production, technology, ability to reinvest in labor-saving devices and a number of other factors. When Congress enacted the Equal Pay Act, it recognized that courts and regulatory agencies lacked the expertise required to make these comparisons, and left the task to the employers and unions. Similarly, the War Labor Board—composed of experienced labor relations practitioners from both management, unions and the public—took the approach that these difficult determinations were best left to the disputing parties.

Additionally, unless the courts were to disregard completely the impact of collective bargaining on wage setting, the "comparable worth" approach would also require them to intrude into the bargaining process—an area which Congress has always protected from excessive government regulation. Because the present labor laws leave collective bargaining to the parties and not the government,[170] courts have no experience in setting wage rates, much less in evaluating relevant economic factors, such as the union's economic strength *vis a vis* the employer, the relative worth of wages and various fringe benefits, the comparative strength of intra-union pressure groups, and the productivity of various workers. Moreover, market factors could not be ignored, unless Congress undertakes the folly of attempting to repeal the laws of supply and demand for labor.

Another valid concern involves the economic effects of implementing the comparable worth approach. Although absolute predictions are not possible, such effects could be extremely costly, especially if applied to entire in-

---

[170] See *e.g., H K. Porter Co. v. N. L. R. B.*, 397 U.S. 99 (1970); *N. L. R. B. v. Insurance Agents' International Union*, 361 U.S. 477 (1960).

dustries or the economy as a whole. *Fortune* Magazine considered these factors and stated:

> There are two ways to correct the imbalance in earnings [between the sexes]. Women can step into higher-income jobs, a commendable process that is, of course, gradually taking place. But if the world could be changed by edict, there is a second method that would work much faster. Women could remain in their customary jobs and men in theirs and employers could be ordered to pay the same wages to all whose work is deemed to be of equal value.
>
> That would certainly correct imbalances rapidly, but the economy would surely be much disrupted in the process. At the extreme, to raise the aggregate pay of the country's 27.3 million full-time working women high enough so that the median pay for women would equal that of men would add a staggering $150 billion a year to civilian payrolls. Such a radical step, of course, seems too preposterous to be taken seriously. But even partial measures . . . would have an enormous impact, undoubtedly aggravated by demands from unionized workers in traditionally male jobs that their pay be increased correspondingly. Higher-paid workers almost always resist any erosion of historic differentials between their pay and that of lower-paid workers.[171]

In short, unlike the Equal Pay Act inquiry, which is restricted to a particular job category, the economic analysis required to set relative wages would be wide-sweeping and totally beyond anything that has been experienced previously by the judiciary or the economy. It is small wonder, therefore, that when Congress passed the Equal Pay Act, it "did not authorize the Secretary [of Labor] or the Courts to engage in wholesale reevaluation of any employer's pay structure in order to enforce their own conception of economic worth."[172]

The existing statutory scheme under the Equal Pay Act and Title VII is fair because it protects the rights of all workers to equal opportunity and compensation without regard to sex. While requiring somewhat difficult factual analyses, it has proven workable because it is based upon factors which do not require subjective judgments about the value of specific jobs. Adoption of the comparable worth theory would upset this measured approach and entangle the judiciary and administrative agencies in issues that would be difficult to resolve and almost impossible to manage.[173]

---

[171] "The EEOC's Bold Foray Into Job Evaluation," *Fortune*, September 11, 1978, 58–59.

[172] *Brennan v. Prince William Hospital Corp.*, 503 F.2d 282, 285 (4th Cir. 1974), *cert. denied*, 420 U.S. 972 (1975), and cases cited in note 49, *supra*.

[173] See Editor's Note on the following page.

EDITOR'S NOTE: After this book was set for final printing, the Third Circuit issued its opinion in the appeal of *IUE v. Westinghouse Electric Corp.*, 19 FEP Cases 450 and 19 FEP Cases 1028 (D.N.J. 1979), *appeal docketed*, Nos. 79-1893 and 79-1894 (3d Cir.), discussed above in footnotes 2, 4 and 131, and on pp. 236–37. In a 2–1 decision, the Court discussed the applicability of the Bennett Amendment to claims of sex-based wage discrimination. The majority judges noted that the case "push[ed them] to the edge of subtle concepts of statutory construction . . ." (slip opinion, page 6). The majority, however, reversed the district court and held that the Bennett Amendment merely incorporates into Title VII the four exceptions set out in the Equal Pay Act. The majority opinion (at pages 23 and 28 of the slip opinion) relies upon and closely parallels the Ninth Circuit's decision in *Gunther v. County of Washington*, which was fully discussed above in footnotes 128, 133 and 137, and on pp. 237-240.

The dissenting opinion in *Westinghouse* advanced a view of the issues that was directly at odds with the majority opinion and which is squarely in accord with the thesis of this paper. The dissent concluded the case was based upon a "comparable work" theory that Congress rejected when it passed the Equal Pay Act. The dissent further stated that Congress did not intend to overrule the "equal work policy" when it adopted Title VII.

Further judicial action in *Westinghouse* can be expected either by way of a petition for rehearing in the Third Circuit or by a request for Supreme Court review. Clearly, the issues in this highly technical and complex area will continue to be the subject of judicial debate and Supreme Court guidance may be forthcoming.

SUPPLEMENTAL READING LIST

Aigner, Dennis J. and Cain, Glen G., "Statistical Theories of Discrimination in Labor Markets," *Industrial and Labor Relations Review*, 30 (January 1977) p. 175.
  A helpful discussion of statistical explanations for the existence of job segregation and the resulting lower earnings.

Allen, Arthur P. and Schneider, Betty V. H., *Industrial Relations in the California Aircraft Industry*, West Coast Collective Bargaining Systems Monographs, No. 8d, (Berkeley, California: Institute of Industrial Relations, University of California, Berkeley, 1956), p. 22.
  A monograph explaining how the Southern California aircraft job evaluation system worked in the post-World War II era.

Becker, Gary, *The Economics of Discrimination*, 2d ed. (Chicago: University of Chicago Press, 1971), pp. 3–17.
  The classic treatise in modern discrimination theory from the point of view of the economist.

Belcher, D. W., *Compensation Administration*, (Englewood Cliffs, New Jersey: Prentice Hall, 1974).
  A comprehensive text on wage and salary administration.

Bergmann, Barbara R., "Occupational Segregation, Wages and Profits When Employers Discriminate by Race or Sex," *Eastern Economic Journal*, (1974), pp. 103–10.

Bergmann, Barbara R., "The Effect on White Incomes of Discrimination in Employment," *Journal of Political Economy*, 79 (March–April 1971), pp. 294–313.
  A discussion of occupational congestion or blockage as a factor in widening income differentials in favor of more mobile groups.

Bergmann, Barbara and Krause, William, "Evaluating and Forecasting Progress in Racial Integration of Employment," *Industrial and Labor Relations Review*, 24, (April 1972), pp. 399–409.
  An exposition and a defense of the random selection theory of employment which would evaluate progress in equal employment on the basis of a parity goal for all races and both sexes.

Bloom, Gordon F. and Northrup, Herbert R., *Economics of Labor Relations*, 8th ed. (Homewood, Illinois: Richard D. Irwin, Inc., 1977).

A textbook containing extended discussion of seniority and wage issues, and the impact of unions and collective bargaining on these and other practices.

Bunting, Robert L., "A Note on Large Firms and Labor Concentration," *Journal of Political Economy*, LXXIV: 4 (August 1966), pp. 404–05.
A paper extending Bunting's original research into a more intensive examination of large firms as an influence upon labor concentration.

Bunting, Robert L., *Employer Concentration in Local Labor Markets* (Chapel Hill, N.C.: University of North Carolina Press, 1962).
A pioneering attempt to test the existence of monopsony in labor markets.

Cook, Thomas D. and Campbell, Donald T., "Inferring Cause from Passive Observation," Chapter 7 in *Quasi-experimentation: Design & Analysis for Field Settings* (Chicago: Rand McNally, 1979).
An excellent discussion of the underadjustment problem in another area of application.

Dempster, A. P., "Statistical Concepts of Discrimination," Statistics Department, Harvard University, (1979).
A careful statement of the problems raised by what Harry Roberts has called "underadjustment", distinguishing underadjustment from incomplete adjustment and exploring subtleties in the statistical definition of discrimination.

Draper, N. R. and Smith, H., *Applied Regression Analysis* (New York: John Wiley & Sons, 1966).
A standard text on regression methodology.

Dunnette, M. D., "Task and Job Taxonomies as a Basis for Evaluating Employment Qualifications," *Human Resources Planning Journal*, Vol. I, 1 (1977).

"The Earnings Gap Between Women and Men," Women's Bureau, Employment Standards Administration, U.S. Department of Labor (Washington, D.C. 1975).

Field, Henry F., et al., "Statistical Study of Equality of Employment Opportunity at United Airlines: Methods and Findings," (Center for Mathematical Studies in Business and Economics, University of Chicago, 1978). (A condensed version has appeared in the *Journal of Contemporary Business*.)

Fox, W. M., "Purpose and Validity in Job Evaluation," *Personnel Journal*, (October 1962), pp. 432–37.

Friedman, Milton, *Price Theory: A Provisional Text* (Chicago: Aldine Publishing Company, 1962), pp. 211–25.
A very thorough technical discussion of the factors responsible for differences in occupational earnings.

Fuchs, Victor, "Differences in Hourly Earnings Between Men and Women," *Monthly Labor Review*, 94 (May 1971), pp. 9–15.
One of the seminal papers on sex differentials (by occupations) in the United States.

Gray, Robert D., *Systematic Wage Administration in the Southern California Aircraft Industry*, Industrial Relations Monograph No. 7 (New York: Industrial Relations Counselors, Inc., 1945).

A monograph reciting how the Southern California aircraft program which significantly affected the thinking of the National War Labor Board, was developed and giving its early results.

Henderson, Richard I., *Compensation Management: Rewarding Performance in the Modern Organization* (Reston, Virginia: Reston Publishing Company, 1976).

Chapter 14 of his standard textbook containing a general examination of union policy and job evaluation.

Heneman, Herbert G., III and Schwab, Donald P., "Work and Rewards Theory." in Dale Yoder and Herbert G. Heneman (eds.), *ASPA Handbook of Personnel and Industrial Relations* (Washington, D.C.: Bureau of National Affairs, 1979), Chapter 6.1, 1-22.

An overview of organizational pay goals and compensation procedures.

Hildebrand, George H., "External Influences and the Determination of the Internal Wage Structure," in J. L. Meij, ed., *Internal Wage Structure* (Amsterdam: North Holland Publishing Company, 1963), pp. 282-90.

An early attempt to consider the ways in which the external labor market influences the internal wage structures of firms and plants.

Job Evaluation (Geneva: International Labour Organisation, 1960).

Jones, Harold S., "Union Views on Job Evaluation: 1971 vs. 1978," *Personnel Journal*, 58 (February 1979), pp. 80-85.

An article reporting on results of a mailed questionnaire survey regarding union officials' views on job evaluation.

Kerr, Clark, "Labor Markets: Their Character and Consequences," *American Economic Review*, Papers and Proceedings, XL: 2 (May 1950) pp. 278-91.

A pioneering article on segmentation in American labor markets; not directly concerned with the theory of occupational wage discrimination.

Krzystofiak, F., Newman, J. and Anderson, G., "A Quantified Approach to Measurement of Job Content," *Personnel Psychology*, 32, 2 (Summer 1979), pp. 341-57.

Lerner, Abba P., *Economics of Employment* (New York: McGraw-Hill, 1951), pp. 20-241.

An interesting method of setting relative occupational wages and salaries to minimize unemployment across the economy.

Levinson, Harold M., *Determining Forces in Collective Wage Bargaining* (New York: John Wiley & Sons, Inc., 1966).

A study examining information about the Southern California aircraft industry wage plan, and discussing patterns of wage negotiations and classifications in other industries.

Livernash, E. Robert, "The Internal Wage Structure," in G. W. Taylor and F. C. Pierson (eds.), *New Concepts in Wage Determination* (New York: McGraw-Hill, 1957), pp. 140-72.

A very good description of what job evaluation accomplishes and how it is conducted in practice.

Madansky, Albert, "The Fitting of Straight Lines When Both Variables Are Subject to Error," *Journal of the American Statistical Association*, 54, 285 (1959), pp. 173–205.

> An early classic in the area of theoretical questions raised by the underadjustment problem.

Madden, J. M., *An Application to Job Evaluation of a Policy Capturing Model for Analyzing Individual and Group Judgment*, Technical Report PRL-TDL-63-15, AD-417-273, Lackland Air Force Base, Texas, (1963).

Madden, Janice Fanning, "Discrimination—A Manifestation of Male Market Power?" in Cynthia B. Lloyd, ed. *Sex Discrimination and the Division of Labor* (New York: Columbia University Press, 1975).

> An interesting attempt to explain sex differentials with monopsony theory.

Mosteller, Frederick and Tukey, John W., *Data Analysis and Regression* (Reading, Massachusetts: Addison-Wesley Publishing Company, 1977).

> A book emphasizing the role of exploratory data analysis in regression studies.

Northrup, Herbert R. and Larson, John A., *The Impact of the AT&T-EEO Consent Decree*, Labor Relations and Public Policy Series No. 20 (Philadelphia: Industrial Research Unit, The Wharton School, University of Pennsylvania, 1979).

> A detailed examination of how the consent decree worked in practice and its results. Included is a critique of the parity goals based upon the random selection theory of employment.

Northrup, Herbert R. and Rowan, Richard L., *Negro Employment in Southern Industry*, Studies of Negro Employment, Vol. IV (Philadelphia: Industrial Research Unit, The Wharton School, University of Pennsylvania, 1970).

> Part One of this work, dealing with the paper manufacturing industry, contains a detailed analysis of job upgrading, and the development of job progression into a formal system after union organization.

Oaxaca, R. L., "Sex Discrimination in Wages," in *Discrimination in Labor Markets*, A. Ashenfelter and A. Rees (eds.) (Princeton, New Jersey: Princeton University Press, 1973).

Oaxaca, Ronald L., *Theory and Measurement in the Economics of Discrimination*, Industrial Relations Research Association Series, (1977).

Raimon, Robert L., "The Indeterminateness of Semiskilled Workers," *Industrial and Labor Relations Review*, (January 1953), pp. 180–94.

> A highly original theory of internal wage structure relative to the external market.

Remick, H., "Strategies for Creating Sound, Bias Free Job Evaluation Plans," *Job-Evaluation and EEOC: The Emerging Issues* (New York: Industrial Relations Counselors, Inc., 1978), p. 91.

Roberts, Harry V., "Harris Trust and Savings Bank: An Analysis of Employee Compensation," Center for Mathematical Studies in Business and Economics, University of Chicago, (1979).

A summary description of studies supervised by the author for Harris Bank in defense of its case against the OFCCP in 1979, providing a detailed treatment of the statistical rationale, including shunting studies and reverse regression and procedures for regression in adversary proceedings.

Robinson, D. D., et al., "Comparison of Job Evaluation Methods," *Journal of Applied Psychology*, 59, (1974), pp. 633–637.

Robinson, Joan, *The Economics of Imperfect Competition* (London: MacMillan and and Co., Ltd., 1933), pp. 292–304.

The classical treatise on monopsony theory.

Sawhill, I. V., "The Economics of Discrimination Against Women: Some New Findings," *Journal of Human Resources* 8, (1973), pp. 383–395.

Schultz, George P., "A Nonunion Market with White Collar Labor," in National Bureau of Economic Research, *Aspects of Labor Economics* (Princeton, N.J.: Princeton University Press 1962), pp 107–46.

A very interesting study of the role of the external market in determining a wage structure for certain types of white-collar labor.

Sherman, Herbert L., Jr., *Arbitration of the Steel Wage Structure* (Pittsburgh: University of Pittsburgh Press, 1961).

A book containing a summary of the steel industry wage classification system and including copies of key arbitration cases arising thereunder, with analyses thereof.

Slichter, Sumner H., Healy, James J., and Livernash, E. Robert, *The Impact of Collective Bargaining on Management* (Washington: The Brookings Institution, 1960).

A book containing the basic and best writing on the relationships of collective bargaining, job evaluation and wage classifications systems. Chapters 19 and 20 are required reading for anyone interested in this subject.

"Statistical Inferences of Employment Discrimination and the Calculation of Back Pay," *OFCCP Statistical Standards Panel Report*, prepared by Applied Urbanetics, Inc., (September 1979).

A useful elementary treatment of employment discrimination, not dealing explicitly with the problem of underadjustment.

Stevenson, Mary J., "Relative Wages and Sex Segregation by Occupation," in Cynthia B. Lloyd, ed., *Sex, Discrimination and the Division of Labor* (New York: Columbia University Press 1975), pp. 175–98.

A highly original effort to achieve occupational comparability so that differentials based upon sex could be isolated.

Stieber, Jack, *The Steel Industry Wage Structure*, Werthun Publications in Industrial Relations (Cambridge, Mass.: Harvard University Press, 1959).

A monograph containing a complete history and analysis of the steel program.

Termination Report of the National War Labor Board (Washington: U.S. Government Printing Office, 1946).

A detailed report on War Labor Board policies and key cases involving job evaluation and wage classification systems contained in Volume I of this three volume work. Later developments are heavily based upon WLB policies.

Trieman, D. J., "Job Evaluation: An Analytical Review," Interim Report to the Equal Employment Opportunity Commission, Washington, D.C., National Academy of Sciences, (1979).

Trieman, Donald J. and Terrell, Kermit, "Women, Work and Wages—Trends in the Female Occupational Structure," in Kenneth C. Land and Seymour Spilerman, (eds.), *Social Indicator Models* (New York: Russell Sage Foundation 1975), pp. 159-71.

A very informative examination of "female" jobs and the various reasons for their existence.

Wolins, Leroy, "Sex Differentials in Salaries: Faults in Analysis of Covariance," *Science*, 200, (May 19, 1978), p. 917.

A concise statement of the bias of "underadjustment,"

TABLE OF CASES